Political Ideas and Political Action

Political Ideas and Political Action

RODNEY BARKER

Copyright © Blackwell Publishers Ltd 2000

This edition first published in 2000

Blackwell Publishers Ltd
108 Cowley Road
Oxford OX4 1JF, UK

Blackwell Publishers Inc
350 Main Street
Malden, Massachusetts 02148, USA

British Library Cataloguing in Publication Data has been applied for

Library of Congress Cataloging-in-Publication Data has been applied for

ISBN: 0-631-22142-5 (pbk)

Typeset by Advance Typesetting, Long Hanborough, Oxfordshire
Printed and bound in Great Britain
by MPG Books Ltd, Bodmin, Cornwall

This book is printed on acid-free paper

Contents

Preface

Rodney Barker

To write about political ideas and political action might look like an attempt to encompass the whole of politics. How after all can politics be understood save as action made meaningful by thought or thought given substance in action? Yet the separation of 'ideas' as something distinct from 'ordinary politics' had for a long time been a feature of much political science. A world that it is increasingly difficult to explain without reference to beliefs, values, and political thinking, has caused a lot of re-thinking. But so well established was this distinction that the growing reaction against it has sometimes displayed the Columbus syndrome: treating as a discovery what for many, the original intellectual inhabitants, had always been familiar. The articles collected in this book do not attempt to cover all aspects of the current state of thinking about thinking in political science. Nor do they reflect a common theory of the relationship between political thinking and political action, nor even a common perception of what those two categories are. Some contributors would in fact question the usefulness of the dichotomy all together. But all the contributions reflect a growing recognition within political science of the central place of political thinking as a dimension, perhaps the single most important dimension, of the activity of politics.

It is an underlying or implied theme of much of the discussion that a simple one way causal chain between one kind of political activity and another misrepresents the complexity of political life. So there is no hierarchy in the arrangement of the articles, from 'high' to 'low' theory, or from 'everyday' political thinking to 'reflection', and apart from the editor's chapter that discusses the recent rehabilitation of political thinking as a necessary dimension of politics, and questions the usefulness of a rigid distinction between ideas and action, they are placed solely by the arbitrary ranking of alphabetical order.

Stefania Abrar, Joni Lovenduski and Helen Margetts in a discussion of municipal policy on violence against women describe the way in which an advocacy coalition model can illuminate the role of belief driven activists in changing the ideas that set the agenda of politics. Steve Bruce, by contrast, looks at some of the disadvantages which can flow from commitment when it takes the form of zealotry, in a discussion of the function in the USA of religious thinking in justifying or sustaining other forms of political action. Andrew Chadwick calls on political science to learn from the theory and practice of historians. He argues that political identity is shaped in the use of political language, 'public discourse', which is neither random nor determined, but a central form of political activity. An analysis of political thinking in the form of ideologies is provided by Michael Freeden in an examination of this particular dimension of political life as 'a series of observable and discoverable practices in the world.' An appropriate response to the existence of many conflicting life shaping, and life expressed, beliefs, is considered in John Gray's discussion of value pluralism. W. H. Greenleaf in a case study of foreign policy presents two levels of thinking about politics: practical and pragmatic which does no more than respond to external events, and theoretical which is removed from those events but can nonetheless be called in aid to support or justify actions taken for quite other reasons. Carol Harlow examines the way in which doctrines of law and the role of the courts have been an inextricable part of the changes taking place in the constitution of the United Kingdom and of the relations of that country to the European Union. James Meadowcroft charts the career of an idea, 'sustainable development' and examines the reasons for its successes and failures. The following essays do not constitute any kind of manifesto. But in a considerable variety of ways they draw attention to politics as an intellectual activity, which is an appropriate reminder for the start of the new millennium.

Acknowledgements

The chapters collected here have been developed from papers first discussed at a seminar at the London School of Economics and Political Science in January 1999. I am grateful to Mick Moran, previous editor of *Political Studies*, for inviting me to edit this book. The advent of word processing has made secretarial assistance unnecessary, but I am grateful to Elisa Roller, Deborah Smith and Tim Walters for valuable administrative help in organizing the January meetings.

R.B.

1

Hooks and Hands, Interests and Enemies: Political Thinking as Political Action

Rodney Barker

I

Thinking and Doing

The familiar and well-established account of politics which describes two spheres, one of thought or ideas, the other of action or practice, is restrictive and distorting. But it has become entrenched in both common speech and political science. In everyday parlance the implication is frequently that the terms represent distinct, even mutually exclusive, forms of life. A man of action is not expected to do very much thinking, a thinker or an intellectual is supposed not to be very useful when the pipes burst or the car has a flat tyre. A similar distinction can be found in political science where a world has been depicted divided between actions, organizations, and practice, and reflection, justification, and normative enquiry. The distinction is made not only in the subject matter of political science, but within the discipline's own manner of operation. There are types of research and enquiry which 'merely' advance understanding, and others which make a practical contribution to the tangible well-being of their societies. The one is presented as reflective, interpretative, passive, the other as engaged, having practical consequences, and an active response to public issues.

This division of politics into two distinct zones needs reconsidering for two reasons. The first is conceptual: the division does not work, it is not coherent, it frequently rests on assumptions which, to sustain itself, it would need to deny. The second is perceptual: the division distorts our vision, and gets in the way of more flexible, illuminating, and historically and empirically sensitive accounts.

The difficulties in moving beyond the ideas/action division however are great. Any altered perspective would need to overcome not only a positivist, or at least positivistic, tradition within political science, but also a scepticism outside it which sees ideas as mere rhetoric, a cover or a justification for other things. Within political science the binary division has the advantages which accrue to familiarity and to neatness. It would be simple and straightforward even if it were not rooted in academic practice. As it is, it has the added strength of tradition. The assumption that there is life, and there is thinking about life, has a long ancestry and a strong hold. A lot of political science assumes that first we do and then we think, or alternatively that we think when no other course is left open to us. Part of the explanation for this division lies in the recent history of political science. The massive expansion, and real achievements, of the study of organizations, outcomes, and processes has employed measurement and the quantitative depiction of behaviour.[1] What can be counted and measured is more amenable to precise formulation and presentation than other forms of human action. Thinking has been increasingly demoted by default. Because so much is described without reference to it, it has become increasingly assumed or stated to be a peripheral, free standing, or insignificant activity.

As well as reflecting the recent past of political science, there are other, and earlier, and more explicitly theoretical foundations for the division. The principal underpinnings are familiar, even if one goes back no further than Marx or the utilitarians. But what is striking is that even there, an ambivalence is evident which destabilizes any simple hierarchy of ideals and action, or thinking and doing. For if philosophers had only interpreted the world, and the point was now to change it,[2] philosophy must be, potentially, a most powerful form of political action.[3] The observation and the recommendation occurred within the world of philosophical criticism, and were clearly not intended merely, or even principally, as a matter of interpretation. Theory was itself, at least potentially, a 'material force'.[4] Utilitarianism led in similar circles.[5] Bentham's objection to imprescriptible natural rights as 'nonsense upon stilts'[6] was raised not because such rights, or the assertion that such rights existed, were purely reflective and of no consequence, but on the contrary because such claims wreaked havoc, and did so from a great height. Natural rights 'hold out a mask for every crime; – they are every villain's armoury – every spendthrift's treasury'.[7] Whether or not ideas could be viewed as occupying a world distinct from that of action, they clearly visited that world, and visited it with consequences which made the distinction of little practical significance. If ideas and action were judged different in their essences, they certainly seemed remarkably similar in their accidents, and, if judged by their consequences, seemed to be members of the same species.

Contemporary arguments which seek to relegate political ideas, and political thinking, to the realm of the charming but insignificant involve similar arrivals at the point of departure. Kenneth Shepsle has argued that ideas are not in themselves important, but are only means whereby politicians explain or justify their purposes to others. They are 'hooks' as he puts it,[8] on which policies are hung. This argument however depends on the very power of ideas which it is intended to discredit. Unless ideas *were* powerful, they would be of no use in trying to gain support for or justify policies.[9] Sky hooks are of no use whatsoever. Shepsle's argument illustrates the way in which the assumption of a distinction between 'ideas' and other features of politics has constantly to invoke precisely what it seeks to deny: the central role of thinking, and the production and use of ideas, in all politics. It is impossible to describe what is labelled an action without reference to what are separately labelled the ideas which inform and justify it, just as it is impossible to isolate what is defined as an idea without immediately speaking of the actions with which it is associated or by which it is expressed and transmitted. Whether or not an analytical distinction can be sustained, a descriptive one cannot.

The argument about the insignificance of ideas frequently has two other components, each of which is equally difficult to sustain. The first makes a distinction between ordinary people, who may be influenced by ideas though elites are not, the second gives an account of the actions of elites in material or objective terms which claims to leave no place for thinking as a formative or influential activity. So the argument turns out to be the familiar one that the true reasons for action are known to an elite, who use ritual, deception, religion, the dignified aspects of the constitution, or whatever, to gain support for their actions amongst the common people. Ideas, in other words, *are* important and powerful, but only amongst ordinary people.[10] The second component is the displacement of the role of ideas in the opposite direction. Ideas, it is argued, do not motivate politicians, but are used to justify or gain support for their policies or their interests. Shepsle writes that his own view 'on the force of ideas is to see them as one of the hooks on which politicians hang their objectives and by which they further their interests'.[11] This responds to the problem of the character and function of ideas by subordinating them to 'objectives' and 'interests'. Each of these is presented as if it were objective and unproblematic. Each is in fact just as difficult as 'ideas'. One devil has been replaced by two, and the expulsion of 'ideas' does no more than make room for two troublemakers instead one. We are left with the question of the character of those objectives and interests, and of how it is possible to describe them or for politicians to act upon them without their being intellectually constructed.[12] Neither of the two principal answers is satisfactory. The first is that the interest of the politician is objective and exists independently of any action of her or his own. This answer must either say that a perception by a politician of an interest different from that which is objectively given is both false and ineffectual, or impossible. The second answer is that interests are socially constructed, and that although they are neither materially shaped nor determined, they are provided for the actor by his or her social location, and may even create the self which the actor believes he or she has. But this is simply the displacement answer performing a slightly different duty. Perception, thinking, is important, but it is the perception which shapes, influences, or determines a person's interest, not his or her own thinking, which matters. Thinking as an independent variable in other words, like the end of the rainbow, is always in the next field.

Doubts and Qualifications: Rationality Revised

Such difficulties have not gone unnoticed. Even amongst those who have seemed most fervently to insist on a division between thinking and doing, there have always been doubts and qualifications. The pure doctrine has to some extent to be constructed from implications and assumptions, rather than read off in all its apparent ruthless simplicity. Even those who remained impressed by the potential of the approach to explain social life have always avoided the possible behaviouralist limitations of rational choice and utilitarian theory. From John Stuart Mill onwards, the mechanistic version of utilitarianism has been rejected. More recently, claims have been made for what has been described as the 'independent force of ideas' or the 'material force of ideas'.[13] To an extent, this argument is no more than an acknowledgement, to which the democratic empiricism of rational choice commits it, of the need to take seriously the fact that the subject matter of the enquiry, people, do themselves take ideas seriously.

Rational choice theorizing has always needed to describe subjective choices. This has been so not only with what Patrick Dunleavy has described as endogenous groups, where membership depends upon an individual having a particular conception of her or his own identity, but with exogenous groups as well, where the conditions and qualifications for membership can be presented as external to the individual actor. Dunleavy describes membership of exogenous groups as depending on the individual actor 'recognizing', 'accepting' and 'knowing' about the existence of the group and of her objective sharing in its identity.[14] But 'recognizing', 'accepting' and 'knowing' are simply the words used by empiricists, and materialists, and indeed some idealists, for belief, thinking, and supposition. The choice of words sustains the belief that thought is the registration of incontestable external and independent truths. Different people, however, know different things and recognize different external circumstances. Once such words have been let into the narrative, action becomes a far more complex matter than simple response, or failure of response, to objective circumstance. Action in part creates the circumstance, and without it the circumstances have no significant social existence.

Recent work, particularly in international relations, has applied these qualifications more systematically to rational choice theory. Judith Goldstein and Robert Keohane, following Weber's railway points operator analogy, have argued that ideas should be seen as 'road maps', Edward Rhodes has argued against allowing theories of bureaucratic power to eclipse the role of ideas.[15] In the study of public policy increasing attention is being given to the 'learning' or 'transfer' of policies as a process distinct from the search for power or the defence or pursuit of interests.[16]

Ideas as Forces

But whilst the dichotomization of ideas and action has come in for increasing salutary criticism, some of the proposed solutions carry disadvantages. The implication or assumption that ideas are things, goods, objects, is open to major objections not least of which is that it implies that they can be active in human life in the manner of the weather, without any necessary human intervention. When Shepsle writes that he prefers to think of the 'convenience' rather than the 'force' of ideas he is making a sound point.[17] The difference between a force and a convenience is the difference between something active by itself, and something which is either an instrument of human action or an aspect or product of such action. Not only is an idea the product of human action, but unless human action continues, the idea has no significant existence. Ideas are not active forces unless they take human shape, and an idea which is not stated, expressed, or published, does not exist. Gramsci's *Prison Notebooks*, or Marx's *Grundrisse*, or the poems of Gerard Manley Hopkins had no significant existence during the long period when they remained unpublished. It made sense to speak of them as political writings or as poems only when they were being read, when, in other words, they were part of the intellectual activity of a reader.

Even when ideas have been expressed, unless they are published, in the broadest sense of that word, they have only private significance. To think privately, whether that action is conducted silently, committed to paper, or recorded, is to speak only to oneself. To think publicly is to think in a way in which others can hear, read, or see.[18] Before ideas can be seen as genies in bottles, they need also to be seen as requiring Aladdin not only to open the bottle, but to employ the spirit within it. So to propose a solution to the difficulties presented by the division of human action into 'ideas' and 'action' by talking of the material force of ideas solves no important problems, and creates or revives new ones.

If ideas cannot be seen as active forces waiting to be discovered and let loose on the world,[19] nor can they be seen as phenomena lurking in the mind waiting to be expressed. Ideas are the products of thinking, not its precursors, and the action of thinking is not to be distinguished from action as such. Political ideas, even one's own, are apprehended only as statements.[20]

An objection can nonetheless be raised on behalf of conceiving of ideas as active forces. If ideas have no independent force, what is to be made of arguments such as E. P. Thompson's about the function of the rule of law in eighteenth century Britain?[21] The answer is that it is not the rule of law as an independent force which constrains peoples' further thinking and acting. Thinking in a certain way has implications for what else you can do and cannot do, and thinking the Rule of Law in a certain way affects what you can readily do next.

There is a further dimension to the problem. Not only is the role of 'ideas' problematic, but so is the identity of the phenomenon to which the term 'ideas' is attached. When Shepsle writes of ideas, what he clearly has in mind are broad justificatory principles, the a priori or in his mind post facto legitimations of policy. A possible consequence of this narrow definition is on the one hand to accord the products of thinking on such matters an autonomous existence, as if the ideas were somehow just there, and on the other to treat such 'grand' thinking as an active and sophisticated intellectual activity, and all other kinds of thinking as a response to or a reflex of material, social, or economic patterns or events. This possibility is tempered by Shepsle's reference to 'Prevalent ideas, from the cruder forms of patriotism to subtle principles of economics'.[22] But the wider the net is cast, the more ideas become characteristic of all politics and impossible to exclude from a consideration of any part of it. And the more narrowly it is cast, the more it makes thinking an elite activity, with all the disadvantages which that entails.

Democratic Empiricism

To deny independent force to ideas is not to deny the centrality of thinking to politics. It is to insist that when we speak of ideas we are speaking of a ubiquitous product or dimension of human action. The recent doubts about the wisdom of abandoning ideas to a kind of upper house of last resort have arisen in part because attempts to explain political life without an account of thinking as a fundamental dimension of political action have come to seem increasingly inadequate. But the doubts may also be a consequence of that democratic empiricism which even if not always expressed in rational choice theory, is implied in it. Inherent to an understanding of political life as rational is a belief that people act rationally, or act as if they were calculating rationally, even if the immediate impression given to an observer is quite different.[23] What people do, in other words, should be treated seriously, and whilst reasons which are not necessarily apparent can be induced to explain their conduct, their conduct cannot be dismissed as either foolish or of no account.

Democratic empiricism places a double obligation on the social scientist. The democratic obligation is to begin with a presumption that just as every one's vote is worth no more and no less than anyone else's, and just as each person has an equal range of rights, so what each person does or says should be treated with equal seriousness. The empirical obligation is to be respectful towards the evidence and deferential in its collection. Evidence should be free range rather than battery reared. A major part of what we recognize as politics and government is not directly of the kind which, in a utilitarian or practical account, would be seen as its main business. A crude count of time would probably find that a great deal of effort is expended, and time spent, on talking, arguing, posturing, rhetoric, ritual, and the culitivation of identity and reputation. But if that is what people do, we are obliged to begin with that.

II

A major objection to conceptions of politics which distinguish rigidly between ideas and action is that they do not accord with the integrated character of political action. It is not that accounts which add in ideas as a distinct and separate variable give them an inappropriate or underplayed role in relation to interests, ambitions etc., but rather that without thinking and hence without ideas those interests and ambitions are inconceivable. Thinking provides the means for redefinitions of identity, interest, and ambitions, though rarely through a rogue or pure idea alone. Action is not simple physical movement, but both expressive of and informed by thinking. Separation may be analytically justifiable, but if it is not the basis for subsequent synthesis or contextualization, it describes artificial and partial entities. If on the contrary action is seen as a human physical event with an intellectual dimension, this involves at least two possible levels of response to the old dichotomy.

The Diffident Response

The diffident response to the division is the material force of ideas with a human face.[24] Ideas are important if for no other reason than that people accord importance to them, and devote time and attention and energy to their communication. Political thinking is itself a form of activity, and neither by its nature nor by its consequences can it be set in an enclosure apart from other forms of human action. But that response leads ineluctably to a stronger response.

The Robust Response: Politics as an Intellectual Activity

There have been plenty of metaphors, organic and mechanical, for ideas. They have been described as lenses which focus the vision.[25] The disadvantage of lenses, like hooks, is that they both suggest something that is external to the actor, that has its own irreducible character, and that can be readily shifted from person to person. But ideas are not best seen as either hooks or lenses. They are part of the person who uses them to cultivate a relationship with the external world, rather than objects in that world. They function as part of the person of whose character they are a major component. Either eyes or hands would be more allusive metaphors. But if they are therefore more usefully seen in metaphor as hands rather than hooks, they are significant as hands only when active. Nor can they be transplanted without assuming a different character, as part of the new wholeness of which they then become a part. *The Hands of Orlac*,[26] in which a murderer's hands, grafted onto the arms of a wounded concert pianist, play havoc with his Schubert and his private life, is not an accurate account of thinking, any more than in fact it is of hands. Ideas are not only the product of human thinking, but they can be apprehended and used only in human thinking. We need to be able to give an account or construct a metaphor which makes sense of an integrated politics in which people construct what they are doing, reflect upon it, and justify or condemn it. This involves the creation of accounts of identity and hence of interests, and of accounts of the values, aspirations and aversions which give those identities normative depth. The relationship between these various kinds of thinking will be organic, rather than causal in a mechanical way.

If thinking is to be seen as a constituting aspect of politics,[27] then there is neither a world out there independent of human action, nor a kind of action from which thinking can be excluded. The social world is created by human action as much as human action is set within it, and human action is both impossible and inconceivable without thinking. Within such an account, action will have one or both of two characters: physical or communicative. It would be directed either at the material world or at other people. Ideas are the product of such action. Action is the creation or maintenance of an individual or social condition that is appropriate to our perception of ourselves. This will involve the telling of stories and the 'staging' of the world. Action is the creation, cultivation and defence of appropriate conditions. It is also the way in which perception exists. There are, in other words, no prior assumptions about the importance, significance, or causal dominance of one form of human activity over another. Reflection is not necessarily prior to practice. It is indeed a form of practice.

Action

An account of human life which treats thinking as the characteristic human activity is of course part of a well established tradition in the social sciences. 'We shall speak of "action" insofar as the acting individual attaches a subjective meaning to his behaviour'.[28] And if action is meaningful behaviour, the meaning does not and cannot precede the behaviour – it is expressed in the behaviour. To act is to do things in a certain way with the expectation of effects, or in accordance with an image of the sort of person it is who is acting. In either case the 'idea' which makes the action appropriate is inseparable from it, and the appropriateness of the action lies either in the fact that it is a mode of acting which is in character, or that it will achieve or contribute to results which are appropriate for the character. This character may be established or in the process of cultivation. This understanding of action differs from that used or implied in rational utilitarian modelling, where beliefs and values are analytically distinct from and chronologically prior to physical movements in relation to other people or to objects.[29] It sees them rather as an aspect or condition of action being action and not simply behaviour.

Political Action

The claim that political thinking is a form of political activity, and that all forms of political activity are meaningful, that action is necessarily composed of intention, communication, and physical impact, is distinguishable from a claim that all forms of action are part of a seamless system, or that they are all part of an interrelated system. It may be accompanied by that claim, but it does not require it.[30] The record of political science suggests, anyway, a far more variegated solution.

Answers have already been proposed for particular parts of the territory. Each account describes a small amount of the terrain, and the relationships, in some directions, between some of the areas of activity. The relationship between normative political theory and ideology;[31] between policy aspirations and pursued policy,[32] between voting and beliefs and ideas, between operative or vocational ideologies, and the management of public business have produced a growing literature. The new institutionalism is a contemporary account which recaptures this insight into the existence of institutions as patterns of ideas and values which are partly external and hence objective to any single individual, but are nonetheless the creation of human action.[33] It is the relation *between* these various kinds of activity which is the problem. But it is not necessary to describe the relationship of everything to everything else. Nor do we have to reduce distinctions by an overbearing emphasis on common denominators.

But the result of an attempt to take account of all these dimensions of human action, and more, is not to privilege the role of thinking, but to dissolve it. The resulting account would not place thinking in the role of a dominant or overarching function. Rather it would insist that thinking, and the production and use of and limitation by ideas is characteristic of all human action. The existing categorizations of organization, coercion, reflection, legislation, persuasion, propaganda, campaigning, administering, judging, would not be jettisoned. But they would be described as each a form, and not a wholly distinct or autonomous or self-contained form, of human action. Such action cannot be understood by means of the old dualism. This will make the task of describing and analysing both more difficult and more unpredictable. It will make it also closer to the complexity of the phenomena of which it attempts to give an account.

What appears to be required is therefore a way of describing politics which takes account of the use of ideas and the role of thinking in *all* political action, and which makes distinctions accordingly. If interests are then to be singled out in a particular piece of analysis, it will not be because they have a given materiality, but because they constitute people thinking in a particular way, and in a way which constructs, cultivates, or sustains a particular aspect of their public identity.

Ideas are not then some singular accompaniment of certain kinds of human social activity, but an integral aspect of all such activity. This does not make less useful the categorization of ideas into principles, ideas about causality, ideas about circumstances etc. But it starts with the recognition that humans are active, constructing creatures, and that their characteristic constructive activity is thinking.

Thinking still has many forms, and a public intellectual is acting in a way different from that of an administrator, or a political propagandist. Experts and intellectuals, equally, are engaged in different forms of action. But all these activities involve thinking and both draw on and produce statements which are heard or read by others as ideas.

Because thinking, or political thinking, is a public activity, it will be constrained and facilitated in varying ways by the social relations in which the thinker is situated. Thinking is not in that respect free and unconstrained. A person whose identity is shaped in part on the shared construction of a religious or national identity, cannot readily think herself a new identity with the ease with which she can think herself a new interpretation of natural or social phenomena. Ernest Barker's balloon theory therefore made the mistake of reducing all ideas to a single currency, one which could be traded without trouble in a college library or an academic disputation.[34] A theory about who you are is more embedded, both personally and socially, than a theory about the operation of legislatures or the behaviour of molluscs.

Interests and Enemies

That what are termed action, thinking, and interests cannot be considered apart from one another, is illustrated in the involvement of all these dimensions of political life in the depiction of enemies. A conception of enemies is the corollary of a concept of friends, and each is part of a concept of interests.[35] But although enemies are objective for the purposes of historical or social science enquiry, they are contingent and subjective at the same time. They can be neither understood nor even identified without conceiving, indeed perceiving, politics as a form of human action and hence as human thinking. Such thinking does not so much precede acts, as constitute them.[36] Politics as action rather than as behaviour, politics as an essentially thinking activity, is most readily evident in this central features of political life.

Perhaps the person who did not have an enemy in the world never existed, because without enemies, existence as a social and human event, is difficult or impossible. Commenting on the cultivation of a Swedish national identity during the Thirty Years War, Erik Ringmar observes that 'the description of the enemy was a mirror image which affirmed the Swedish identity by defining its opposite: the Swedes knew what they were when they knew what they were *not*.'[37] There has always been a recognition within political science of the role of enemies.[38] For Adam Ferguson, society was given vigour and cohesion, and civilization made possible, by animosity and hostility to other societies.[39] For Carl Schmitt politics was structured on the identification of enemies and the consolidation of alliances with friends.[40] Anthony Crosland commented on the psychological necessity of enemies, and the distress and disturbance caused when the reality, or location, of the enemy was questioned: 'A people enjoying full employment and social security has lost its dreams, and lost the need to struggle; and the activists in consequence feel restless and frustrated. That is why they resent revisionist thinkers who compel them to face the new reality, and try to delude themselves that all the old enemies – capitalist barons, Wall Street, exploiting profiteers – are still there, waiting to be attacked.'[41]

Accounts of the way depictions of enemies and identities are constructed, cultivated, and expressed describe also the relation between perception and conception, aims and means, aspirations and understanding. What we want, and what we can achieve, are aspects of what we are, just as the unacceptable *and* the impractical are indicated by those against whose difference we mark out our own character. Enemies and allies, and the cultivation of identity, give an account of social life which relates interests and values as aspects of an organic whole. Interest becomes a perception, created, cultivated, or received. Enemies define themselves in part only: we create, define, and choose our enemies as well. In so doing we create, define, and choose our interests. What my interests are and what I value are alike part of what I am. Without such an identity I can have neither interests nor values. Interests are an aspect of identity, hence the particular character of their objectivity.

III

An account which, seeing politics as an activity, describes the use of enemies in the construction of political life, can illuminate politics at the close of the chronological twentieth century. An account of recent changes in the taxonomy of politics that employs a conventional distinction between ideas, or thinking, and action, is inadequate for two reasons. Either it restricts the account to one aspect or dimension of the phenomena it is explaining, or it divides thinking and acting, or both. The end of socialism and conservatism is a phenomenon expressed in all forms of politics. The end of the short twentieth century cannot be discussed only as an intellectual reflective event, or only as one of 'practical' politics.

Political identity draws sustenance from the depiction of enemies, and political thinking cultivates both alien and fraternal identities. When the managerial communist regimes of the USSR and eastern Europe abdicated after 1989, one of the frequent descriptions of what had happened was that this was a vindication of or a victory for the western way of life. A form of politics, which was a form of thinking about and accounting for and describing and justifying and creating human action had won in the competition with a rival. But victories are seldom simple, nor is a story of success in political conflict an adequate account of what frequently occurs. It is identity which enemies both challenge and create – not just physical security, but the way in which we think of ourselves and of the world. Hobsbawm, amongst many others, makes the point: 'we have all been marked' by the impact of the Russian Revolution of 1917, 'inasmuch as we got used to thinking of the modern industrial economy in terms of binary opposites, "capitalism" and "socialism" as alternatives mutually excluding one another'.[42] In the chronological twentieth century, for many people in Western Europe and North America, there have been two principal perceived threats. Now both have gone and identity is in suspension or flux.

The political actions to be described in an account of the aftermath of the short twentieth century range from the publishing of statements to the construction of governments, from the formulation of new ways of making claims on behalf of political parties to changes in the allocation of resources of money, time, and personnel by governments. A related series of changes requires description: shifts in the landscape of political discussion, the polarities of party politics and policy discussion, and the location and identity of friends and enemies. The changes in the way political reflection or advocacy are carried out cannot be separated from other kinds of actions.

The removal of enemies creates fluidity, and there has been a search for new locations and new enemies. The disappearance of Russian Communism has displaced one devil, and the owners of the house are now casting around for new ones. The existence of the Soviet Union provided not simply a standard enemy, but a polarity which, depending where one located oneself on it, gave a choice of both allies and antagonists. Capitalism and socialism, totalitarianism and democracy, markets and planning, were all available as grid references on the political map. With their waning, other markers were established: denial of identity, egregious identity, faith, fundamentalism, poverty, greed. The work of political thinkers has become, amongst other things, an attempt not just to map but to create the new terrain.

Since human generations do not coincide neatly with historical ones, the actors in the aftermath of the short twentieth century are frequently those who had been part of the politics of the former era. The politics of the aftermath is thus a politics of movement and an attempt to construct new accounts of location and purpose. This phenomenon can be viewed in all forms of political life, from the organization and justification of institutions to the elaboration of analysis and advocacy. New enemies are identified and described in order to clarify identities which the disappearance of old enemies have eroded or evaporated.

It might be argued that the new enemies did not need to be identified: they forced themselves upon the consciousness of those whom they threatened in a manner that demanded recognition. But that is only part of the story. The nature of the threat was to culture and identity as much as to physical security or even physical well being. As such it required that the enemy be not only acknowledged, but described. Action, choice, self-description, were involved. At the same time as the world was being reconfigured by the disappearance of managerial communism, the power of central government and the ascendancy of new right thinking in western europe both provided a new enemy for political liberals and the left, and was complemented by their re-description of their own character, aspirations, and aversions. In the area of political analysis and advocacy, writers as different as Paul Hirst in a discovery and examination of early twentieth century English pluralism,[43] John Gray in a long march from market liberalism through green conservatism to an accommodation with New Labour,[44] Andrew Gamble, or Hilary Wainwright in two very different selective uses of and accommodations with the work of F.A. Hayek,[45] can be observed in peripatetic search for redescribed identities, as old enemies are rehabilitated, redescribed, or made redundant, and new aspirations and aversions are described.

One of the enemies now described was one that would have been recognized by many of the left before the Great War: 'the despotic tendencies built into the British constitution'.[46] But precisely because enemies, to be identified, and whatever their objective reality, have also to be chosen and described, the descriptions varied as did the political identities of the describers. For John Gray, as for Herbert Spencer a little over a century before, it was as if the hostile principles had remained much the same, but the persons and institutions who had embodied them had shifted and changed places. A belief in 'the limitations of reason' which was grounds for being enthusiastic about the arguments of F. A. Hayek in the the 1980s,[47] was associated, ten years later, with a furious assault upon the New Right which claimed Hayek as one of its chief intellectual inspirations, as representing 'the triumph of an ideology'.[48] For both Andrew Gamble and Hilary Wainwright, the passing of the high point of the influence of the New Right made possible a selective use of the arguments of Hayek. Wainwright could praise 'the distinctive importance of "everyday" or uncodified knowledge'[49] in a manner which would have been less easy when that knowledge seemed to be solidly part of a major antagonist, the right wing liberal commendation of the subtle understanding embodied in markets. For once enemies are replaced, their inheritance can be redistributed.[50]

None of these changes is as fully understood as it can be if it is seen as no more than a reaction to objective circumstance. The circumstances themselves were both constituted by action, and understood by means of accounts which were not themselves determined. Political action was constructed neither by whim nor of necessity, but in creative representation.

IV

Thinking Politics and Thinking about Politics

New ways of thinking about politics are both the condition of and a feature of new ways of conducting politics. Thinking 'about' politics is to that extent better described as thinking politics. The account suggested here is more readily expressed by an organic metaphor than by a mechanical one. This has implications for the status of laws, models, and theories. They give accounts of possibilities: possible actions. But they do not make robust predictions about sequences of events.[51] They are likely, though, to predict constitutive relationships of characteristics and actions to each other. The disappearance of the uniting enemy is accompanied by the disappearance of the uniting utilitarian paradigm. A polarized politics facilitates an analysis of politics which is similarly homogeneous. The more varied the forms of political action described, the more varied and flexible the analyses are likely to be.

Where to?

The peril which lies in the path for those who deny the usefulness of established distinctions, is that they risk having to describe everything, a responsibility of which the old divisions sensibly absolved them. Some of the critics of taking political thinking too seriously have, either explicitly or implicitly, advanced the difficulties in so doing as a reason for not trying. Shepsle, discussing one of the examples he employs in his 'hooks' argument, asks whether the ideas were 'in fact the motivation for the veto or were they just cosmetic? Hard to say, and this is precisely the problem with offering the force of ideas as an explanation.'[52] Very possibly, but problems ought to be seen as an incentive to further enquiry, not a deterrent. The simplicity of a solution does not recommend it if it works only by leaving difficult relationships out of account. The difficulty of explaining relationships is not a reason for leaving consideration of them to one side.

What I am proposing is not a new theory, nor the adoption of a new perspective on causality whereby politics can be described from the point of view of some one fundamental or over-determining factor, structure, or process. Something more modest is envisaged: a shift of emphasis, so that even though many of the existing conceptions and existing patterns of description remain, the account is given fuller dimension and, without pursuing homogeneity, greater interconnectedness. The words that are used to describe politics cannot be replaced. Much can be achieved if it is taken as a working assumption that analytical distinctions like ideal types should not be mistaken for adequate images of politics. That will guarantee neither easy or even possible answers, nor a simple or straightforward set of research programmes. But it will widen the focus of political science at the same time as increasing its unpredictability. That is a prospect which is entirely appropriate for the end of a century in which political science has grown up in symbiosis with democracy, and for the the beginning of a century in which all options, especially the ones we have not yet observed or described, are likely to be open.

Notes

An earlier version of this chapter, as well as being discussed with members of the seminar of contributors to this book, was presented to a seminar at the London School of Economics, and I am grateful to colleagues there, especially to Chun Lin and Erik Ringmar, for their comments

1   Desmond King has explained this characteristic of recent political science in the UK and the USA as in part a result of the political context within which funding for the social sciences originated. D. King, 'The politics of social research: institutionalizing public funding regimes in the United States and Britain', *British Journal of Political Science*, 28, 3 (1998), 415–444.

2   Karl Marx, 'Theses on Feurbach, XI', in David McLellan (ed.), *Karl Marx:–Selected Writings*. Oxford: Oxford University Press, 1977, p.158.

3   See Michael Freeden in this volume, p.302–322.

4   Karl Marx, 'Towards a Critique of Hegel's "Philosophy of Right"' in McLellan, *Karl Marx: Selected Writings*, p.69.

5   It could be argued that rational choice theory is dependent on mind. But it frequently assumes a mind with a mechanical and universal manner of operation that can be both observed and predicted.

6   Jeremy Bentham, 'Anarchical Fallacies' in J. Bowring (ed.), *Works*. London: Simpkin, Marshall, 1843, vol. 2, p.501.

7   Bentham, 'Anarchical Fallacies', p. 524, quoted Nancy L. Rosenblum, *Bentham's Theory of the State*. London: Harvard University Press, 1978, p.56.

8   Kenneth A. Shepsle, 'Comment' in Roger Noll (ed.), *Regulatory Politics and the Social Sciences*. Berkeley; University of California Press, 1985, pp.231–7 ('ideas don't effect changes, people do'), a remark which has the same logical character as the more familiar 'guns don't kill people, people do'. (Until recently, a seemingly devastating riposte to that argument was, 'try using a cucumber next time you're at the OK corral'. However, the following report weakens the case: 'A man who held up a bank in Glenties, Co. Donegal, with a cucumber has been given a six-month suspended jail sentence. James Conway held the cucumber, hidden by a plastic bag, like a weapon when he demanded IR£100.' *The Independent*, Thursday 15 October 1998, p.7.)

9 As Stefan Collini long ago pointed out, 'It is one mark of the cynic that he sees other people's expressions of their principles as a kind of smokescreen for their putative "real interests", but even were he always correct it would not follow that the study of such statements was devoid of explanatory power. Even the most disingenuous legitimation involves an appeal to existing characterisations' Stefan Collini, *Liberalism & Sociology: L.T Hobhouse & Political Argument in England 1880–1914*. Cambridge; Cambridge University Press, 1979, p.10.

10 Reviewing Green and Shapiro's *Pathologies of Rational Choice Theory*, Stewart Wood and Iain McLean make the damaging concession that the attack on rational choice theory and voting is justified, and that while it 'makes little sense to argue that voters are rational calculators, it makes a lot of sense to argue that legislators and lobbyists are', *Political Studies*, 43, 4 (1995), p. 706.

11 Shepsle, 'Comment', p.233.

12 Christopher Hood has commented that 'the further we move from "harder" to "softer" versions of the "primacy of ideas" approach, the harder it will be to distinguish "ideas" from "interests" '. Christopher Hood, *Explaining Economic Policy Reversals*. Buckingham; Open University Press, 1994, p.7.

13 John Kurt Jacobsen, 'Much ado about ideas: the cognitive factor in economic policy', *World Politics*, 47, 2, (1995), p.283.

14 Patrick Dunleavy, *Democracy, Bureaucracy and Public Choice: Economic Explanations in Political Science*. Hemel Hempstead; Harvester Wheatsheaf, 1991, pp. 54–7.

15 Judith Goldstein and Robert O. Keohane (eds), *Ideas and Foreign Policy: Beliefs, Institutions, and Political Change*. Ithaca: Cornell University Press, 1993, pp. 13–14; Edward Rhodes, 'Do bureaucratic politics matter? Some disconfirming findings from the case of the U. S. Navy', *World Politics*, 47, 1, (1994), 1–41.

16 See for instance Diane Stone, 'Learning lessons and transferring policy across time, space and disciplines', *Politics*, 19, 1 (1999), 51–9; David Dolowitz and David Marsh, 'Who learns from whom: a review of the policy transfer literature', *Political Studies*, 44, 2 (1996), 343–57; Desmond King and Randall Hansen, 'Experts at work: state autonomy, social learning and eugenic sterilization in 1930s Britain', *British Journal of Political Science*, 29, 1(1999), 77–107 ; John Greenaway, 'Policy learning and the drink question in Britain: 1850–1950, *Political Studies*, 46, 5, (1998); Peter Hall, 'Policy paradigms, social learning, and the state: the case of economic policy-making in Britain', *Comparative Politics*, 25, (1993), 275–96; C. Radaelli, 'The role of knowledge in the policy process', *Journal of European Public Policy*, 2, (1995), 159–83; A. Hann, 'Sharpening up Sabatier: belief systems and public policy', *Politics*, 15 (1995), 19–26; Peter John, 'Ideas and interests; agendas and implementation: an evolutionary explanation of policy change in British local government finance', *Journal of Politics and International Relations* 1, 1 (1999), 39–62.

17 Shepsle, 'Comment', p. 234.

18 As Randall Collins argues when casting doubt on the importance, or frequent existence, of philosophical 'isolates' and as Andrew Chadwick argues in this special issue. Randall Collins, *The Sociology of Philosophies: a Global Theory of Intellectual Change*. Cambridge MA: Belknap Press/Harvard University Press, 1999.

19 Christopher Hood uses the image of ideas as meteors, 'hitting the world of public policy with sudden and devastating effect'. Christopher Hood, *Explaining Economic Policy Reversals*. Buckingham: Open University Press, 1994, p.5.

20 And perhaps as statements which are immediately they are made seen as in some sense beyond the maker of those statements, who is now the observer. 'When the mind is like a hall in which thought is like a voice speaking, the voice is always that of someone else.' Wallace Stevens, quoted John Burnside, *A Normal Skin*. London: Jonathan Cape, 1997, p. vii.

21 E. P. Thompson, *Whigs and Hunters*. London: Allen Lane, 1975, p. 263; 'And the rulers were, in serious senses, whether willingly or unwillingly, the prisoners of their own rhetoric; they played the games of power according to rules which suited them, but they could not break those rules or the whole game would be thrown away.'

22 Shepsle, 'Comment', p. 235

23 Robert Keohane comments of rational choice accounts of human action that they are 'a theoretically useful simplification of reality rather than a true reflection of it'. Robert O. Keohane, *After Hegemony: Cooperation and Discord in the World Political Economy*. Princeton: Princeton University Press, 1984, p. 108, quoted in Goldstein, and Keohane (eds), *Ideas and Foreign Policy: Beliefs, Institutions, and Political Change*, p.5. But the insight cannot stop there. If people act as if they were rational, and if all rational action has this quality, then even the most un-utilitarian actions must be analysed to discover what metaphor of rationality, and what understanding of the thinking of the actors, would render them comprehensible.

24 I have argued this myself elsewhere. Rodney Barker, *Political Ideas in Modern Britain in and after the Twentieth Century*. London: Routledge, 1997, pp.4–6.

25 Jacobsen, 'Much ado about ideas', p.293.

26 Karl Freund, *The Hands of Orlac* (1934).

27 This can be compared with the comment of Ball, Farr and Hanson that 'politics is a linguistically constituted activity', Terence Ball, James Farr and Russell L. Hanson (eds), *Political Innovation and Conceptual Change*. Cambridge: Cambridge University Press, 1989, p. ix.

28 Max Weber in Guenther Roth and Claus Wittich (eds), *Economy and Society*, two volumes. London: University of California Press, 1978, p.4.

29 See for instance the account in Keith Dowding, *Rational Choice and Political Power*. Cheltenham: Edward Elgar, 1991, p. 23.

30 As Margaret Archer puts it, ideas and interests are 'not separate entities, only analytically separable ones'. Margaret Archer, *Culture and Agency: The Place of Culture in Social Theory*. Cambridge: Cambridge University Press, 1988, fn. 86 p. xiii quoted Jacobsen, 'Much ado about ideas', p. 309.

31 Michael Freeden, *Ideologies and Political Theory: a Conceptual Approach*. Oxford: Clarendon, 1996.

32 Goldstein and Keohane, *Ideas and Foreign Policy: Beliefs, Institutions, and Political Change*; Robert D. Putnam with Robert Leonardi and Raffaella Nanetti, *Making Democracy Work: Civic Traditions in Modern Italy*. Princeton: Princeton University Press, 1993; Rhodes, 'Do bureaucratic politics matter?'; Abrar, Lovenduski and Margetts in this volume, pp.239–261.

33 It is an account less removed than might at first appear from Hayek's Darwinian account of the evolution of institutions.

34 Conflicts between groups depended upon ideas, he argued, and 'one can deflate a bubble idea with a prick of logic'. E. Barker, 'The discredited state', *Political Quarterly*, February1915, p.113.

35 The sociological theory of exclusion deals with a similar and related observation. See for instance Frank Parkin, *Marxism and Class Theory: a Bourgeois Critique*. London: Tavistock, 1979.

36 'Once we have rejected the notion of a transcendental "real self", however, it seems difficult to make any form of references to "real reasons" behind an action.' Erik Ringmar, *Identity, Interest and Action: a Cultural Explanation of Sweden's Intervention in the Thirty Years War*. Cambridge: Cambridge University Press, 1996, p.60.

37 Ringmar, *Identity, Interest and Actioni*, p.165.

38 And not only within political science. Edmund White points out the observation, by novelists as varied as Kurt Vonnegut and Philip Hensher, that rulers and politicians choose to have enemies in order to consolidate the identity of their own societies. Edmund White, 'Sinister blandishments', *London Review of Books*, 20, 17, 3 September 1998, p.18. A similar reading can be made of the wars presented, by cinema, to the subjugated population of *1984*.

39 Adam Ferguson in Vincenzo Merolle (ed.), *The Correspondence of Adam Ferguson*. London: Pickering, 1995.

40 Carl Schmitt, *The Concept of the Political* (translated and introduced by George Schwab, with a new foreword by Tracy B. Strong). Chicago IL: University of Chicago Press, 1996.

41 C. A. R. Crosland, *The Future of Socialism*. London: Jonathan Cape, 1956, p. 100.

42 Eric Hobsbawm, *Age of Extremes: the Short Twentieth Century 1914–1991*. London: Michael Joseph, 1994, p.4

43 Paul Hirst (ed.), *The Pluralist Theory of the State: Selected Writings of G. D. H. Cole, J. N. Figgis, and H. J. Laski*. London: Routledge, 1989; Paul Hirst, *Associative Democracy: New Forms of Economic and Social Governance*. Cambridge: Polity, 1994; Paul Hirst, 'Introduction', *The Collected Works of Harold Laski*, 10 volumes. London: Routledge; Paul Hirst, *From Statism to Pluralism: Democracy, Civil Society and Global Politics*. London: UCL Press, 1997.

44 John Gray, *Hayek on Liberty*. Oxford: Blackwell, 1984; John Gray, *The Undoing of Conservatism*. London: 1994; John Gray, *After Social Democracy*. London: Demos, 1996; John Gray, *Endgames*. Cambridge: Polity, 1997; John Gray and David Willetts, *Is Conservatism Dead?* London: Profile Books, 1997; John Gray, *Beyond the New Right*. London: Routledge, 1993; John Gray, *Post-Liberalism: Studies in Political Thought*. London: Routledge, 1993; John Gray, *Enlightenment's Wake: Politics and Culture at the Close of the Modern Age*. London: Routledge, 1995.

45 Andrew Gamble, *Hayek: the Iron Cage of Liberty*. Cambridge: Polity, 1996; Hilary Wainwright, *Arguments for a New Left: Answering the Free Market Right*. Oxford: Blackwell, 1994.

46 Hirst, *The Pluralist Theory of the State*, p.6.

47 Gray, *Hayek on Liberty*, p.113.

48 Gray, *Beyond the New Right*, p.5.

49 Wainwright, *Arguments for a New Left*, p. 261.

50 The life and survival of institutions can be observed making similar journeys, none more dramatic perhaps than that of state security organizations such as MI5 in the UK, who having lost their defining enemy with the collapse of managerial communism in the Soviet Union, soon lost its replacement with the cessation of political violence in Northern Ireland, and had swiftly to bring on the understudy's understudy in the shape of international crime and drugs.

51 This is a point raised in relation to constructivism in international relations theory by Jeffrey T. Checkel, 'The constructivist turn in international relations theory', *World Politics* 50, 2 (1998), 324–348.

52 Shepsle, 'Comment', p.234.

2

Feminist Ideas and Domestic Violence Policy Change

Stefania Abrar, Joni Lovenduski and Helen Margetts

The extent of influence of feminist ideas and efforts on domestic violence policy has been the subject of some contention. For example Hanmer, Radford and Stanko argue that by 1989 it appeared that '... the police and caring professions have responded ... to feminist criticisms of the 1970s, but have done so in a way which has completely negated feminist definitions, politics, research and provision of support services'. In their view the wide and radical aims of feminist advocates to shift official thinking about domestic violence and to insert feminist practices into policy have not been met. Institutional analyses of the development of domestic violence policy since the early 1970s would, with their emphasis on formal policy making roles tend to concur with this statement. However, if an approach that focuses on the impact of ideas on policy change is used, a different picture emerges; one of feminist driven change. The advocacy coalition framework is such an approach. Using the belief systems of public officials and policy advocates as its starting point, policy oriented learning as its motor of change and policy change as its measure of success the advocacy coalition framework is a pluralist approach to public policy analysis, with a built-in recognition that policy is carried out by a huge and complex array of networked actors.

The advocacy coalition model was developed in the USA and the available evidence from other polyarchies suggests that it will have most utility for policy areas that exhibit pluralistic characteristics.[1] Domestic violence policy is just such an area, complicated by the involvement of actors at different levels of the political system who have different priorities, constraints and traditions including professional values and organizational cultures. These include national and local political elites, national and local officials, regional authorities including the health services and the police, experts and activists. At local level policy delivery is typically the provenance of several agencies. Complex institutional patterns of activity are made more opaque by the nature of domestic violence that is also termed as violence or abuse by known men and spouse abuse.[2] The part played by feminist ideas and the belief systems of relevant officials is central to the policy. Treatment of domestic violence involves a constant struggle to traverse boundaries of public and private, bringing into play a concern with gender relations that has not traditionally informed the study of public policy. The 'radical' feminist policy advocates who brought the issue into the public sphere and keep it there have been unwilling to compromise on their understanding of the causes of, and solutions to, the problem. Action oriented feminist experts are and have been particularly interested in understanding violence at home in a women-centred way, a pre-occupation that is reflected in reports, books, public statements and projects.

Feminist scholarship offers a further reason to adopt the framework. Feminists have noted significant similarities and interconnections between feminist action inside and outside the state. Brownhill and Halford[3] insist that in practice 'people are constantly meeting, consulting or working jointly and resources may constantly change hands'. Eisenstein[4] and Stetson and Mazur[5] observe that feminist advocacy functions most effectively where it has a beachhead in the policy making and implementation institutions. Ideally this takes the form of women's policy machinery, that is agencies with responsibility for sex equality, but also useful are feminist individuals in strategic positions in the important institutions. In her discourse based study of feminist accounts of the state Watson[6] reminds us that it would be wrong to assume that institutional political agendas are monolithic and uniform. Within any institution a range of sympathies will exist and feminist policy advocates have been skilful at exploiting them. Such observations combine to suggest that a policy approach that is sensitive to ideas and belief systems and tracks the policy influence of opposing advocacy coalitions operating across the boundaries of the state will be the most useful in describing policies where feminist coalitions have endeavoured to influence public policy. We argue that such a lens is provided by Paul Sabatier's advocacy coalition framework, 'a descriptive framework outlining what to consider when examining policy change'. Capable of dealing with mess, the framework is a sensible tool for use in an area of research that is currently at the stage of systematic (thick) description of its object. It uses the concept of belief system as 'the template on which change is measured, both with respect to the beliefs of different coalitions and the actual content of public policy'.[7] In this chapter we apply the framework to the making of domestic violence policy in two British localities from the 1970s to the mid 1990s. The case studies demonstrate that by 1995 a significant and effective feminist advocacy apparatus was located around the issue of domestic violence, that considerable feminist influence had been at work and that an identifiable 'traditionalist' opposing coalition was located at various levels of government.

This chapter is in four parts. First, we summarize the advocacy coalition framework as a lens for viewing public policy. Second, we give an account of domestic violence policy in Britain, outlining the roles of two opposing coalitions – feminists and traditionalists. We argue that the concerted nature of the feminist 'advocacy coalition' creates an opposing coalition from the diffuse assortment of state actors involved in domestic violence policy making and implementation, a coalition that favours the status quo and is resistant to feminist approaches. Third, we illustrate our points with a detailed exploration of policy change in two localities. Finally, we offer a concluding assessment of the relative influence of the feminist advocacy coalition on domestic violence policy.

The Advocacy Coalition Framework

The advocacy coalition framework is a theory of policy change and learning. As described by Sabatier and Jenkins-Smith in 1993 it requires a perspective of at least ten years, a focus on policy subsystems, an intergovernmental dimension and the conceptualization of public policy as both analogous to and based upon a belief system capable of establishing value priorities and causal assumptions. The elements of this framework seem especially pertinent to domestic violence policy. For example, the long time span is important because changes in domestic violence policy have taken place only after sustained effort by activists over a significant period of time. Sabatier and Jenkins-Smith argue that for any policy problem (termed policy sub-system), the actors involved in dealing with the problem can be aggregated into a number of advocacy coalitions who 'share a set of normative and causal beliefs and who often act in concert'.[8] Not everyone in a policy subsystem will 'belong to' an advocacy coalition or share its belief system. There will almost certainly be a category of actors termed 'policy brokers' whose dominant concerns are with keeping the level of political conflict within acceptable limits and reaching some 'reasonable solution', for example civil servants. In any subsystem there may also be advocates who do not belong to a coalition, for example, researchers who have skills to offer, but no particular policy stance. By contrast the coalition will consist of those who prioritize policies that arise from their belief system. In Sabatier's analysis, belief systems are not homogenous, but stratified and hierarchical, building upon previous arguments that beliefs are important and complex yet structured dimensions of policy-making.[9] They include what Sabatier terms deep core beliefs, policy core beliefs and secondary aspects. Deep core beliefs are normative and ontological axioms such as beliefs about human nature, the value and priority of freedom, security, power, health. Policy core beliefs are policy propositions such as whether to use market mechanisms or government action to produce policy. Secondary aspects are institutional decisions about policy. Deep core beliefs are hypothesized to be stable and virtually impossible to change from within the subsystem; they are susceptible only to major external influences. Policy core beliefs are difficult to change and secondary aspects are amenable to change under certain circumstances.[10]

In addition to the timeframe, the most important components of the framework for our purposes are its taxonomy of belief systems and its assertion that it is belief systems that drive and constrain policy change which will arise from competition between opposing advocacy coalitions located within and around state institutions. The model has obvious application to the analysis of feminist ideas on domestic violence policy because it incorporates the notion of long term interests, it is driven by beliefs and learning and it can be adapted to explain feminist engagements with state institutions, for example with the police, with women's policy agencies and with individual feminists located in various government institutions. It enables the identification of the part played by feminist core beliefs about the causes and nature of domestic violence and demonstrates the unchanging nature of such beliefs among feminist advocates and, in specific localities and time periods, their role in bringing about policy change. We will suggest that in the case of domestic violence, the traditionalist coalition was prepared, under pressure, to change its policy core beliefs, probably in order to maintain its deep core beliefs. Under the circumstances we describe policy core beliefs will change because of the importance of deep core beliefs, an observation that may have important implications for the application of the framework.

Domestic Violence Policy

New knowledge about domestic violence was part of the outcome of the consciousness raising groups that characterized the 1970s women's liberation movement. The resurgence of feminism created a climate of public opinion that was receptive to thinking about the problems of women who wished to escape violence. British feminist interest in male violence to women and children in the home and family is long-standing. Nineteenth century feminists were concerned about 'spouse abuse' which they thought was largely the product of male alcoholism, hence the slogan 'marry only men who have taken the pledge'. In the 1970s the issue was taken up again by feminists who gathered information on violence at home and became involved in successive campaigns about this issue. According to most accounts this was the issue that split British feminism at the end of the 1970s. At that time British feminist movements were often characterized as divided into two broad wings, socialist feminists who (to simplify) believed male violence to women was the product of capitalist structures and institutions and radical feminists who argued that it was in men's nature to mistreat women. Over time the argument became more sophisticated and divisions blurred, but socialist feminists never accepted the essentialist analysis of domestic violence and radical feminists never quite abandoned it. Versions of this nature–nurture dispute continue to underpin debates in feminism. Parallelling their theoretical disagreement was a functional division of labour in which the main feminist actors on issues of male violence were radical feminists. Other feminists, while supportive of campaigns and action research tended to concentrate their activities in other areas.

From the 1970s onwards a coalition of feminists including local and national experts and activists involving traditional and new feminist women's organizations sought to alter legislation and practice on domestic violence. The advocates consisted of a diverse and informal coalition of activists involving new feminist groups such as the Women's Aid Federation, Rights of Women, Justice for Women, Southall Black Sisters, the Zero Tolerance campaigns and Women Against Violence Against Women as well as the long established groups that are included in the Women's National Commission. Strategies included lobbying, campaigns, research, reports, the establishment of alternative institutions and cultural production such as novels, plays, television documentaries and films. A particularly relevant development was the growth of the women's studies movement providing a means of amassing, assessing and communicating knowledge and beliefs about domestic violence to successive generations of activists. Such knowledge constituted a substantial part of the technical information that was used by feminist advocates.

The Advocacy Coalitions

Feminists

In this array of actors the outlines of two advocacy coalitions of the kind envisaged by Sabatier can be detected: feminists and traditionalists. The feminist advocacy coalition consists of municipal feminists, radical feminist groups, the feminist sections of the women's movement, academics and experts, individual feminists located in relevant agencies, the political parties, local councils, Parliament, the civil service and central government. Although it is possible to conceptualize it as a national coalition, its strength and effectiveness varies significantly by locality. As the framework predicts, the feminist advocates' belief system is deep rooted. The coalition is constructed around individuals who share a deep core belief about the patriarchal nature of gender relations and the empowering, women-centred approaches necessary to solve the problem of domestic violence. It is a core belief of feminist advocates that the distinction between public and private life denies protection to women. Personal security and bodily integrity is systematically more likely to be denied to women than to men. Women are vulnerable not only in public but also at home. Their lack of safety has profound effects on their quality of life and affects their rights and capacities as citizens. Crucial to the radical feminist belief system is the view that the problem is caused by men who, as a group, benefit from violence to women. Women's fear of violence and lack of security underpin the male dominance of gender relations. Radical feminists point to the considerable incidence of organized and deliberate abuse of women and children and argue that the great scale of the problem means that its cause is located not in individual male traits but in crucial aspects of maleness. Policy core beliefs follow logically. Solutions, they argue, must be women-centred, and must address fundamental institutions such as the family and heterosexuality.[11] Although short term measures are useful and necessary to address current victimization, long term and radical strategies are needed to eliminate male violence to women. Such strategy must be empowering, giving women both autonomy and safety without turning them into victims or prisoners. Empowerment in this context means that treatment must enable women to become confident enough to break away from or change violent relationships. Emotional and psychological support are needed as well as economic support. In other words women are the experts and the best judge of when to leave. Violent men should be made to leave the family home in order to render it safe for family members. All women who flee violence should have a place to go. Women who say they are fleeing violence should have absolute rights to financial, housing and other support and should receive the support of women who have had similar experiences. They should not have to deal with men. The appropriate policies will be multi-faceted, wide ranging, will engage many areas of policy making and face to face provision should be offered only by women. They will crosscut established functional divisions of government and require huge efforts of co-ordination. Feminist academics and researchers play an important role in the coalition:

> ... we have managed to survive as an explicitly feminist research unit ... to stand almost in the middle of a triangle between academia, the statutory sector and the voluntary sector ... have connections, input, networking and I think we are very much seen by individuals and organizations as a point that you go to if you need information, if you want to find out other groups doing certain things... We are always connected up to various networks of women ... are actually physically doing research with them ... or working in a local authority context ...[12]

The feminist core theoretical stance has not shifted, despite the passage of time. The belief system is the foundation of feminist advocacy about the issue of domestic violence. [Table 1]

From the early 1970s the focus of the feminist advocacy coalition expanded and by the 1990s it explicitly sought to influence housing and social service departments, the criminal justice community, the health services, politicians and other decision makers, experts and general public opinion. That bundle of policy makers had apparently little in common but was united by a 'status quo' approach to the treatment of domestic violence which in some central government cases resulted in a refusal to recognize the policy area at all.

Traditionalists

The particular nature of the feminist coalition has had the effect of defining another coalition, characterized principally by its resistance to prioritizing the domestic violence issues, and sometimes by its opposition to the feminist coalition. This coalition may be thought of as the traditionalists. Traditionalists have a core belief system centred on patriarchal notions of sex roles; the chastisement of wives[13] was legally supported until the nineteenth century and rape within marriage was only recognized as a crime in the 1990s. (Table 1) Whilst the legal rights of men to beat their wives has been formally removed, the values that support it remain deeply embedded in the culture. There is a considerable residue from the days of legal sanction and public approval of wife beating. Punch and Judy shows, epigrams, popular songs and doggerel of various kinds reflect its sanction. 'Many people know and use the expression "rule of thumb" in their everyday conversation. What they may not realize is that one origin of the expression derives from the right of a man to beat his wife with a stick, provided it was no thicker than his thumb'.[14]

De facto tolerance of violence to women was masked by a core belief in the sanctity of family life. In evidence to the 1975 Parliamentary Select Committee on Domestic Violence, the Association of Chief Police Officers expressed the view that '... we are, after all, dealing with persons "bound in marriage", and it is important, for a host of reasons, to maintain the unity of the spouses. ... Every effort should be made to reunite the family.'[15] The professional values of the police, government officials in housing, social services, the judiciary and so on are major determinants of policy core beliefs. The professionals make the dominant definitions of issues and problems. Such definitions determine what requires explanation, treatment and remedy and where responsibility rests. Police, medical staff, government officials, social service professionals and other public officials may be identified as part of the traditionalist coalition. In the 1970s their policy core beliefs included the views that domestic violence was a private matter and should be treated differently to 'stranger assault'. It was not regarded as appropriate work for the police, nor was it an appropriate matter for criminal law. Then appropriate policy was a matter exclusively for the professionals who were the experts, not for feminists who were unreliable extremists, nor for survivors who may have acted unreasonably in leaving their partners. The traditionalist coalition although dominant was diffuse and therefore susceptible to intervention by the more coherent, more highly motivated feminist coalition, particularly during a period of changing attitudes and widespread institutional reform.

Table 1: Domestic Violence Policy
Beliefs of Feminist coalition and Traditionalist coalition – Deep Core, Policy Core and Secondary Aspect

Belief system	Feminist Advocacy Coalition 1975–1995	Traditionalist Coalition 1975
Deep core	Public private distinction denies protection to women. Male violence reflects unequal power relationships. Right to personal security and bodily integrity more likely to be denied to women than men. Violent behaviour is in male nature. Men benefit from male violence to women. Home and family are places of potential danger.	Family life is a private matter. Families are important. Home and Family are safe.
Policy core	Violence to women is a political matter. Most violence to women is by known men. Solution must empower women – Refuges provide emotional support, renew self confidence. Women only delivery of policy – sufferers of domestic violence should not have to deal with men. Survivors of violence and feminists are experts. All women must have somewhere to go – open door policy is essential. Women have right to go where they please.	Violence to women is normally stranger assault. DV is a private matter. DV should be treated differently to stranger assault. DV 'not police work'. DV not a matter for criminal law. There is no such thing as 'DV policy'. Families should be reconciled. Professionals – social services, police, health workers are the experts. Professionals deliver policy. Professionals determine need. Violent behaviour is individually learned. Men 'protect' families from violence. Men are not to blame – DV attacks often warranted or provoked. Families should stay together. Women should stay at home and off the streets if they want to be safe.
Secondary aspects (decisions)	Refuges run by residents. DV should have crime status and response priority. Feminists should staff DV units. Women centred multi-agency policy is remedy. Survivors decide when to leave, return home. Resources should be specially targeted to survivors. (e.g. Women's Aid)	Complaints not recorded. Complaints not treated. Long response time. Formal non-arrest policies. No referral to other agencies. Lighter sentences and lower fines than stranger assault. Independent corroboration of homelessness is necessary to get benefit. Resources should be allocated through mainstream providers. (e.g. Victim Support)

In this configuration the feminist coalition sought to get the value of feminist approaches and expertise recognized, for example by the police or central government personnel. Only then would they have their desired influence on policy. That is feminist policy success could occur only where the opposing coalition's policy core belief system was modified, a situation identified by Sabatier as difficult but not impossible to achieve.

The policy subsystem and policy change

An examination of the development of domestic violence policy between the 1970s and 1990s shows evidence of significant policy change. There is no single public organization with responsibility for domestic violence policy; responsibility spreads across a wide range of agencies spanning central and local tiers of government and public, private and quasi-governmental sectors. At national level, Parliament, the Home Office, the DHSS, the cabinet sub committee on women's issues, the shadow Women's Minister and various legislators considered and/or made policy on domestic violence. These agencies are under pressure from nationally mobilized campaigns, experts and professionals. At the local level, policy on domestic violence is delivered by the criminal justice system, housing authorities, social services, the health service and the voluntary sector. Statutory authorities have considerable discretion in this area which allows widely varying local policies.[16]

Women's mobilization on the issue of domestic violence led to innovative policies clearly grounded in feminist core belief systems, highlighted by the development of refuges. To escape violence at home women need safe alternative accommodation, a need that was met by the establishment of safe houses or refuges. The first refuge was set up in 1971 and by 1975 there was a national network of refuges run on women-centred principles. The refuges aimed to offer personal security to women escaping violence and to enable them to look after their children and to decide on their own future. To find and develop feminist ways of working was a central concern of the refuge movement, which was committed to the management of the refuges by the residents rather than by public officials. Many refuges were staffed by feminist activists; others were managed by voluntary organizations. Their funding was provided by a combination of central and local government and public and private sectors. Linking with local agencies was acknowledged to be essential from the start. To be effective, the activists had to establish relationships with local police forces in order to ensure that women needing their services were referred to the refuges. From that baseline, policy developed during the 1980s, with different patterns of change and engagement with public officials in different localities. Feminist principles were a challenge to the local housing and social service officials, hence uneasy working relations with local authority professionals characterized the early years.[17] More difficult were relations with the police whose values and culture made them especially unsympathetic to intervention in domestic disputes, even where serious assaults occurred. A related problem was the reluctance of the judiciary to accept women's evidence, to make convictions in this area.

At national level, the central government department with prime responsibility for domestic violence policy is the Home Office which has varied in its interest in and

prioritization of the problem. As well as drafting legislation the Home Office over-
sees the police, funds research on crime, is responsible for immigration policy
(which is especially important in relation to violence in ethnic minority and
migrant communities) and funds projects and parts of the voluntary sector. The
Department of the Environment is responsible for housing policy and the DHSS for
the benefits on which women's escape from violence may depend, but although
the resources allocated by these two departments are crucial to good policy, the
Home Office has been the dominant department. After 1989 it recognized the functional overlap that remedy in this area involves by financing multi-agency initiatives, but it did not make long term funding available.18 Home Office policy early
in the 1990s was contradictory. It funded numerous small-scale initiatives under
its Safer Cities Programmes and by 1995 it had funded 11 multi-agency projects on
domestic violence. However, after 1991 support for feminist, women-only groups
such as Rape Crisis and Women's Aid declined while finance for Victim Support, a
mainstream, mixed sex organization increased. This caused considerable anxiety in
the feminist community where there was a feeling that the work of Victim Support
filtered funds away from the provision of direct emergency services and marginalized the views of the women who needed them.

Police policy on domestic and sexual violence has been one of the prime sites of
feminist contestation of the definition of crime. Police are major actors in this area
of policy and domestic violence is potentially an important part of police work.
Evidence to the Select Committee in 1975 indicated that between one quarter and
one third of all calls to the police concerned 'domestic occurrences'.[19] Prior to the
1980s police forces treated domestic violence as a private family affair and left
women without legal recourse or protection. But the 1980s crisis in British policing
made some forces more responsive to feminist demands for policy change. Discourses of 'new community policing', considerable vocal critique from women and
the desire to project an image of the police as protectors of women and children led
to a turn about in police responses to violence against women. Force orders in 1985
and Home Office guidelines concerning violence against women in 1986 and 1990
began to meet some of the criticisms from feminists working on violence to
women. Good practice ideas about inner city crime, sexual violence and domestic
assault were imported from North America where costly class action suits brought
by feminists were compelling police to treat domestic violence as a crime and
were incentives to police co-operation with feminists to develop women-centred
responses to domestic violence. By the late 1980s British policing policy on sexual
and domestic violence had changed, it was both officially acknowledged and
treated as a crime. The first police domestic violence unit was set up in London in
1987. By 1989 further units were established in West Yorkshire, Manchester and
Birmingham. These units were staffed largely by female officers. Variations in
police practice have, however, been widely noted. Local police forces have considerable discretion and interpret policy and guidelines in different ways. The attitudes of individual Chief Constables are particularly important to the exercise of
discretion. A 1990 Home Office Circular recommended that specialist units be set
up to deal with domestic violence and provide follow up services and support for
survivors. The circular emphasized that the primary concern of police officers
should be the safety of women and children and the arrest of the violent man.

Also crucial to policy delivery are local authorities, especially housing officials and social services. Local authorities act as gatekeepers for housing waiting list applicants, as landlords to tenants experiencing domestic violence, as a general source of housing advice and have clear responsibilities in the provision of housing for women escaping violence in the home. The Homeless Persons Act 1977 and the Housing Act 1985 required local authorities to secure accommodation for unintentionally homeless persons in priority need. According to this provision women experiencing domestic violence, particularly those accompanied by their children could be given priority eligibility for housing. Case law further refined the duty to secure 'permanent' housing and the Women's Aid federation successfully lobbied to get those living in temporary accommodation such as hostels or refuges defined as homeless.

Local authorities also determine whether refuges are adequately funded, whether they can remain open and whether their open door policy is a practical reality. Practice varies widely by authority. Some local authorities lead well funded and managed multi-agency responses whilst others deny domestic violence is a problem in their community. A few have developed good practice guidelines together with training, information and education campaigns. Most have produced a leaflet on how to get help. Our research indicates that the most 'feminist' and most developed policies are multi-agency initiatives with a number of officers in dedicated posts. Although such initiatives occurred almost exclusively in Labour controlled areas, many Labour authorities had only minimal policies, suggesting that partisan explanations could offer relatively little illumination of varying practices. However surveys in the 1990s showed wide variations amongst local authorities,[20] overall lack of written policy[21] and virtually non-existent provision for unmarried women experiencing domestic violence.

The definition of domestic violence itself was a major point of disagreement between the coalitions and a cause of local variation. Some authorities adopted a women-centred definition, accepting the statements of women leaving violent partners as evidence of priority need, whilst many, possibly most, required women to take out injunctions as a condition of receiving permanent rehousing.[22] Pressure on housing stock due to the 1988 Right to Buy legislation and increasingly limited allocations of social housing led many local authorities to adopt narrow interpretations of the homelessness legislation and to restrained use of their discretion in domestic violence cases. In this climate a House of Lords decision in 1995 (R v London Borough of Brent, *ex parte* Awua) reinterpreted a local authority's duty to mean securing 'suitable' accommodation rather than 'suitable permanent accommodation'. The Housing Act 1996 amended this position slightly by stipulating a temporary – two year – duty to rehouse. The 1996 act removed domestic violence as an indication of a priority need category and called into question the homelessness status of women in refuges. Most importantly it increased the discretion of local authorities. These elements of the Act are regarded as legislative expressions of the Conservative demonization of lone parents after Peter Lilley's 1992 speech attacking teenage mothers for, amongst other things, bearing children in order to jump housing queues. Our interviews indicated that the 'pro family' ideology of the Conservative right in the early 1990s was so extensive that no policy that could be seen to assist marriage breakdown would be encouraged by central government, even where the breakdown was caused by criminal assault in the home.

Policy Change in Two Localities 1975–1995

The large constellation of actors, both governmental and feminist, involved in domestic violence policy suggests that there will be variations in policy as it operates on the ground, both by locality and over time. The relative influences of the two coalitions cannot be analysed without looking at particular localities and particular time periods. Accordingly we analyse policy in two localities: a provincial city, Radicalton and an inner London borough, Progressiveham. The authorities differ in their structure, culture, feminist presence and the way they implemented local government reform between 1979 and 1995. Radicalton is a provincial Metropolitan authority under Labour control throughout the period of Conservative local government reform. Although some streamlining had taken place, there was comparatively little structural change in its institutions by the time our fieldwork was completed. Radicalton set up a council women's committee in 1981 following local feminist activism that had been strong since the 1970s. Progressiveham was a modern, recently decentralized Labour led council with a national reputation for initiatives to promote changes in gender relations. A women's committee was set up there in 1981 but, unlike Radicalton, this council was not influenced by a local, autonomous feminist movement. Policy change occurred in both authorities, but to differing extents.

Policy Change in Radicalton

Radicalton offers an example of policy change in the local authority and in the police. Change was driven by a strong coalition of feminist policy advocates. Radicalton at the end of the 1970s became the site of substantial feminist mobilization around issues of male sexual violence, activity that was strengthened by a widely publicized series of brutal sex murders in the area. Locally the murders became a psychological landmark that drew a wide spectrum of women into political action. Angered by police advice to stay home as a means of ensuring their safety, women gathered in widely publicized 'reclaim the night' marches. In addition a local campaign was organized to secure the release of two Radicalton women imprisoned for killing their drunken and abusive father in self defence. The atmosphere was alive with women's anger and issues of male sexual violence to women were at the forefront of local preoccupations. Thus, when the council women's committee was established in 1981 feminist community representatives prioritized the issue of male sexual violence to women. The council sponsored conferences on sexual violence and feminists on the committee gained access to the police via the council police committee. This enabled the women's committee to work on the 'no crime' status domestic violence then had with the police. The chair of the women's committee described the initial meeting with the police as 'staggering … we all came out thinking "good god". The bit … that always sticks in my memory was the Chief Inspector sitting there saying, "you see, the man in the street is not interested in domestic violence". And we said our concern is the woman in the street and she is.'

Feminist researchers and academics played a central role in demonstrating the legitimacy of their concerns about domestic violence in Radicalton. These experts were well established in national feminist circles and their arguments and research were central to national debates. They were also linked into local networks, working alongside community activists to collect information on the incidence of sexual violence against women. One influential feminist academic was particularly important. She had been there a long time and ran a popular and influential women's studies course on gender and violence. She educated a group of women who have stayed on in Radicalton and play a part in local feminist policy advocacy.

Important to later developments was the continuing access of feminists to the police which over a number of years included action to shift attitudes, via training, the exchange of expert information and research. In the 1980s the force underwent a serious legitimacy crisis due to race problems, the miners strike and media exposés of the police treatment of rape victims which led to the introduction of rape suites in police stations. In Radicalton rumours were going around that the reason police could not catch the serial sex murder was that he '… was a policeman, he had to be a policeman because why else couldn't they catch him? Or it had to be somebody the police were protecting, perhaps he was a special', evidence of a negative reputation that was damaging to police work. In this atmosphere a catalyst came when a man who had murdered his partner was released on bail leading to a local campaign that further embarrassed the police who had already suffered a loss of legitimacy over their repeated failures to solve the serial murders and more generally to provide safety for local women.

Meanwhile feminist advocates began to realize that in order for arrest to become an answer to domestic violence, other parts of the criminal justice community such as the courts, the probation services and the Crown Prosecution Service would have to be brought on board. Bowing to public pressure the police allowed feminist researchers, funded by the local council, to investigate the force's responses to domestic violence. The recommendations of the research were that the police should not only treat domestic violence as a crime but should also participate in multi-agency co-operation over domestic violence. The recommendations were strongly supported by the Chief Constable who persuaded local constabularies (meeting in police forums) to accept his endorsement of the research. This personal backing symbolized a new commitment by the police to multi-agency co-operation and, most importantly, their recognition that the police alone could not remedy domestic violence. The feminist experts were then commissioned to evaluate the ensuing projects.

The first step was the establishment of an inter-agency working party on domestic violence chaired by the chair of the women's committee and including the police, representatives from local authority departments and the voluntary sector. Members of the inter-agency working group were also able to lobby inside their own agencies. The role of the local council women's committee was crucial, first in establishing a dialogue between agencies and feminists and later in establishing the Radicalton Inter Agency Project (IAP). The chair of the women's committee at the time of the project's inception had been a student on the women's studies programme taught by one of the experts who led the research on the policing of domestic violence. Soon she secured funding from the three council committees most directly involved with women who experienced domestic violence (Housing, Social Services and Equal Opportunities) for a full time worker to develop inter-agency work. A co-ordinator was appointed who had wide experience of the domestic violence issues and of the voluntary sector. By that time the local profile of domestic violence was such that securing funding was easy. The establishment grew.

The IAP is a local example of an early effort to produce 'joined up' policy. Its aim was to develop women-centred policy in the agencies that deal with women experiencing domestic violence. Because the project was undertaken during local government reorganization and restructuring, part of its work is to deal with the confusion and uncertainty generated by the devolution of power to local agencies. For example influence in the local education department was held up by difficulties about how equal opportunities work would be funded in schools with local management. Once funding arrangements were clarified the IAP was able to link domestic violence work to child protection policies. In the health service the reorganization of budgetary structures in purchaser provider relationships made it difficult for the IAP to identify the part of the service it needed to influence. According to the co-ordinator

> we did not know who we wanted, we did not know who we were supposed to have, did we want a policy worker from community mental health or someone who is interested in purchasing services? … or from Accident and Emergency? It was a nightmare.

There were three elements to the work of the IAP: an interagency forum, a comprehensive domestic violence training scheme and the development of good practice guidelines with agencies through such devices as the Good Practice Pilot Project. The IAP aimed to change attitudes and beliefs by training all relevant workers and establishing special education health and court based projects in the area. Training over the years has, according to one of the feminist experts, become 'one of the most challenging programmes that I have ever seen in this country and our trainers are incredibly politicized and the whole structure that has been developed around the trainers is excellent. So on that level we have moved on aeons, light years into creating a very feminist base and centre for debate, discussion and growth.'

The IAP did not confine work to its participating departments; it targeted relevant agencies and attempted to ensure their participation in meeting its goals, working at several levels of its target agencies. For example where policy was not yet formulated, it worked at front line service delivery level as a means of changing practice. In Accident and Emergency services for example one IAP worker spent time in the hospitals to 'get to know senior … nurses and actually spend time that way, it was about winning their trust and through that actually starting to develop the work'.

Micro policy change was an important part of IAP strategy. In the 'Good Practice' project, multi-agency approaches were followed with intensive community development schemes. The IAP co-ordinator worked to get the agreement of staff in all relevant agencies in one part of the city to be trained by the project. The cumulative impact of the training and community development in a small geographic area has had significant results in awareness of women's possibilities for autonomy and self determination. Notably

> ... there is a difference in this part of the city of [Radicalton] in terms of people's understanding, in terms of the workers' understanding. It is interesting, what a number of women are doing who have been on the programme, who I have spoken to, are saying that it has made them re-assess the nature of their relationships, their heterosexual relationships and it has made them rethink whether or not they are involved in a violent relationship. There are women who are saying 'my husband is not violent, he does not hit me, it is not about that, but I am starting to understand much more about the ways in which I am controlled and the ways in which I do not have the freedom to choose to do what I want to do'.

It is possible to identify some of the officials at the local level in Radicalton as what Sabatier calls 'policy brokers', strategically placed to form linkages between coalition advocates. Personnel with access to other organizations were deliberately placed on steering groups and committees. For example, one member of the interagency project's steering group was the women's officer from social services with close access to the departmental management team, useful in overcoming past problems with accessing social services and probation offices. Many interviewees stressed the importance of incorporating within feminist networks people at sufficiently high levels to give women's committees access across the policy-making structure.

Changes of personnel due to local government restructuring had advantages and disadvantages. On the one hand turnover may have made IAP goals more difficult to achieve. Since the main aim of IAP work was to educate professionals on domestic violence issues, a frequent turnover of staff was highly disruptive. New staff often arrived with traditionalist belief systems. An IAP worker commented 'We have just constantly had to go back over the same ground, constantly getting the same stuff about should we not be talking about violence to adults here, shouldn't we be talking about men who are abused, should we not be talking about elderly men?' On the other hand, turnover also had the advantage that obstructive individuals eventually left. For example, the restructuring of the Crown Prosecution Service meant that an unsympathetic Chief Prosecutor was replaced by two younger prosecutors anxious to make the service more accountable and open to the public.

The growing strength of the IAP was emblematic of changes in the participating departments. Scrutiny of such changes indicates the strategic significance of different components of the feminist advocacy coalition. In housing, for example, change resulted both from the presence of senior women in the department who were committed to improving domestic violence policy and the acceptance of domestic violence as a legitimate policy area by women politicians. The catalyst appears to have been lobbying by senior women (one of whom had been a founder member of the IAP) in the department for the establishment of a women's officer post. The advocates were backed by the women's committee itself. Women's Aid and the local Asian women's refuge had long been funded by the authority, hence officials were well aware of domestic violence issues. When the women's officer was appointed, the male director of the housing department immediately placed her in charge of drafting a domestic violence policy and an allocations policy. Her policy covered all housing provision and incorporated Women's Aid good practice guidelines for a women centred policy privileging women's word as proof of violence rather than demanding legal and criminal proof. Also incorporated was the DOE Code of Guidance on the 1985 Housing Act. Initially the chair of the council Housing Committee blocked the policy, but when the chair was replaced, the housing director took the policy to the committee again, via the tenancy subcommittee which, as a smaller committee, allowed for a more sympathetic reading and the possibility of informed discussion. Agreement in the subcommittee meant that the policy appeared as a minuted note on the Housing Committee agenda where it could be agreed with little debate. To the surprise of the officers in charge of presenting the new policy, the document was met with enthusiasm:

> The liberal democrat started by saying 'excellent document, very clear, very easy to understand, should have had it years ago'. I thought 'I am dreaming.' Then Conservative councillor [x], a woman, said, 'I used to work in a refuge years ago, excellent, it is a clear policy'. I am thinking 'no way.' The Labour councillors just looked gobsmacked ... and that was it. They said it was really good and they were supportive. It was accepted at the next housing committee meeting and went out with a circular from the director as policy to be implemented.

The training has produced results, producing political change across a wide range of local agencies.[23] The project co-ordinator reported in 1995 that she was beginning to see the results of five years work:

> just the other day there was a criminal prosecution that was taken forward and the CPS prosecutor was absolutely brilliant. Apparently, the magistrate who was there gave this man 80 hours of community service, which is, I think, unheard of in domestic violence cases, and a fine. We think he is one of the magistrates that have been brought through our training programme. The different agencies are actually starting to support each other, it is wonderful.

Although more intermittent, policy oriented learning also took place in the police. New policies introduced after the research included training on intervention for domestic violence, the development of management information systems to collect statistics and produce annual surveys and reports on domestic violence in the area. Special units staffed by women police officers were established to deal with domestic violence and child protection and became repositories of expertise on violence against women. Evaluation research indicated that women calling on the police to assist them in dealing with domestic violence began to get a sympathetic response.

Our research suggests that the ability of local feminists to challenge police practice fluctuates over time; the attitudes of Chief Constables are central in determining policy priorities. Turnover at this level first brought in a sympathetic Chief Constable who was very interested in domestic violence policing and committed to the IAP. His replacement showed no interest in the issue and feminist advocates felt they had lost influence. One policy setback was the dilution of the specialist domestic violence units in the early 1990s. In line with police 'equal opportunities policies' and because the units were seen in the police as a backdoor through which women were entering the CID, the units were changed to mixed sex staffing despite objections by the IAP. And when the new units proved less effective at dealing with domestic violence the IAP felt that it had no influence: '... there's resistance ... basically we have lost the police in terms of domestic violence ...'. By 1995 the units were named 'Sexual Abuse and Child Protection Units' and one half of a 'vulnerable persons post' was allocated for domestic violence victimization cases. The Chief Constable was overt in his resistance. According to the IAP co-ordinator 'he said we are going to treat all victims of crime in the same way, they are all going to get appropriate treatment and there is not going to be any priority for victims of interpersonal crime ...'. However, other organizational changes in the police mitigated the setback. Devolution after 1994 moved considerable decision making away from Chief Constables to Divisional Commanders and the IAP was able to locate a sympathetic Divisional Commander who has spent two days on one of their training programmes and has agreed for them to train probationers and their trainers in one Radicalton police division.

By the mid 1990s the Inter Agency Project was one of the most comprehensive and successful in the country. Located partly in the voluntary sector and partly in the local authority it was able to obtain funding from a variety of sources and to be autonomous while having political backing from the local authority. Funding for 11 workers was secured, with the Home Office making the lead contribution of 25 per cent of the projects total funding. The Inter Agency Project also received money for short term action projects and central government section 11 money (for the employment of black workers).

The IAP enabled networking in Radicalton, in the interagency project itself and within and between other organizations and institutions. Over time awareness of domestic violence has grown throughout the area. According to a departmental women's officer:

> The profile that the issue has got in the city now, it is almost like, in the department we have done policy ... a lot of workers in the department have gone through interagency training, there is a tremendous kind of network around that. I have represented the department on the service planning team for women experiencing violence within the community care process, so again that has fed into the network in terms of the health authority and good practice there.

The advocacy coalition is maintained and continued partly by a core of key women who are present in multiple networks.

Policy Change in Progressiveham

Although less substantial than in Radicalton, policy change in Progressiveham was also evident. Feminist initiatives received considerable councillor support, but effects on Housing and Social Services were more limited in this very decentralized borough. As in Radicalton policy oriented learning in the police took place, but it was more restricted. The Progressiveham feminist advocacy coalition had less of a local grass roots base and was more concentrated in authority agencies than was the case in Radicalton. It had more often relied upon the initiatives of a few strategically situated individuals. Individual women police officers in the locality were helpful as were some high profile local feminist councillors. A local university employed feminist experts on sexual violence who contributed to policy change. Through such contact and through participation in national networks Progressiveham feminists were integrated into the advocacy coalition, and directly linked with the Radicalton project including cross representation on multi agency steering committees.

As in Radicalton the role of the council women's committee backed by a women's unit was central to policy oriented learning and change. The Progressiveham women's committee prioritized women's safety issues from its foundation in 1981, but few of the initiatives taken in the early 1980s survived until the later part of the decade. There was no active borough based women's movement pressuring the council to take the lead on domestic violence policy and co-ordination. Rather progress in the borough was the by-product of increasing pressure on the Metropolitan police by feminists in the Greater London Council, in various London-wide pressure groups and in the media to offer more effective policing of domestic violence. This led most notably to the Metropolitan Police Force Order in 1987 and a commitment to the establishment of Domestic Violence Units in police stations across the city. Pioneering multi-agency work by Radicalton attracted the attention of local advocates who were effective in persuading Progressiveham to adopt the multi-agency approach.

At council level the women's committee acted to raise the reputation of the problem. A survey of domestic violence in the area showing that a high percentage of local women experienced domestic violence shocked councillors, but did not at first lead to change. The establishment of the women's unit in 1988 enabled pressure to develop. A report was produced detailing inconsistency in council provision for women experiencing domestic violence. However, the Director of Housing and Social Services, whose department was targeted by the report, was unsympathetic and able to ignore its recommendation for the appointment of staff with responsibility for the issue. In 1990 a local female police officer encouraged the women's unit to revive a domestic violence working party that had existed in the early 1980s. Further action came in 1991 with the establishment of a Home Office Safer Cities project that enabled the women's unit to secure temporary funding for a Domestic Violence Coordinator post based in the unit. The post was filled by a worker with a background in Women's Aid who linked the women's unit to voluntary sector expertise.

Full funding for the post was provided by the council two years later. Council support resulted from a combination of factors. The rising profile of domestic violence nationally was important, but so was the work of the coordinator who was particularly effective. A further incentive was the presence in the borough of a high prestige Home Office funded action research project, Domestic Violence Matters, which lasted for three years and was located in one of the borough's police stations. The project was developed with collaboration by London-based feminist academics, the Progressiveham police and the Safer Cities coordinator for the borough.

The role of the co-ordinator was to develop good practice and policy, provide training and facilitate the borough-wide domestic violence working party established by the council in 1990. In her dealings with external agencies she sought to influence policy through training and guidelines to front line service deliverers to whom she has access via the working party which appears to be the nexus of inter departmental work. The women's unit also secured representation on the Safer [Progressiveham] Strategy Group, a multi-agency group of senior decision makers, but we did not find evidence of policy change there.

By 1990 links with the criminal justice community were established. These were developed in 1991 by Domestic Violence Matters. The project had a co-operative relationship with the women's unit, but relationships with the police were not straightforward. The local police were regarded as difficult by feminist advocates who worked in the Domestic Violence Matters unit. The advocates reported a continuing reluctance by the police to record domestic violence as a crime or to adopt procedures to deal with repeat victimization. Domestic Violence Matters was an intervention project in which a unit of experienced domestic violence professionals were located in two Progressiveham police stations to undertake crisis work with survivors. When Home Office funding ended, the police maintained only token levels of staffing in the units. During the course of the project, although there was some appreciation of the unit's role in reducing the burden of work in the station, it was also seen by police as interfering 'with something that is not our business.' 'Lesbians ... probably as trouble makers who are a load of ugly feminists who should be shot at dawn, quite frankly.' Unit staff reported that their civilian status made them outsiders, unable to integrate with police cultures. 'We do not fit in with their culture and what we do is tip toe around them, bend over backwards, swallow our tongues, we are very diplomatic, we sacrifice what potentially might be a great pleasure in telling them exactly what we think of them, just for good relations, they do not do it, they have no notion of subtlety ... we do not call it training because that would antagonize them, you cannot tell them anything they do not know...'

Thus feminist advocates doubted the success of the project. However, it was evaluated by a nationally respected feminist researcher and expert who regarded its significance rather differently.[24] Domestic Violence Matters was intended to be proactive, offering assistance to women in all domestic violence situations. It also aimed to produce cultural change in the police. The evaluator thought that the project was trying to do two very large and opposing things: change police culture and prioritize women. Her analysis is that it inevitably prioritized women and that three years was far too short a time to change police culture. Moreover, by separating strategic from practical work in its structure, Domestic Violence Matters limited the policy change that could occur. The project became a political football within the police and within the council. Nevertheless, in their day to day work, project workers were creating a climate of change by raising issues and keeping staff in other agencies involved. Its effects were significant and the evaluator thought it a positive outcome when the project secured external funding and carried on with two workers.

In both localities policy oriented learning was evident in the council, in key departments of the authority and to a lesser, but nonetheless significant extent in the police and health services. Both established multi-agency structures to treat problems of domestic violence. These involved multi agency, professionalized fora that facilitated policy oriented learning across coalitions in Radicalton but not in Progressiveham where the feminist advocacy coalition was weaker. The case studies suggest that the Home Office, the Metropolitan Police and the Police Authority in which Radicalton is located may have experienced policy oriented learning.

We have demonstrated that, in the mid 1990s, there was a significant and effective feminist advocacy apparatus located around the issue of domestic violence, including national and local organization, a set of publicly funded policy development projects, an extensive and widely accepted expertise, knowledge and literature and a well integrated network of policy minded feminist advocates. Evidence of policy change included new laws, official circulars, guidelines and practices in a variety of state and professional agencies. Although not fully accepted anywhere, there were few relevant arenas in which the radical feminist definition of the problem and its solution had not gained some ground. There is evidence that a feminist advocacy coalition existed and was effective.

Discussion and Conclusions

The story of domestic violence policy shows how a network of radical feminists can influence policy in organizations as traditional, conservative and hierarchical as the police, albeit only in some localities and at specific periods of time. Such a development is a proud testament to the role of ideas and beliefs in policy change in unlikely circumstances. The advocacy coalition framework would not have predicted this adjustment of core policy beliefs, but has proved useful in highlighting the conditions that facilitated change.

Our research supports Sabatier's assertion that the probability of policy-oriented learning across belief systems of different coalitions is likely to be increased through the presence of a professionalized forum. The feminist coalition in the field of domestic violence consists of a distinctive mix of experts, practitioners, interest group activists and academics operating on a national as well as a local basis. As one academic observed:

> ... the practitioner conferences, those are in the main the ones we prioritize, that we get asked to speak at, it is much more important to me to go to some domestic violence forum conference or Zero Tolerance conference than to the BSA for example, because those are the people who can make a difference in women's and children's lives, and do make differences, often negative differences so we are in contact often with policy makers at that level. ... we want to do research that is useful. It is not for its own sake, it is to contribute to debate to policy and practice development ... it matters enormously to me to have women from groups that are providing a service, tell me the things that I write, they find really helpful and that they have used it to discuss something.

This unusual relationship between the academic and practitioner community has had the effect of professionalizing the policy area, which may have helped to reduce conflict as well as to strengthen links among members of the coalition, thereby reducing the number of different belief systems in the policy subsystem.

Sabatier's framework stresses the importance of policy brokers in achieving learning across advocacy coalitions. By identifying some of the actors in domestic violence policy as such policy brokers, we can start to explain why feminist advocates have an important role even where circumstances are inauspicious. In central government, as one official put it, 'women who work in ... [a department] ... who every now and again will be moles, off the record will tell you what is going on in the internal debates with ministers, what the current line is, it is very important information for women on the outside to have, because it means you can think about strategy, think about targeting particular issues more or less ...'. At the local level in Radicalton policy brokers were strategically placed; steering groups and committees incorporated personnel with access to other organizations. Committees provide the crucial links to other organizations.

But the policy instruments allow considerable agency discretion and this translates into widely varying local practices, raising questions about how to explain local differences. Change was more extensive in Radicalton which had a well-established IAP and a well funded and co-ordinated domestic violence policy sector. Resistance from the police remained significant, but a good deal of change was apparent and there was evidence of repeated interactions between feminist advocates and the police. Interaction was initially facilitated through factors external to the policy sub system – the perceived loss of legitimacy of the police in dealing with violence toward women, which allowed feminist expertise a new legitimacy. But once interaction began, and such actors as the police became used to dealing with feminist activists, then one of the policy core beliefs of the traditionalist coalition – resistance to feminism and women's centred approaches – became more likely to break down. As a result Radicalton's policies could be sustained when national government financial support was withdrawn. In Progressiveham policy change was apparent, but it was less secure. Interagency work was not so well funded and contact with the police was more variable, insufficient for accumulation effects to kick in. Some of the features of Progressiveham might be explained as London effects. The absence of a borough level feminist movement reduced the prospects for the development of feminist advocacy and the restricted competence of borough government by comparison to metropolitan government limited the reach of local components of the advocacy coalition and increased the dependence of policy change on national initiatives. Nevertheless Progressiveham, like Radicalton, was able to find local funding to replace national Safer Cities funding of a domestic violence coordinator. Moreover, the local police station continued their Domestic Violence Matters unit, albeit on a reduced basis.

The key concepts of the advocacy coalition framework; policy oriented learning, coalitions built around belief systems and the nature of policy change, are useful in analysing the domestic violence policy change we have described. The policy subsystem includes pressure groups, civil servants, politicians, professionals and experts working via conferences, campaigns and debates, statutes, laws and policy directives of various kinds. An advocacy coalition of feminists inside and outside the government has functioned for at least twenty years. It would be difficult to argue that the coalition was 'in power' in the policy subsystem but, allowing for local variations, it was influential. It had an impact on different levels of

Table 2: Domestic Violence Policy Beliefs of Traditionalists 1975 and 1995

Belief system	Traditionalists 1975	Traditionalists 1995
Deep core	Family life is a private matter. Families are important. Home and Family are safe.	Family life is a private matter. Families are important. Home and Family are safe.
Policy core	Violence to women is normally stranger assault. DV is a private matter. DV should be treated differently to stranger assault. DV 'not police work'. DV not a matter for criminal law. Families should be reconciled. Professionals – social services, police, health workers are the experts. Professionals deliver policy. Professionals determine need. Violent behavior is individually learned. Men 'protect' families from violence. Men are not to blame – DV attacks often warranted provoked. Women should stay home and off the streets if they want to be safe.	Home and family must be protected and policed. Feminists are also experts. Public policy is needed on domestic violence. Domestic violence is a crime. Women decide when to leave violent men. Women are needed to deliver DV policy.
Secondary aspects	Complaints not recorded. Complaints not treated. Long response time. Formal non-arrest policies. No referral to other agencies. Lighter sentences and lower fines than stranger assault. Independent corroboration of homelessness is necessary to get benefit. Resources should be allocated through mainstream providers. (e.g. Victim Support).	Arrest policy. 'Normal' fines and sentences. Complaints treated and recorded. Multi agency approach. Evaluation by feminist experts. Training by feminist experts. Government funding of projects. Regular police / refuge contact. Housing rights for survivors (until 1996).

government and a variety of local agencies and organizations, largely without deviating from its members' deep core and policy core beliefs that domestic violence is caused by patriarchy and must be treated by women-centred, empowering approaches. The traditionalist coalition on the other hand altered its policy core beliefs but maintained its deep core beliefs. (Table 2)

Our case studies indicate that one partial explanation of policy change is that an accumulation effect of interactions between local policy actors and the feminist advocacy coalition on domestic violence affected the belief systems of officials, influencing some of them to accept feminist definitions of the problem and its solutions. By the mid-1990s both Radicalton and Progressiveham had experienced considerable policy change. Change in these and other localities reflected and probably contributed to wider changes in the policy subsystem, most notably alterations in policy core and secondary aspects of traditionalist belief systems (Table 2). Arguably the changes in traditionalists policy core beliefs resulted from their need to keep faith with their deep core beliefs. In order to maintain a patriarchal deep core belief in the traditional family, in order to 'save' the family, it was necessary to alter policy core beliefs and therefore policy. Feminists were able to insert their views into this process. Such an explanation also shows why feminists found no discernible change in the deep core beliefs of traditionalists.

The focus in this chapter has been on the involvement of the feminist advocacy coalition in domestic violence policy making and the role played by belief systems. We are aware that the changing role of the less coherent and self-conscious traditionalist coalition in the policy area should be given more detailed consideration. Resistance to feminist proposals appears to come partly from a set of beliefs about gender relations that is deeply embedded in the dominant culture, partly from professional values that lead to 'ownership' of the policy, and partly from the beliefs of senior national politicians far removed from this area of policy making. These elements at times compete. In part the traditionalist coalition is defined by its resistance to the feminist coalition. In part the influence of the feminist coalition in some localities and time periods might be explained by its superior motivation and strong belief system. A further possible explanation is that the deep core beliefs of traditionalists required them to alter their policy core beliefs. It may be that it is in the nature of deep core beliefs that they will lead to changes instead of stability in policy core beliefs, an outcome that has implications for the advocacy coalition framework. This chapter has concentrated on understanding the feminist advocacy coalition. Understanding the opposing coalition would involve identifying and detailing the exact nature of opposition to women-centred policies – a valuable exercise for future feminist research.

About the authors

Joni Lovenduski, School of Politics and Sociology, Birkbeck College, Malet Street, London WC1E 7HX, UK; email: *j.lovenduski@pol-soc.bbk.ac.uk*

Helen Margetts, School of Public Policy, UCL, 29/30 Tavistock Square, London WC1H 9EZ, UK; email: *h.margetts@ucl.ac.uk*

Notes

This chapter is based on research from the Gender and New Urban Governance (GNUG) project which was funded by the ESRC Local Government Programme, award number L1311250304901. The chapter was written by Joni Lovenduski and Helen Margetts on the basis of research undertaken by Stephania Abrar. We are grateful to Adam Smith for his comments on an earlier version of this chapter and to the very useful comments made by the other contributors to this book. We are also grateful to Patrick Dunleavy for discussions of and insights into this topic during the course of the GNUG project.

1 W. Parsons, *Public Policy: an Introduction to the Theory and Practice of Policy Analysis*. Cheltenham: Edward Elgar, 1995, p. 201.

2 Some experts object to the use of the term domestic violence when what is really meant is violence to women. Domestic violence is violence in the home and family and may affect any family or household member. Here we use the term in its everyday usage and mean violence to women.

3 S. Brownhill and S. Halford 'Understanding women's involvement in local politics', *Political Geography Quarterly*, 9, 4 (1990), 396–414.

4 H. Eisenstein, *Gender Shock: Practising Feminism on Two Continents*. Sydney: Allen and Unwin, 1985.

5 D. Stetson and A. Mazur, *Comparative State Feminism*. London: Sage, 1995.

6 S. Watson, *Playing the State*. London: Verso, 1990.

7 P. Sabatier and H. Jenkins Smith, *Policy Change and Learning*. Oxford: Westview, 1993, p. 55.

8 Sabatier and Jenkins Smith, *Policy Change and Learning*, p. 23.

9 G. Majone, *Evidence, Argument and Persuasion in the Policy Process*. New Haven: Yale University Press, 1989; R. Putnam, *The Comparative Study of Political Elites*. Englewood Cliffs: Prentice-Hall, 1976.

10 The advocacy coalition framework allows a large number of actors to be clustered together in a policy subsystem. In practice both advocates and brokers have an interest in subsystem maintenance and differences between them are part of a continuum. (Sabatier and Jenkins-Smith, 1993, p. 27) The dynamic of change is policy-oriented learning which includes the incorporation of technical information and the development of strategies to influence public policy. A distinction is made between learning within and learning across coalitions. The former is relatively unproblematic. However, productive debate is relatively unlikely to occur across coalitions because it may lead to the alteration of policy core aspects of a coalition's belief system. Once established, policy is unlikely to be revised so long as the coalition that instituted it remains dominant in the subsystem.

11 L. Kelly, 'Violence Against Women: a Policy of Neglect or a Neglect of Policy', in Sylvia Walby (ed.), *New Agendas for Women*. Basingstoke: Macmillan, 1999.

12 Expert interview. The GNUG project conducted over 100 interviews with experts and advocates between 1993 and 1995. By agreement with respondents interviews have been anonymized. Unless otherwise indicated quotations are drawn from interview transcripts.

13 The law allowing the chastisement of wives in Britain was repealed in 1829.

14 E. Malos and G. Hague, *Refuges and the Movement Against Domestic Violence*. New Clerical Press, 1993, p. 35.

15 L. Smith, *Domestic Violence: a Review of the Literature, Home Office Research Study 107*. London: HMSO, 1989, p. 42.

16 External instability has characterized the development of domestic violence policy which has taken place over a period of enormous changes both in the patterns of women's lives and in the structure and management of local government. Local government changes led to high levels of staff turnover, unpredictable budgets, changed and reduced statutory functions for local agencies, privatization of traditional public functions etc. Change in London's political system has been particularly dramatic since 1985. Until then London was run by a single strategic authority, the Greater London Council (GLC), while the delivery of services was the responsibility of 33 local councils covering the capital. In 1985 central government abolished the GLC and devolved its authority to the 33 local authorities. Since that time a variety of boards, committees, and offices has been created to deal with London wide issues whilst the boroughs have had to deliver services in their areas while experiencing major restructuring. The rest of British local government has also experienced restructuring which has taken the form of a succession of centrally directed management initiatives in which decentralization, downsizing, job losses, the introduction of purchaser provider splits, privatization and severe budget cuts and loss of areas of autonomy have been characteristic features. These changes greatly affected the framework in which domestic violence policy is made and delivered. As well as changes in urban institutions, agencies are also affected by policy changes on a central level, for example, reforms of the probation service, changes in housing legislation, changing spending priorities. In Radicalton 'right to buy' policy had less impact on women's access to social housing than in many other localities.

Where suitable housing stock has been depleted, the council has arrangements with local housing associations to choose tenants for 75 per cent of their housing in exchange for rights to build on local authority land.

17 J. Lovenduski and V. Randall, *Contemporary Feminist Politics*. Oxford: Oxford University Press, 1993.

18 S. Abrar, 'Feminist intervention and local domestic violence policy', *Parliamentary Affairs*, 49 (1996), 191–205.

19 Malos and Hague, *Refuges and the Movement Against Domestic Violence*, p. 40.

20 Malos and Hague, *Refuges and the Movement against Domestic Violence*.

21 J. Bull, *Housing Consequence of Relationship Breakdown*. Department of the Environment, London: HMSO, 1993.

22 Bull, *Housing Consequence of Relationship Breakdown*.

23 Abrar, 'Feminist intervention and local domestic violence policy,' p. 196.

24 No name given in order to preserve the anonymity of Progressiveham.

3

Zealot Politics and Democracy: the Case of the New Christian Right

Steve Bruce

This chapter uses the example of the Christian right in recent US politics to reflect on (a) the advantages and disadvantages of religious motivation for political activity, and (b) the structural constraints that modern democracies place on religiously-inspired politics.

The Christian Right

The Christian Right (CR) of the 1980s owed its existence to two Catholics and a Jew. Richard Viguerie, Paul Weyrich and Howard Phillips were three conservative activists who were responsible for the organizational planning and fund-raising behind a number of new conservative groups in the late 1960s and early 1970s.[1] They believed that, beyond the common stock of the economy and foreign policy, there were many socio-moral issues that could serve as the basis for an organized conservative movement. They were also innovators in seeking to build a movement independent of the main parties. Although the Republican party was always its first choice, the point of the new right was to mobilize previously uninvolved conservatives. One obvious audience was the conservative Protestant milieu, and Viguerie, Phillips and Weyrich persuaded Jerry Falwell, a popular fundamentalist Baptist preacher from Lynchburg, Virginia, to lead an organization they named the 'Moral Majority'.

The Moral Majority and related organizations such as Christian Voice and the Religious Roundtable worked on a number of fronts. They sensitized conservative Protestants to political issues and to their need to get involved. America was depicted as a country in decline because it had turned its back on the religious values that had made it great. The politicizing was carried out through Falwell's *Old Time Gospel Hour*, through campaign rallies, and through mailings to people who in some way or another had expressed support for conservative issues. Conservative Protestant pastors were encouraged to preach on the subject from their pulpits and to arrange voter registration drives. This latter part of the campaign was crucial. In Britain registration is easy and obligatory; in many parts of America, it is awkward. Especially in the South, where the system was arranged to discourage blacks from voting, many white fundamentalists did not register or vote. They responded to the wider world by trying to ignore it, a position with ample justification in the pietist tradition of Protestantism.

In the late 1970s, the CR was successful in turning religious and moral issues into campaign topics. In the 1978 mid-term elections, specific candidates were targeted.

If someone had voted for abortion or equal rights for women, or voted against school prayer, their transgressions were made known to the voters. In broadcasts, handouts and rally speeches, liberals were depicted as being anti-religion, anti-family, anti-America, and anti-God.

The greatest success of the CR was its contribution to the 1980 presidential election of Ronald Reagan. Long a standard bearer for the right, Reagan happily adopted the rhetoric of the Christian Right, though he was not known for his personal piety. What made the contrast ironic was that his opponent, Democratic incumbent Jimmy Carter, was a born-again Christian who agonized over the public application of his faith. Rhetoric triumphed over substance. Reagan won in 1980 and again in 1984 by concentrating on the economy and America's prestige abroad. He very successfully engineered an economic boom, and played a major part in the collapse of the Soviet Union but he did very little to promote CR issues. Congress refused to act on the Moral Majority agenda and Reagan declined to push it.

Reagan's success created a problem for the CR. Although its leaders repeatedly bewailed moral decline and threats to the traditional family, and distinguished between the President (a good man) and Congress (a bad thing), such analysis sounded rather unconvincing with a conservative in the White House. During the Reagan years, CR leaders found it increasingly hard to raise funds. In 1987, faced with a major hole in his income, Falwell closed down the Moral Majority and retired from electioneering.

Falwell's place was taken by Pat Robertson, a Pentecostal minister who had made two major innovations in religious broadcasting. In styling itself as a current affairs programme, his *700 Club* had been a departure from the traditional televangelism formats of the church service or the evangelical crusade. And rather than just buying time on existing channels to air his show, he had created his own Christian Broadcasting Network (now the Family Channel). Like other more popular televangelists, Robertson had been cool towards Falwell's initiatives. When he finally committed himself to the Christian Right, instead of seeking only to influence candidate selection, platforms and voting patterns, he decided to run for president.

Robertson's 1988 campaign for the Republican party nomination was extremely helpful to analysts in providing a wealth of opinion poll and voting data from which we can infer a great deal about the popularity of CR positions.[2] To summarize, a well-organized and well-funded campaign back-fired. Robertson spent more money than any other candidate and failed to win a single primary. The more people considered his candidacy, the more anti-Robertson feeling outstripped pro-Robertson sentiment. Even those who should have been most sympathetic had their doubts: many fundamentalists were unhappy with such overt mixing of religion and politics. In one poll, self-identified conservative Protestants, by a margin of 42–25%, said that Robertson's status as a former clergyman made them less, rather than more, likely to support him. Many preferred a secular politician who had some of the correct positions to a born-again televangelist who had them all. In a poll which was confirmed by the voting patterns in the southern states primaries, southern fundamentalists and evangelicals divided

44 per cent for George Bush, 30 per cent for Bob Dole and only 14 per cent for Robertson.[3]

In the aftermath of his drubbing, Robertson concentrated on building Christian Coalition, a grass roots organization similar to Falwell's Moral Majority but (reflecting the denominations of their leaders) drawing more on Pentecostals and charismatics than on Baptist fundamentalists. By 1992, it claimed 350,000 members in 750 local chapters and, in those areas where Robertson supporters had performed well in the primaries, it achieved some influence in the Republican party. However, this could not sustain a second Robertson campaign. One early 1993 poll of Republican voters showed only 2% endorsed another Robertson run; far fewer than favoured the other 1992 losers.[4]

Support from such organizations as Christian Coalition helped some moral conservatives win Republican party nominations but this rarely translated into overall victory and was often reversed once liberal Republicans realized they could not take their hegemony for granted. Virginia, home of Robertson's CBN, was the site of a vicious 1994 battle for the soul of the Republican party. Christian Coalition supported Oliver North, famous for his role in the Reagan administration's illegal use of funds to arm the Nicaraguan Contras. North won the primary for the Senate but liberal Republicans ran an independent candidate in the full contest and thus ensured that Democrat Chuck Robb held his seat. Two years later, the liberal Republican and sitting senator John Warner, much demonized by the religious right, defeated the next Coalition-sponsored candidate.

Within the party nationally, the CR was no more successful. Pat Buchanan, the religious right's favoured candidate, was defeated by George Bush in 1992 and Bob Dole in 1996. Buchanan did well enough in 1992 to force a morally conservative platform on the national party but George Bush and his running mate Dan Quayle suspected that the platform would be unpopular and openly briefed journalists on their disagreement with the anti-abortion stand.[5] The swing to the Republicans that gave them a majority in both the House and the Senate in the mid-term elections of 1994 brought a number of moral conservatives to office but few commentators believed that socio-moral issues were important in that swing. At the same elections, CR-inspired referenda in Oregon and Colorado to restrict homosexual rights were defeated. In the 1996 presidential primaries, the winner of the Republican nomination Senator Bob Dole defied the Buchanan camp and refused to endorse their moral agenda. In that round of elections a number of prominent CR-supported candidates lost. In Louisiana, the anti-abortion Woody Jenkins lost to the 'pro-choice' Mary Landrieu, who became the first woman elected to the Senate. In Colorado and Louisiana, referenda designed to give parents control over the primary school curriculum were heavily defeated.

Furthermore, whatever success the religious right had within the Republican party was nullified by the party's failure to win the presidency. Despite repeated exposure of his sexual indiscretions, the Democrat Bill Clinton won in 1992 and was re-elected in 1996. Republican attempts to impeach Clinton in 1998 back-fired and that year's mid-term elections saw a number of leading conservatives losing their seat and Newt Gingrich, on whom much CR hopes rested, losing his position as Speaker of the House.

What does the Christian Right Want?

The aspirations of the Moral Majority, Christian Coalition, and other religious right groups can easily be listed although it is sometimes difficult to draw a clear line between what the CR wants and ambitions which it shares with secular conservatives. Most generally, the Christian Right wants its religion and its religiously-inspired social mores given pride of place in the operations of the state. Particularly, the CR is anti-abortion and pro-traditional family. It is opposed to the acceptance of homosexuality as a legitimate lifestyle and to the Equal Rights Amendment for women.[6] It is in favour of public prayer in schools, at present judged by the Supreme Court to violate the constitutional separation of church and state. The background desires translate into strategic considerations. Religious right activists recognize that educational policy acts as an obstacle to the promotion of their goals and therefore they want to see greater local control of course content and teacher selection so that, for example, they can promote 'special creation' as a legitimate alternative to evolution as an account of the origin of species. Where they are not strong enough to influence public education they want tax tuition credits to allow parents more easily to pay for the private education of their children in 'Christian' schools (which in this context generally means fundamentalist schools although the issue brings them into alliance with the Catholic Church).

In addition to the above, the CR shares the more general conservative desire for a strong defence programme, an assertive foreign policy, unrestricted right to gun ownership, lower taxation, a curb on unions, the removal of restrictive business legislation, a reduction of welfare spending, and a general reduction in the power of central government.

The Nature of the Christian Right

Falwell insisted that the Moral Majority was not a political organization, and Ralph Reed, its director, asserted the same of Christian Coalition. This could only be true if we confine 'political' to 'political party'. Falwell and Reed also insisted that their organizations were not religious, which could only be true if we confine 'religious organization' to 'church'. There are two good reasons why CR leaders wish to avoid the 'religious' tag. In the first place, the confusion of church and political campaign organization would create problems with tax status. More importantly, movements such as the Moral Majority needed the support of conservatives who were not Baptist fundamentalists, and hence Falwell had to distance his religious from his political activities in order to court the widest possible base for the latter.

In practice, however, the Moral Majority was Baptist fundamentalist. Analysis of over 1,000 respondents to the 1980 CPS National Election Survey shows that at least a third of those who were defined as 'ardent supporters' of the Moral Majority were Baptists. Equally important, an equal proportion had been raised in the South.[7] In contrast, three-quarters of Jews surveyed were hostile to the Moral Majority. In a survey of Texas support for the new Christian right, less than 10% of Roman Catholics expressed support for the Moral Majority.[8] As one would expect from the looser association of both his career and his television show with any one denomination, Pat Robertson's Christian Coalition has enjoyed a wider base but it still appeals primarily to conservative Protestants and regularly signals this by referring to the number of affiliated congregations as an index of its popular support.

The narrow religious base from which the religious right recruits should not surprise us. Moral Majority was led by Baptist fundamentalists; Christian Coalition by fundamentalists and charismatics. Gospel shows (and the mailing lists which they generate) formed a major part of the movement's infrastructure. But the narrow base was also a consequence of the negative connotations that fundamentalism has for other social groups. The Texas survey showed that many members of ethnic minority groups strongly agreed with most of the value positions of the Moral Majority but were still hostile to the movement and the explanation for that seems to lie in the white supremacist past of conservative Protestants. Although there had been considerable changes in the attitudes of Southern Baptist whites towards blacks, Hispanics, Catholics and Jews, there was enough in the voting records of leading conservatives to lead many people to suspect that the old racist right was not far beneath the skin of the new right. The Helms solution to the liberal humanism of the national culture is a return to 'states' rights': the old justification for racial discrimination in the South. Viguerie's quest for a third party conservative presidential candidate had led him to support such racists as George Wallace and Lester Maddox. It is also noteworthy that in Christian Voice's 1983 report card on how legislators voted on various supposedly 'moral/family issues', all of the black representatives failed the new Christian right's test, as did 32 out of 37 Jewish representatives.[9]

Finally, we should note that while the political positions of the CR organizations can be separated from their religious justification, it is a religious world-view that has produced such positions. Falwell, Robertson and other ideologues are keen to re-cast that religious tradition in the broadest possible terms, but the America to which they wish to return is a Protestant America and there is very little in the mythology of 'one nation under God' to which Catholics, Jews and Mormons can attach their aspirations; the founding fathers, after all, were white Anglo-Saxon Protestants.

The Impact of the Christian Right

It is difficult to evaluate the impact of the Religious Right. It is certainly the case that Moral Majority, Christian Coalition and the like raised a lot of money and spent it on voter registration drives, electioneering, running general issue campaigns, and lobbying. For example Christian Coalition spent $5.9 million lobbying Congress in the first 6 months of 1996. What is not as clear is that any of this had much impact.

Naturally such organizations wish to claim great influence (especially when fundraising) but such claims are almost invariably contestable. For example, four leading liberal Senators who were targeted by the CR in 1980 were defeated but, as Lipset and Raab point out, the swing against these Democrats was the same as the swing against the Democratic Party in states where CR organizations had not been active.[10] Surveys of religious and political attitudes have produced conflicting results. According to Johnson and Tamney 'Religious issues, such as being a member of the Christian Right and taking a stand against abortion, were found to have no impact on the 1980, 1984, and 1988 presidential elections'.[11] Another survey by Himmelstein and McRae showed that those people who voted Republican for the first time in 1980 were not 'social' or 'moral' conservatives, as Viguerie claimed, but simply people who did not like Democratic incumbent Jimmy Carter.[12] On the other hand, Miller and Wattenberg claim a strong connection between religious fundamentalism and having voted for Reagan.[13]

My impression is that analysts have been far too willing to accept at face-value the claims that CR organizations have made about their own success. Many commentators were previously oblivious to the strength of conservative Protestantism in the Bible Belt. When it forced itself to their attention, they over-reacted. Only now, 20 years after the rise of the NCR, are balanced assessments being made. In contributing to that assessment, I will concentrate on court decisions, legislative action, and electoral power.

The Christian Right and the Law

We can summarize the Christian Right's judicial and legislative record under what Garvey has called its 'defensive' and 'offensive' agenda.[14] The movement has achieved most with what are clearly religious claims in the private sphere (for example, trying to protect religious schools from state regulation) and it has usually succeeded by following failures in court with legislative action to give specific protection. Thus in 1979, after a state court upheld a scheme for regulating private schools, the North Carolina state legislature passed a law enacting that 'in matters of education … No human authority shall, in any way whatever, control or interfere with the rights of conscience', a view that very many people outside the NCR could readily endorse.[15] What Garvey calls the fundamentalist 'defensive agenda' has also had some success in claiming rights such as access of religious groups to public facilities for private activity. In 1990, the Supreme Court upheld the federal Equal Access Act against objections that it was unconstitutional in bringing religion into the public sphere. A Moral Majority officer commenting on that case said:

> For the first three years of our existence we framed the issues wrong. We pushed for school prayer but we framed the issue in terms of how prayer in schools is good. But some people feel that prayer in school is bad. So we learned to frame the issue in terms of 'students rights'. … We are pro-choice for students having the right to pray in public schools.[16]

In 1995, in Rosenberger v. University of Virginia, the Supreme Court overturned a judgement that the University had been right to deny a Christian student group funding for an advocacy publication, when non-religious advocacy groups had been funded. In a 5–4 decision, the Court ruled that the Court of Appeal had been guilty of 'viewpoint discrimination' and that such funding did not violate the establishment clause of the Constitution.

So far the CR has only successfully deployed appeals to fairness on a very narrow ground. Attempts to use equity as a principle for requiring schools to balance the teaching of evolutionary accounts of the origin of species with equal time for 'creation science' alternatives have failed. With by all accounts very little thought for the consequences, the Arkansas legislature passed an equal time bill. The American Civil Liberties Union took the bill to the courts in 1981 to argue that it was an unconstitutional requirement to support a particular religion. The creationists had to persuade the judge that someone who did not accept the authority of the Bible would none the less find their account as compatible with the evidence and with scientific method as that of the evolutionists. They failed miserably to present a case that was consistent, let alone plausible. The bill was struck down.[17] A very similar bill from the Louisiana legislature was taken to the Supreme Court where, by the very considerable margin of 7 to 2, it was judged unconstitutional.[18]

The fairness principle was also employed to argue that 'secular humanism' (a supposedly coherent package of beliefs united mainly by their lack of support for traditional Christian propositions) was a religion and that even-handedness required that, if Christian values and perspectives were to be banned from schools, so too should the secular humanist alternatives. With assistance from Robertson's National Legal Foundation, over 600 fundamentalists filed suit against the Alabama State Board of Education, charging that the Board had violated their constitutional rights. Judge W Brevard Hand found for the plaintiffs but the unanimous verdict of the three Appeal Court judges was that he was wrong in accepting that all knowledge could come in only two forms so that anything which was not patently Christian must be secular humanist. The Appeal Court applied the narrower test of whether the textbooks at issue taught an identifiable philosophy of secular humanism and concluded that they did not. As with the creation science cases, the fundamentalists had some initial success in presenting themselves as a disadvantaged minority but lost the argument as soon as the apparent symmetry between theism and humanism was scrutinized in detail.

Finally on the equity argument, it is worth noting a Tennessee judgement with clear implications for its limits. In overturning the judgement of a lower court, the Sixth Circuit Appeals Court unanimously stated that requiring children to read books which did not endorse their beliefs or even challenged them was not an infringement of their constitutional rights: the lower court had failed to distinguish between simply reading or talking about other beliefs and being compelled or persuaded to adopt them.

On two other matters of Christian Right interest, the courts have recently failed to deliver. In June 1997, the Ohio Appeals Court struck down a scheme to provide poor people with vouchers worth £2,500 to pay for their children's education in private schools. It judged that, because the vast majority of private schools in Ohio were religious foundations, such support amounted to the state subsidy of religious activity.

Also in 1997, the Supreme Court struck down one of the Christian Right's few Congressional legislative victories. Following a 1990 decision in Oregon v. Smith, which made it easier to apply general laws to religious groups, various CR organizations (with the support of mainstream churches) lobbied Congress to pass the 1993 Religious Freedom Restoration Act. This required that the courts and government agencies show 'compelling interest' before they apply general statutes to churches. The particular case before the Supreme Court concerned a church in Boeme, Texas, which had been refused planning consent for new buildings on the grounds that it was in a historic preservation zone and that the secular enterprises in the same location would have been similarly denied consent. The Boeme church argued that the RFR Act gave it immunity from planning laws. As is often the case with Supreme Court decisions, it is a little hard to make general inferences from this decision because the RFR Act was dismissed on the ground, not that it gave an unfair advantage to religion, but that, in passing such a broad act, Congress had over-reached itself.

One recent decision which the Christian Right has welcomed is the Court's reversal of the 1985 *Aguilar v. Fenton* decision that prohibited the use of state funds to provide mandated secular services (such as special education) in religious schools. Justice O'Connor, a Reagan appointment who has often been the swing vote between hard and more moderately conservative decisions, wrote that we should 'no longer presume that public employees will inculcate religion simply because they happen to be in a sectarian environment'. In his dissent, Justice Souter, a Bush appointee, feared that reversing the previous position would 'authorize direct state aid to religious institutions on an unparalleled scale'.[19]

What of the CR's 'offensive' agenda? In 1986 the Supreme Court held that the Due Process Clause did not protect homosexual sodomy. However, in so doing the Court was explicitly returning the issue to the elected branches of government to deal with 'and there the tide is running against fundamentalist homophobia. States are with increasing frequency repealing or refusing to enforce their laws against sodomy'.[20] Indeed Hawaii is considering recognizing same-sex marriages.

In the late 1980s the Supreme Court made three significant decisions on abortion. It expressed unhappiness about the trimester rules laid down by Roe. It allowed the government to restrict public funding for abortions. And it permitted states to require that minors notify their parents before having abortions. Despite having a conservative majority, the Court has very pointedly declined to outlaw abortion. It has simply handed the issue back to the legislatures, where the fundamentalist record is at best mixed. Louisiana and Utah have enacted restrictive time laws. Iowa, Minnesota and New York have restricted public funds for abortions. Arizona, Arkansas, Michigan, Mississippi, North Dakota, Nebraska, South Carolina and Tennessee have enacted laws designed to ensure parental consent or notice for minors, or informed consent for adults. On the other side of the balance, attempts to restrict abortions have failed in Alabama, Florida, Idaho, Illinois and South Dakota. And Maryland and Connecticut have passed laws designed to preserve the right to abortion in the event of Roe v. *Wade* being overturned. Furthermore, the Court has protected the basic right to abortion where state laws have been too restrictive. Parental notification laws have only been permitted where there is a judicial 'by-pass': a judge is able to waive the requirement if the minor is suffi-ciently mature or if telling a parent would not be in the girl's best interest. In 1997, by 8 votes to 1, the Court decided that a Louisiana attempt to weaken the judicial by-pass was undue interference with a girl's abortion rights. The few restrictions on abortion that Reagan enacted by executive order were all reversed by Clinton within days of his inauguration in 1992.

Finally, a major part of the offensive agenda was concerned with competition over what, after the model of Weber's 'ethnic honour', we might term 'religious honour': the assertion of 'the excellence of one's own customs and the inferiority of alien ones'.[21] The CR wants public support for acts of religious worship and for the symbols of its distinctive religious culture. Despite the appointment by Reagan and Bush of five conservative justices, the Supreme Court has followed the precedents of the earlier courts in refusing to permit government support for such acts and symbols. Equally noticeable is that the lower federal courts, heavily packed with conservatives by Reagan, have proved little more sympathetic.

Politics and Elections

As we can see from the cases that find their way to the Supreme Court, Christian Right organizations have succeeded in promoting bills through legislatures in areas with strong conservative traditions, but they have made very little headway in Congress. Even the 1994–96 Congress, with a Republican majority in both houses, failed to deliver much. Despite its expensive lobbying, Christian Coalition had seven of the ten planks of its 'Contract with the American Family' wholly rejected. The partial successes concerned Internet pornography. In announcing his retirement as director of Christian Coalition, Ralph Reed claimed four major achievements: welfare reform, the Communications Decency Act (a blanket anti-pornography measure), the Defence of Marriage Act (an anti-gay rights measure), and the Partial Birth Abortion Act.[22] The first of these was not a specifically CR issue and within a year was unravelling. The second was voided by two federal courts. The Defence of Marriage act has yet to face any serious tests but is thought unlikely to prevent moves to recognize same sex unions such as that being contemplated by Hawaii. The abortion act was vetoed by President Clinton.

As the conflicting studies already mentioned show, it is not easy to judge CR impact on elections. Proponents of competing evaluations can readily list any number of contests from 1980 to 1996 to show either that Christian Right support helped win or helped lose seats. On one side we have spokesmen for the American Coalition for Traditional Values saying that Roger Jepsen of Iowa lost his senate seat in 1984 to a Mondale Democrat because he turned his back on the religious groups which had supposedly helped him win in 1978.[23] On the other side, we have reports that Virginia got its first black governor in 1990 because his white opponent was vocally 'pro-life' until he discovered it was costing him the election.[24] Abortion is also thought to have delivered the Western Massachusetts seat to a Democrat for the first time in its history; the Republican was against it. Some commentators blame the defeat of George Bush in 1992 and Bob Dole in 1996 on the fundamentalist party platform. Pat Buchanan's supporters argue that Bush and Dole lost because they showed insufficient commitment to that platform. But whichever explanation of defeat one prefers, the fact to be explained remains defeat and not victory. We should also note that, as of early 1999, the clear front-runner for the Republican nomination to succeed Clinton is the liberal George Bush Jnr, who has gone out of his way to distance himself from conservative socio-moral positions.

It is possible to be impressed by figures such as those used to describe Christian Coalition. In 1997 it was estimated to have 1.9 million members, 125,000 participating churches and annual revenue exceeding $27 million. But it is easier to be impressed by how little the Coalition has achieved with all that money and support.

What the CR has done best is to infiltrate the Republican party. In 1994, *Campaigns and Elections* magazine surveyed Republican party leaders state-by-state for their assessment of the CR's influence in their organizations. Of 52 states (and the District of Columbia), 18 reported the Christian right to be 'dominant', 13 described its influence as 'substantial', and 20 gave it as 'minor'.[25] However, to return to a point made repeatedly, such entrism is of little value if the final product is rejected by the electorate. Like the militant left's influence on the British Labour Party in the early 1980s, the Christian Right's effect on the Republican party is to shift it away from the middle ground that it needs to occupy if it is to win major elections.

None of this is intended to deny the obvious point that in small political units where conservatives are numerous, the CR can achieve legislative and electoral success. As I have argued at length elsewhere, in contrast to the much more monolithic structures of the old world, the federal structure of the USA permits locales a considerable degree of freedom.[26] However, as we move up from the city and county to the congressional district and the state to the federal government we move to units of greater cultural, social and political diversity and we see the potential for such pressure groups as the CR steadily diminished. The congressional structure is 'centripetal'. Any enthusiast may introduce a bill in the House of Representatives but to have any chance of becoming law, it must attract broad-based support. It must then pass the Senate which, by giving two votes to every state irrespective of size, acts as a brake on regional and sectional interests. That senators are elected by the entire state rather than by a small congressional district means that they are much more likely to be moderates after the style of Virginia's John Warner than true believers such as Ollie North. Finally, bills have to be approved by the President, who answers to a national electorate, and they can only get past his veto with two-thirds support from Congress.

Furthermore, the centripetal structure of the courts, and the fact that many socio-moral issues concern fundamental rights, means that the final judgement will often lie with the cosmopolitan centre and not with the locale. Judge Brevard Hand's district of Alabama might be sympathetic to fundamentalist criticism of secular humanism but his views will always be subordinate to those of either the Supreme Court or, in so far as the Court returns such issues to the legislative branch of government, to a larger electorate.

One may argue, as Falwell and others have frequently done, that the CR has re-established the respectability of conservative socio-moral positions and the right of fundamentalists to be taken seriously. It is certainly the case that the 1980s saw considerable publicity given to CR activists and their views. However, while such exposure ensures a vigorous debate, it only guarantees victory in that debate if it is the case that the previous liberal hegemony was achieved by stealth.

To conclude this very brief review, the CR began with a great many advantages. It had ready access to the mass media through the products of televangelists such as Falwell and Robertson. It had the mailing lists of televangelism organizations to reach its potential supporters. It was led by some extremely skilled self-publicists.

It was able to make use of the excellent existing networks of conservative Protestant pastors. Nonetheless, it failed to achieve significant progress on items that were specific to its agenda (as distinct from those ambitions such as increased defence spending which were shared with mainstream conservatives). It is always possible to argue that the CR acted as a brake: that without it, America would have become more liberal. But unfortunately claims for influence of this sort are untestable and have to remain in the realm of speculation. All we can do is look at the wish list, look at what was achieved and compare the two. The future may yet prove me wrong but it is worth referring again to the Clinton impeachment and the November 1998 elections. What should have been the CR's finest hour ended in humiliation for Newt Gingrich, its most prominent elected politician.

Personal Motives and Social Functions

I would like now to draw attention to features of the Christian Right and its environment that, had they been properly attended to in, say, 1980, would have led to a realistic assessment of the movement.

It is useful to separate the accidental from the essential. It was certainly no help at all that two very prominent television evangelists were caught with their pants down and their hands in the till. Jim Bakker, who had worked for Pat Robertson before becoming a star in his own right, was accused of sexual misdemeanours in 1987 and was eventually sent to prison for swindling supporters of his PTL ministry out of $150 million.[27] In 1988 and again in 1991 Jimmy Swaggart was exposed as a hypocrite when he was caught consorting with prostitutes. Though he eventually cleared up his finances, Jerry Falwell came very close to the courts and had some of his college premises seized by creditors in the 1991.[28] Although these indiscretions did not dent the faith of core supporters of television evangelism, they created considerable embarrassment for CR organizations at just the time when they were doing their best to broaden their appeal.

Fascinating though such sleaze is, my main concern is to identify those problems which were not accidental but which instead tell us something general about the link between religion and politics in modern America.

The Advantages of Zealotry

What most journalists had right was the commitment of CR activists. Conservative Protestantism is a system of beliefs that encourages enthusiastic support. It supposes a simple world of good and evil; it asserts certainty and castigates doubts; it divides people into believers and apostates; and it requires believers to spread the Word. The beliefs produce an appropriate social psychology: conservative Protestants are generally highly motivated to support their beliefs. Most will spend 10 or more hours a week in church-related activities and most will give a tenth of their income to church work. Hence when such people can be persuaded to become politically active they form a powerful resource. This is reflected in the enormous funds CR organizations have been able to raise in small amounts. It is also reflected in the success the CR has had in taking over branches of the Republican party.

The Disadvantages of Zealotry

What is less often observed is that the motivational advantages have corresponding weaknesses. Dogmatism and certainty make for a powerful group when its members are united but they also promote divisions. The social psychology that drives the purists to split into ever smaller groups is a product of the core theological proposition that every person has an equal ability to hear God's truth, to interpret the Word. In organizational terms, conservative Protestants tend to 'independency'. Even when fundamentalists join together in supra-congregational organizations (such as Falwell's network of Baptist fundamentalists) the organizational ties are weak and are frequently broken. Of course, conservative Protestants are united by core beliefs but, unlike the more 'churchly' Protestant forms of Lutheranism, Presbyterianism or Anglicanism, fundamentalism and Pentecostalism have no *theological* commitment to over-arching organizations to restrain their fissiparous tendencies.

Many of the early exaggerations of CR influence stemmed from over-looking this point. All too often it was assumed that the Christian Right could win the support of almost all evangelicals, fundamentalists and pentecostalists. It was not until the late 1980s that it became common for commentators to point out that there were major differences within and between these groups, not only about religious beliefs and socio-moral issues but also about the appropriateness of various ways of campaigning on those things about which they did agree.[29]

It is also worth noting that CR activists lack a particular source of cohesion that is central to other forms of conservative Protestant politics. Commentators often elided US fundamentalism with other right-wing political movements such as Paisleyism in Northern Ireland and the Broederbond in South Africa and failed to notice the salient differences between the part played by religion in the politics of ethnic conflict and state formation and the role it can play in the politics of pressure groups competing within a stable democratic nation state.[30] It simplifies, of course, but we can think of the difference in terms of the classic distinction between ascribed and achieved identity. Ulster Protestants have a history of religio-ethnic conflict with Irish Catholics as long as their sojourn in Ireland (more than 300 years). To be born a Protestant is to be placed in one camp on an historic battlefield. That the fundamental issue of the border and sovereignty has not been resolved means that religious and ethnic identity remain firmly wedded. One can abandon one only by abandoning the other and at considerable cost; people are killed for rejecting their ascribed identity. The casual use of the phrase 'culture wars' to describe US arguments over socio-moral issues deflects us from the cardinal point that the conflicts that motivate involvement in the CR are not pressing on the participants, are a product of individual choice, and such choices can be altered at little personal cost.

Furthermore, and this is important for understanding the fussiness of American fundamentalists, identity based on ethnicity can encourage a more tolerant attitude than does identity based on individually-appropriated ideology. Especially in circumstances of ethnic or national conflict, one demands little of those in one's own ethnic group other than that they do not reject their ascribed identity and fraternize with the enemy. Groups based on achieved identity tend to demand a great deal of consensus and be quick to expel those who do not maintain the rather exacting list of ideological or behavioural requirements.

Certainty and dogmatism, combined with a belief in the possibility of miracles, form a precarious base for political activism because they create unrealistic expectations and thus generate their own sources of disappointment. This simplifies, of course, but there is almost an inverse relationship between the energy which people can bring to a cause and their ability to sustain their support for that cause over long periods of only slight achievement (and the achievements are bound to appear slight because of the heightened expectations which provoked the original mobilization). Hence the pattern of rapid organizational growth and decline. Some great disaster is predicted, large numbers are mobilized to prevent it, and equally quickly they fall away.

What drives the zealots to political action also hinders their ability to make the compromises that democratic politics requires. Their tendency to fall out among themselves has a corresponding external weakness in their inability to form alliances with others. What was abundantly clear to the leaders of the Christian Right (and to such vociferous opponents within fundamentalism as Bob Jones III) was that the 'moral majority' was not a majority and could only achieve its goals through alliances with other groups: conservative blacks, Catholics and Jews. This in turn requires flexibility, a willingness to cut deals and overlook aspects of the beliefs of one's allies, that is quite at odds with the key premise of most varieties of conservative Protestant. They identify themselves by contrasting their supposed consistency across all spheres of life with the liberal Protestant acceptance of a division between the public and the private. The CR requires its supporters to alternate between religious thinking (in which only born again Bible-believing fundamentalists are saved) and political thinking (in which one seeks to mobilize around a shared Judeo-Christian heritage or, even more broadly, around conservative values). While leaders such as Falwell, Robertson, and Reed manage to alternate, many of the foot soldiers cannot. There was thus always a paradox at the heart of CR activities. The reason for getting involved in politics is the belief that confining religiously-derived values to the private world and to voluntary associations is an offence to God. The mark of the true Christian is the desire to re-establish God's righteous kingdom on earth and to protest against error. Yet in order effectively to pursue that agenda, the true Christian has periodically to overlook the heresies of Romanism, Judaism and every other form of Protestantism.

Two problems result from this. The first is that many fundamentalists could not sustain their political involvement for long. In 1984 and again in 1986 I interviewed many fundamentalists in Virginia and South Carolina and found in their conversation recurring statements of disillusionment with the compromises of the political process that they had become involved with in 1979 or 1980. I would not claim this fully explains the following data but it is worth noting that despite voter registration drives, fundamentalists (37%) were more likely than evangelicals (34%) and non-evangelicals (26%) to have abstained from the 1984 presidential elections.[31]

Even if Christian Rightists can set aside Paul's injunction to 'Be ye not yoked with unbelievers', the unbelievers may not be so accommodating. Many potential allies remain deeply suspicious of CR groups. Catholics can easily remember that the people who now solicit their assistance in anti-abortion crusades are the same people who previously campaigned against them. Tamney and Johnson's work shows Middletown Catholics no keener on religious involvement in politics than liberal Protestants.[32] Catholics had good reasons to be suspicious: the Ohio Moral Majority chapter preceded a meeting to discuss alliances with non-fundamentalists groups with a talk on 'The Roman Catholic Church: Harlot of Rome!'.[33] The alliance between the Archdiocese of New York and Pat Robertson's Christian Coalition to put out voter guides for the 1993 New York school board elections was an interesting departure but there are two reasons to doubt that this signals the start of a genuinely cross-confessional movement. First, as it usually tries to do, the Church has set the agenda for its members. Second, it has become involved in a city where it is in a strong position and thus has little reason to fear that a CR campaign will become an anti-Catholic campaign. The first point reminds us of the institutional strength of the Catholic Church and suggests a model of operation which, because it offends against the individualistic conscience assumed by democratic politics in a pluralistic culture, is unlikely to be very popular, even with many of its own members. The second point suggests geographical constraints on Protestant-Catholic alliances.

There have been enough instances of CR leaders making off-hand anti-Semitic remarks to give Jews cause for concern. In a crass introduction to a pro-Zionist speech, Falwell told his audience: 'A few of you here don't like Jews. And I know why. He [sic] can make more money accidentally than you can on purpose'.[34] In addition there is something a little unsavoury in conservative Protestant interest in Zionism. Falwell and Robertson support Israel, not because they have Jewish interests at heart but because they believe Israel has a date with divine providence on the fields of Armageddon!

The reluctance of black conservative Protestants to become involved (even if they overlooked the liberal economic and anti-statist agenda of the CR) can be readily understood if one considers that one of the unstated but obvious purposes of the independent Christian schools attached to many white fundamentalist churches is to maintain racial segregation.

The motivational weaknesses of zealotry are exacerbated by the CR's very limited ability to set the political agenda. Many social scientists forgot this and were misled by concentrating on attitude surveys that showed considerable sympathy for some CR agenda items. There are very many considerations that intervene between an opinion, attitude, belief or value and action predicated on such mental states. Insufficient attention was given to the need for opportunities to act and the relative costs of different courses of action. American fundamentalists, pentecostalists and evangelicals are not much of a religious muchness nor are they socio-economically homogenous. The call to think as members of Moral Majority or Christian Coalition is a call that competes with the other sources of identity and action and the extent to which it takes precedence is largely determined by a public agenda over which those groups have little control. Bill Clinton became president because more people were concerned about the weakness of George Bush's economic policy then were concerned about Clinton's support for promoting the rights of women and homosexuals. Falwell sold hundreds of thousands of a video called *Bill and Hilary's Circle of Power* in which opponents of the Clintons accused them of involvement in assassinations.[35] Clinton was re-elected in 1996 because the economy was booming.

This brings us to a paradox at the heart of movements that seek to elevate single-issue pressure group politics into broad party campaigns. To keep their supporters focused on the common cause requires activists to stress their single issue but this backfires because it further alienates non-supporters (who suppose that the candidate or the activists have nothing to offer on other matters). Indeed, it seems clear that single-issue candidates alienate even those who support their stand on the single issue. Polls during Robertson's election campaign showed that even many of those who shared his socio-moral positions and his religion were less rather than more likely to vote for him because he was a televangelist and an ordained cleric. A defeated Christian Right congressional candidate understood this:

> Lynch said he suffered from the dilemma facing all Christian Right candidates. Such candidates begin their campaigns emphasizing moral issues because that gets them volunteers and financial support. But, the media tags Christian Right candidates as moral issue candidates and plays up their positions on such issues; for instance, interviewers spend all their time on moral issues. The result is that Christian Right candidates cannot get across their secular message.[36]

A further problem with zealot politics is that its dynamism provokes opposition. The extravagant claims of influence made by the CR aroused those who had previously seen little need to defend what they held dear. The triumphalism and dogmatism of the fundamentalists who for a decade controlled the procedures for approving school textbooks in Texas motivated liberals to campaign successfully for a complete overhaul of the book selection procedures. Bills designed to force schools to give equal time to creation science made some headway until leading scientists realized that they could not take for granted their cultural hegemony but had to win the arguments. Robertson's campaign for the Republican party presidential nomination showed that his campaigning stimulated his opponents more than it mobilized his supporters. And, to return to the previous point, liberal anti-CR campaigns were often very effective in labelling CR-supported candidates as single-issue people. They were also effective in preventing leading CR activists effectively deploying religious rhetoric for their 'home boys' and then switching to a secular justification when addressing a wider audience. Organizations such as People for the American Way recorded the religious rhetoric and made it widely available to audiences to which the Falwell and Robertson had hoped to present a very different image.

Much more could be said about the social psychology of conservative Protestantism but the above contains enough to make the case that the motivational advantages enjoyed by fundamentalism as a source of political activists have matching disadvantages which are exacerbated by the political environment of a modern democracy. The attitudes and beliefs that can make evangelicals, fundamentalists and Pentecostalists excellent 'storm troopers' prevent them functioning well as trench warriors and besiegers. They become disappointed easily, they fight among themselves, they fail to sustain alliances, and they are poor at pragmatic compromise.

Pluralism, Democracy and Social Necessity

In this second section of theoretical considerations, I would like to turn to what could grandiosely be called the 'functional pre-requisites of modern democracy'. Many of the exaggerations of CR influence stem from inappropriate comparisons between the Christian Right and religio-political movements elsewhere, often in countries with quite different economic and political structures. The grouping of the Moral Majority with Iranian Fundamentalism and Protestant Unionism in Ulster confused rather than illuminated. The more one stresses continuities between Islamic fundamentalism and the CR, the more one loses sight of the fact that social structure sets the conditions for individual action. The United States is a culturally pluralistic affluent industrial democracy with a complex and stable civic society. Egypt and Iran are not.

It is my case that the Christian Right is constrained by some very general features of modern societies that cannot be readily imagined away. It is clear that sympathy for particular aspects of the CR programme (respect for the claim that funda-mentalists are as legitimate a minority as homosexuals, for example) is tempered by disquiet about the overall project. Here I would draw attention not to the position or popularity of specifically anti-CR movement organizations such as People for the American Way (though that is important) but to two more subtle indicators; one from the actions of the general public and one from the responses to the CR of a pivotal elite. Consider again the responses to Robertson's run for the presidency. What is significant is not that liberals voted against him but that many evangelicals, fundamentalists and Pentecostalists, who shared his religious beliefs and many of his particular platform positions, declined to support him. My own interviews and my reading of the gulf between widespread support for what we might call CR-friendly attitudes and actual support for CR-promoted candidates suggest that there is among American voters a clear understanding that there were dangers to mixing religion and politics.

Consider also the judgements of the Supreme Court. The CR explanation of all that is bad about America includes the proposition that unrepresentatively liberal justices have by-passed the legislative arm of government to impose unpopular decisions on the American people. Yet almost two decades of a Supreme Court dominated by conservatives appointed by Reagan and Bush (and of federal courts similarly staffed) has produced very little change in the decisions made on issues of concern to the CR. The explanation is that once in office judges and justices tend to temper their own ideological preferences with a sense of public opinion and social necessity. One organizational interest is the need to maintain the authority of the judiciary; the justices appreciate that too frequently over-turning previous decisions will undermine the legitimacy of the courts. But they also share with those conservatives who do not vote for CR candidates an implicit understanding of the wider implications of endorsing the CR agenda.

Most Americans are reasonably content with the present place of religion in public life. Most think religion a good thing and have some of it themselves. But they also appreciate its potential for conflict and are content with the general accommo-dation that modern America has reached in its interpretation of the constitutional requirements. Great liberty should be permitted to the individual and the family in the private sphere and the price of that liberty is something approaching neutrality in the public arena. Ordinary Americans may not often consciously articulate their happiness with the public-private divide but they regularly endorse it when they vote against referenda which they see as religious meddling and when they refuse to translate their general dislike for, say, abortion, into support for single-issue anti-abortion candidates.

My argument is that what in the end restrains the Christian Right is the implicit recognition by many Americans, found as much among the common people as among the justices of the Supreme Court, that the separation of church and state and the location of religion in the private sphere are not historical accidents. They are functional pre-requisites for a modern democratic society which happens to be culturally heterogeneous and which places great stress on individualism.

To see what would have to change for the Christian Right project to succeed we need not consider the wilder extremes of lifestyle experimentation and liberal excess. We need only contemplate the following. About 70% of American women work. The chances of a first marriage ending in divorce are 50:50. Almost a quarter of American families are headed by a single parent. Most middle-aged Americans have experimented with soft drugs and many middle-class Americans still smoke dope. Extra-marital and pre-marital sexual intercourse are commonplace.

Conservative critics see the social changes they dislike as being the consequences of deliberate choices. William Donohue, for example, blames it all on 'the new freedom ... a socially reckless force standing in the way of true liberty'.[37] The main causes of that social irresponsibility are 'rights mania' and reliance on big government and his detailed discussions of these pathologies consist mainly of exegesis of the views of philosophers, social theorists and political activists who advocate specific rights. 'Moral codes, which are by their very nature restrictive, are cast as the enemy of freedom'.[38] Yet the opening sentence of the main part of his text suggests a very different explanation: 'The contemporary idea of freedom ... is the result of a long series of political, economic, social and cultural changes ...'.[39] There is not room here to take one by one the aspects of the modern world that Donohue dislikes and trace their causes to see to what extent they are the intended consequence of deliberate action or the unintended outcomes of changes which no-one much desired. All that is necessary for my case is to believe (a) that much of the new freedom and consequent cultural variety is an unintended consequence of individual autonomy and prosperity; and (b) that many of even those changes for which conscious authorship can be identified are now largely irreversible.

One brief way of making this case is to note the poverty of the solutions which conservatives themselves offer to what they perceive as the evils of modern America. For example, the best that most can suggest as a response to America's high divorce rate is to teach Christian values in schools. I do not wish to suggest that this prescription is insincerely offered but it does seem to have more to do with one cultural group wishing to assert the superiority of its values than with any reasonable hope of effectiveness. Insofar as there is faith in the remedy, that faith draws its strength from faith in the religious sense. It is not just rhetorical habit that explains why Falwell and Robertson quickly go from analysing social vices to promoting religious revival: their solutions are implausible unless God takes a hand. Only if the sexually active teenagers on the end of a badgering about traditional moral values are brought under conviction of sin and undergo a born-again experience will exhortation produce deep and shared commitment to those values.

But the social and cultural diversity of the United States is now such that it is very difficult to see how a sufficient consensus can be created to reverse pluralism. Individual autonomy is both a cause of, and a necessary accommodation to, social and cultural diversity. Even if (as I suspect) the sovereign consumers of late capitalism mistake the extent of their freedom, they are profoundly attached to that illusion and show little sign either of being willing to subordinate themselves in an ideologically cohesive community or of being able to agree on what should be the shared values of such a community.

If we begin with a view of modern social structures which pays appropriate attention to the functional prerequisites of culturally plural democracies, we come to an estimate of the Christian Right in America which is in line with the evidence. Our societies permit (and in some places even encourage) the maintenance of distinctive religious worldviews and thus encourage socio-moral contests but they also create a structure (the division of the life world into public and private spheres) and a culture (universalism and tolerance) that of necessity restrain such contests and require that they be fought on universalistic ethical and public policy principles. In modern democratic culturally plural societies, no socio-moral interest group can plausibly promote its case on the grounds 'that the Bible (or the Koran or the Book of Mormon) says so'. Instead it must argue that equity or reason or the public good says so. So the CR promotes, not Christian values, but 'family' values. But in replacing divine authority with mundane reasoning, the CR swaps its strongest suit for its weakest. It asks to be judged by secular criteria and on those it must lose.

The spokesmen of the Christian Right believe that many of those features of the modern world that they find objectionable (in particular, the secular nature of the public world) are either contingent or negotiable and hence can, with the right sort of political pressure, be changed. My concluding point is that much of what the Christian Right dislikes about the USA is a near-inevitable consequence of cultural pluralism in a democratic industrial democracy.

Conclusion

This chapter has aimed to make two simple points from the recent career of the Christian Right in the USA. First, political movements that mobilize conservative Protestants have an advantage over secular movements in that their supporters tend to be highly motivated and disciplined. However, that bonus comes with inherent disadvantages. The social psychology of the zealot creates difficulties with long-term involvement and cooperation with potential allies. In particular, zealots are not good at the compromises that are essential for a minority to enjoy lasting success in a democratic society. Second, modern culturally plural democracies have a number of characteristics that are so difficult to imagine away that we can almost describe them as 'functional pre-requisites': separation of public and private spheres; tolerance of diversity in the private sphere; and the widespread imposition of universalism on the public sphere. It is these, rather than any conspiracy to promote 'secular humanist' values, that prevent the CR achieving its goals. And insofar as the majority of the politically active people of the United States are, with varying degrees of consciousness and detail, aware of these pre-requisites, the progress of the CR will be confined to establishing the right to be tolerated as one cultural minority among many.

About the author

Steve Bruce, Department of Sociology, University of Aberdeen, Edward Wright Building, Dunbar Street, Aberdeen AB24 3QY, Scotland; email: *s.bruce@abdn.ac.uk*

Notes

1 J. L. Himmelstein, 'The New Right', in R. C. Liebman and R. Wuthnow (eds), *The New Christian Right.* New York: Aldine, 1983, pp. 1–30.

2 J. M. Penning, 'Pat Robertson and the GOP: 1988 and Beyond', in S. Bruce, P. Kivisto, and W. H. Swatos Jr (eds), *The Rapture of Politics: the Christian Right as the United States Approaches the Year 2000.* New Brunswick: Transaction, 1995, pp. 105–22.

3 L. Barnett, 'The electability test', *Time*, 29 February 1988, 13.

4 C. Wilcox, 'Premillenialists at the Millennium: Some Reflections on the Christian Right in the Twenty-First Century', in Bruce *et al.*, *The Rapture of Politics*, p. 31.

5 C. Cleary, *America: a Place Called Hope.* Dublin: O'Brien, 1993, p. 99.

6 D. W. Brady and K. L. Tedin, 'Ladies in pink: religion and political ideology in the anti-ERA movement', *Social Science Quarterly*, 56 (1976), 564–75.

7 E. H. Buell, 'An Army that Meets Every Sunday? Popular Support for the Moral Majority in 1980', paper given at Midwest PSA meeting, Chicago, April 1983, p. 22.

8 A. Shupe and W. Stacey, *Born-again Politics: What Social Surveys Really Show.* New York: Edwin Mellen, 1982, p. 41.

9 B. Fishman, *American Families: Responding to the Pro-Family Movement.* Washington: People for the American Way, 1984, p. 86.

10 S. M. Lipset and E. Raab, 'Evangelicals and the elections', *Commentary*, 71 (1981), 25–31.

11 S. D. Johnson and J. B. Tamney, 'The election of a traditional-family-values candidate', *Review of Religious Research*, 38 (1996), 97.

12 J. Himmelstein and J. A. McRae Jnr, 'Social conservatism, New Republicans and the 1980 election', *Public Opinion Quarterly*, 48 (1984), 595–605.

13 A. H. Miller and M. P. Wattenburg, 'Politics from the pulpit: religiosity and the 1980 elections', *Public Opinion Quarterly*, 48 (1984), 300–12.

14 J. Garvey, 'Fundamentalism and American Law', in M. Marty and R. S. Appleby (eds), *Fundamentalisms and the State.* Chicago: University of Chicago Press, 1993, pp. 28–48.

15 Garvey, 'Fundamentalism and American Law', p. 40.

16 A. D. Hertzke, 'Christian Fundamentalists and the Imperatives of American Politics', in E. Sahliyeh (ed.), *Religious Resurgence and Politics in the Contemporary World.* Albany: State University of New York, 1990, p. 70.

17 L. Gilkey, *Creationism on Trial: Evolution and God at Little Rock.* Minneapolis: Winston, 1985).

18 Supreme Court of the United States, 85-1513, 19 June 1987, pp. 13–14.

19 *Religion Watch*, July–August 1997, 2.

20 Garvey, 'Fundamentalism and American Law', p. 41.

21 M. Weber, *Economy and Society.* New York: Bedminister, 1968, p. 391.

22 'Reed resignation from CC Reveals a Split in the Ranks', www.atheists.org, 1997.

23 J. McLaughlin, 'The evangelical surge', *National Review*, 20 (1984), 13.

24 P. Brogan, 'Abortion issue returns to muddy political and legal waters', *Herald*, 27 July 1991.

25 L. R. Stains, 'Religion as politics', *USA Weekend*, 16–18 September 1994. For an excellent summary of CR attempts to take over the GOP, see M. C. Moen, *The Transformation of the Christian Right*. Tuscaloosa: University of Alabama Press, 1992.

26 S. Bruce, *The Rise and Fall of the New Christian Right*. Oxford: Oxford University Press, 1988.

27 G. L. Tidwell, *Anatomy of a Fraud: Inside the Finances of the PTL Ministeries*. New York: John Wiley, 1993; J. Barnhart, *Jim and Tammy: Charismatic Intrigue Inside PTL*. Buffalo, Prometheus, 1988.

28 L. J. Davis, 'Other people's money: being a tale of Jerry Falwell, Charles Keating, and the pursuit of Christian booty', *Mother Jones*, 93, www.mojones.com, 1997.

29 For a good example of such research, see C. Wilcox, 'Religion and the preacher vote in the South: sources of support for Jackson and Robertson in the Southern Primaries', *Sociological Analysis*, 53 (1992), 323–31 and *God's Warriors*. Baltimore: Johns Hopkins University Press, 1992.

30 These and other differences are pursued in S. Bruce, *Conservative Protestant Politics*. Oxford: Oxford University Press, 1998.

31 T. G. Jelen, 'The effects of religious separatism on white Protestants in the 1984 presidential elections', *Sociological Analysis*, 48 (1987), 30–45. See also T. G. Jelen, *The Political Mobilization of Religious Beliefs*. New York: Praeger, 1991.

32 J. B. Tamney and S. D. Johnson, 'Church-state relations in the 1980s: public opinion in Middletown', *Sociological Analysis*, 48 (1987), 1–16.

33 C. Wilcox, 'America's radical right revisited', *Sociological Analysis*, 48 (1987), 46–57.

34 F. Conway and J. Siegelman, *Holy Terror*. New York: Doubleday, 1982, p. 168.

35 D. Lauter, 'Culture of hate', *The Guardian*, 7 July 1994.

36 S. D. Johnson, J. B. Tamney, and R. Burton, 'Factors influencing vote for a Christian Right candidate', *Review of Religious Research*, 31 (1990), 300.

37 W. A. Donohue, *The New Freedom*. New Brunswick: Transaction, 1990, p. 15.

38 Donohue, *The New Freedom*, p. 5.

39 Donohue, *The New Freedom*, p. 15.

4

Studying Political Ideas: a Public Political Discourse Approach

Andrew Chadwick

How do parties, groups and movements construct shared frameworks of understanding? Answering this question must involve some analysis of the role played by political ideas. They are an inescapable fact of political life. Yet, as with most inescapable facts, controversy has raged over how they should be studied.[1] This chapter presents a framework for the empirical analysis of ideas. It aims to strike a balance between the presentation of a set of general assumptions, and a recognition that any framework must engage with particular evidence from the historical context under investigation, especially the processes through which ideational communication occurs. Elements from a variety of perspectives are combined to provide a 'public political discourse' approach, which: appreciates the importance of communication through the media; provides justifications for specific sources of evidence to be used; and places ideas in context. My main concern throughout is in developing a useful framework of explicit assumptions about how to study political ideas. It is not my intention to delve deeply into the philosophical roots of its elements, nor do I seek to provide a blueprint that is bought wholesale or not at all. It represents only one approach among countless possible others. Rather, my aim is to raise awareness of the fact that the assumptions which are brought to the study of political ideas are important determinants of the kinds of analyses we see produced. These assumptions need to be stated and defended, with a recognition that they obscure as many possibilities as they reveal.

This chapter emerges from a partial sense of dissatisfaction with recent methodological debates in history, a field which has, since the 1980s, experienced a wave of revisionism. The shift has involved a widespread reappraisal of earlier class-based interpretations of politics and a reassertion of the importance of ideas, usually defined as 'discourses'. The examination of these, and the organizational structures of parties, movements, and the state, has gone hand in hand with a new sensitivity to the means through which historical evidence is mediated, along with the emergence of postmodernist approaches to political identities. Written from the perspective of one who enjoys having a foot in both disciplines – history and political science – this chapter is intended to suggest to the political science community the ways in which some of the interesting developments in historiography over the past 15 years, if developed in the directions outlined here, might contribute to an understanding of the relationship between political ideas and political action. Although analysis of how ideas, parties and movements interrelate has always been a core concern of political scientists, it is interesting to note how few of the controversies that have raged in history have flowed into political science's mainstream. Yet historians, often condemned by all social scientists for being 'atheoretical', have recently provided a rich and suggestive combination of theoretical discussion and empirical research.

It is valuable at the outset to consider briefly what has usually been meant by the terms 'discourse' and 'discourse analysis'. Basic definitional usage differs sub-stantially across disciplines. In mainstream linguistics first, the dominant definition implies a focus on the interpretation of coherent units of spoken or written language, and the emphasis is on the formal analysis of such texts. It is mostly concerned with language use in action – in everyday conversation, or in classrooms or courtrooms, for instance.[2] Second, during the last 20 years 'critical discourse analysis' has sought to forge links between mainstream linguistics and critical social theory in order to comprehend the role played by language use in producing asymmetrical power relations and social and political identity. Still employing a practical focus on language use in action, it typically seeks to link the formal features of texts with social and political contexts, and often broadens out the definition of text to include symbolic representations which may appear alongside the written and spoken word.[3] Third and finally, in the hands of theorists such as Foucault and Derrida, the terms are less easy to pin down, but there is a general level of agreement that they are used to understand how the totality of social relations is constituted by language and this does not necessarily require close analysis of written and spoken texts in the manner of formal linguistics. Indeed, in this vision, the concept of a 'text' can refer to any or all social and political phen-omena.[4] On the whole, revisionist historians have taken their inspiration from the third of these three definitions. I would argue that their neglect of the other two, but particularly the second – critical discourse analysis as the interrogation of text and context which draws upon both linguistics and critical theory – has proved a source of weakness. Norman Fairclough, a writer at the forefront of the develop-ment of critical discourse analysis as a distinctive field, recently criticized discourse analysts from outside linguistics for their failure to recognize that the 'texture' (form and organization) of texts should be viewed as equal in importance to their 'content' – an insight which I shall explore later in this essay.[5]

It is difficult to deny postmodernism's influence on the social sciences during the last 20 years, and the study of politics is no exception. Yet here the postmodernist approach has had a much greater impact on political theory than it has on what can be termed empirical studies. It is undoubtedly the case that postmodernism has so far failed to inspire research agendas that involve an established interface between evidence and theory. These observations do not assume a divide between the 'real' world of empirical work, and the 'less real' world of political theory. It is simply to assert that, as far as research is concerned, there have always been different forms of *practice*, and each form has its own conventions. Those who have adopted a postmodernist approach to politics have so far been less inclined to perform the characteristic practices of empirical political scientists and historians: using the 'archives', interviewing, 'thick description', and so on.[6]

The results of this retreat into theory are intriguing, especially in the light of recent developments in the related field of media/cultural studies. There the preoccupation with language and discourse has impacted on the mainstream, and has strongly informed empirical modes of research practice. In short, in both history and media/cultural studies, there has been a fruitful balance between theoretical coherence and 'making sense of the world' through empirical investigation. This is not to argue that postmodernist approaches have become hegemonic in either of these disciplines. Far from it. But it is to state that negotiations with the approach have been informed to a much greater extent by the usage of empirical research practice rather than claims to theoretical 'purity'.

The discipline of political science is therefore left in a curious situation. Recent work in the fields of historical and media/cultural studies have demonstrated that the chief concerns of the approach raise some important and interesting questions. It would be rash to say that both of these fields have taken a 'linguistic turn'; more accurate to describe it as a linguistic 'scenic route', a journey less direct, with less certainty of arriving at a precise location, but one all the more interesting for it. The linguistic scenic route has raised more questions than it has answered, but it has opened up a new range of possibilities from which political scientists engaged in 'empirical' types of research practice might learn. I turn now to a discussion of the new historical postmodernism.

Historical Postmodernism

The debate over the 'linguistic turn' in history has raged since the publication of Stedman Jones' essay on English Chartism in 1983.[7] Stedman Jones is acknowledged to be the first to introduce linguistic theory to social history, though his remarks were initially tentative and cautious. This, along with a lack of immediate further clarification, soon led to a number of important critiques which stress: the misappropriation of linguistic theory and the superficiality of the approach;[8] the similarity between it and 'traditional' histories of 'political thought';[9] or the implications for a history seeking to establish causal explanations.[10] It has also been argued that the methodology of Patrick Joyce, another major contributor to the postmodernist historiography, is merely eclectic, since it privileges the discourse of 'populism', thereby replacing one all-embracing category of explanation – 'class' – with another.[11] Nevertheless, Joyce's work has been at the forefront of the recent assault on traditional history. He wishes to give more prominence to 'the actual terms in which contemporaries talked about the social order, and to the means through which they communicated their perceptions'.[12] This involves a marked reluctance to impose preconceived judgements on political utterances. Instead, a sensitivity to the ways in which individuals and groups actually discussed their social and political positions brings into focus 'extra-proletarian identifications'; in other words, political identities which did not stem from recognition of a position in an economically-determined class structure. 'Class', as the major conceptual inspiration for social history since the 1960s, is not completely removed from the scene: it is acknowledged that elements of class identity have often been present which contradict and conflict with other identities. But the overwhelming emphasis in this approach is placed upon the limited role of social and economic structures (as traditionally understood) in determining political discourse.

Historians influenced by the 'linguistic turn' have therefore attempted to apply generalizations about the constitutive role of discourses in the creation of political identity. The established tradition in social history has come under attack from an approach which rejects the view that ideas emerge 'automatically out of the "objective" economic and social interests of groups', and that parties, pressure groups and movements are the 'passive beneficiaries of structural divisions within society'.[13] Historical postmodernism views political organizations as active participants in the creation of political alliances and shared discourses. In order to understand how coalitions of support are constructed, attention must be paid to expressions of political discourse. This points toward a 'recognition of the contested and constructive role of argument and ideas in the establishment of successful political strategies'.[14] The central core of historical postmodernism is originally derived from a structuralist interpretation of language as generative of human consciousness, and therefore of political identities. Rather than language reflecting a prior social existence, it is said to create that very existence. Language is not a reflection of processes more 'real' than itself. Rather, existence is to be understood as produced by and within language, which in turn is said to exist as a system of differences. This interpretation originated with the Swiss structural linguist, Saussure.[15] The arbitrary nature of words, and their use in different, 'encoded', ways are studied for how meaning is constructed *within* texts. Meanings are said to be the product of the differences internal to the system of signs rather than the relation between language and an extra-linguistic 'context'. In the hands of post-structuralists, it is the idea that language is anterior to what we experience as 'reality', and the lack of control over how languages are used, for example, by authors of texts, which has had a destabilizing effect on traditional history. The notion that we are able to 'read' texts as unproblematic expressions of authorial intent has been decisively rejected. All we are able to achieve is a sensitivity to the 'encoded' nature of language, attainable through 'decoding'. Along with this goes an assumption that texts are open to an infinite number of readings. This does not occur as a result of a reader's position in the social and economic structure, but is due to the ambiguities, openness and 'polysemic' character of the text itself.

It would be a mistake to argue that these historians have accepted all of the post-modernist 'project'. Work has tended to focus on the production of social and political identities through the examination of discourses in particular historical periods. This is, in a sense, why the work of Joyce and others has been criticized for its often traditional appearance 'on the page'. Nevertheless, it *is* the case that postmodernist historiography can be accused of throwing the baby out with the bath water. For in its rejection of a social existence outside of language, it becomes impossible (because unnecessary) to consider the interrelations between texts and contexts, between texts and the ideas contained within them, and the *uses* to which ideas are put by individuals, groups and classes; in essence the *communication, reception and mutation* of ideas. As I will argue later, a 'dialogical' conception of political discourse comes closest in providing the necessary balance between these three areas. It is possible to take the recent interest in language, and develop it in more fruitful ways.

First, however, I want to focus on the debates over the meaning of discourse in the new history. In Joyce's influential work *Visions of the People: Industrial England and the Question of Class, 1848–1914*, for example, there are at least two definitions at work. In the first section of the book, which is mainly concerned with politics and work, it is used to refer to 'bodies of utterance of a relatively formal, public sort, often associated with institutions'. This is clearly the realm of the printed word, the pamphleteer, political intellectual, newspaper columnist, or platform speaker. The second sense in which discourse is used – in relation to art and culture – refers to the 'symbolic, less formal and less public, often assumed and unspoken ways in which the social world is given form by people'. This second sense is much more inclusive, taking in mannerisms, gesture, clothing, and patterns of consumption: in short, 'culture', broadly defined.[16] The ambiguity surrounding the meaning of discourse in the new history presents several important difficulties, but by far the most damning criticism is that the approach does not live up to its expectations because it has paid too much attention to formal discourse (Joyce's first definition), and not enough attention to the broader, symbolic definition. It has been argued that much of the work inspired by the linguistic turn seems to focus on coherent public expressions, which are seen as linked directly to the fortunes of existing political institutions, such as pressure groups and political parties.[17]

These are important criticisms. There is no escaping the fact that the study of language presents the problem of mediation. As Friedman has argued:

> The past is ... triply mediated – first, through the mediations of those texts, which are themselves reconstructions of what "really" happened; second, through the fragmentary and partial survival of those textualizations which are dependent upon the politics of documentation and the luck, skill, and persistence of the historian-as-detective who must locate them; and third, through the interpretive, meaning-making gaze of the historian.[18]

If this is assumed, then a necessary component of a credible approach to the study of political ideas must include some appraisal of the implications of differing patterns of mediation. It is arguable that mainstream work, whether of a 'narrative' or 'analytical' kind, has generally belonged to the genre of 'realism', in which the synthetic and constructed nature of research becomes masked by the seemingly unproblematic use of particular kinds of source material, as the *definitive* sources. This is then joined to a simple concept of referentiality in which the historical narrative is a straightforward 'reflection' of the 'real'. But this paradigm ignores the necessarily intertextual nature of writing, the fact that all histories are positioned alongside other histories, and that even the ideas which are studied are themselves histories of a kind.[19] Highlighting the contingency of historical explanation as it relates to source materials can open up avenues of explanation which have previously been neglected or simply ignored. There is, in short, no such thing as the 'definitive' source. Being aware of the constraints imposed by the selection of source material is not about getting the story straight; it is, in Kellner's witty formulation, about 'getting the story crooked'; alerting the reader to the contingency and unavoidable assumptions which are a part of all intellectual inquiry.[20] The neglect of this simple point is one of the reasons why those who study ideas in action have often found it difficult to answer the criticism: why did you look at *that* particular expression? If this deserves an answer, the study of ideas must involve some explanation of the sources of expression, and the hierarchies of evidence which are a crucial component of any research. How can this insight be developed?

Ideas and Communication Practices: a Taxonomy

In the study of political ideas more generally many begin by asserting their import-ance simply because they exist. This is a start, but it does not go very far in the direction of deciding precisely which sorts of ideas are more important for par-ticular purposes. A way forward can be found if we appreciate that ideas are dependent upon communication practices. If they are to win support, ideas must be communicated to audiences, and audiences must be receptive. The rather vague definitions as they are used in both mainstream political science and postmodernist historiography suggests the need for a basic taxonomy of the main communication practices. The problem may be defined as one of levels of abstraction and com-munication. It is possible to generate such a taxonomy using two basic questions:

1. What are the principal styles of argument which characterize the communi-cation practice?

2. What are the dominant media of communication which characterize the com-munication practice?

This provides at least three types of communication practice: ideas as philosophical discourse; ideas as public political discourse; and ideas as symbolic discourse.

Ideas as Philosophical Discourse

First, there are ideas communicated by the practice of philosophical discourse, in which certain concepts enjoy status because they may be seen as 'perennial'.[21] Arguments about the nature of 'the state', for example, rely on a distinctive mode of reasoning about 'the state' which has a long ancestry. Political philosophers are at one remove from the political arena, and enjoy the fruits of idle speculation. Indeed, such practices have been celebrated in the mainstream of the normative tradition, especially by those who have used Aristotle's response to those who questioned the utility of philosophy when he wrote that 'to be constantly asking "What is the use of?" is unbecoming to those of superior mentality and free birth'.[22] Communication at this level occurs mainly through narrowly circumscribed channels – works of political philosophy – whose main audience is literate, highly educated and familiar with the demands of the genre. The practice of philosophical discourse is thus confined to a small minority during any given period.

This does not, however, mean that the concepts discussed are always so confined: ideas as philosophical discourse may often radiate out into other areas of com-munication. Nevertheless, it is difficult to go as far down this path as Rawls when he argues that 'Political philosophy does not, as some have thought, withdraw from society and the world. Nor does it claim to discover what is true by its own distinctive method of reason apart from any tradition of political thought and practice'.[23] To accept this would be to lose the necessary distinction between modes of communication which is being established here. Put very bluntly, do the typical voter, the typical government minister and the typical philosopher enjoy the same daily diet of reading? The answer will usually be 'no'. It may sometimes be yes, but only to a certain extent; and I would argue that it is the differences in diet to which those who study the power of political ideas must be sensitive.

It is most often assumed that ideas as philosophical discourse are 'independent variables', that they influence political 'action', and that it is therefore acceptable to assume all of this, and study ideas in their 'purest' forms. Debate exists over the exact method to be employed: for instance, should the approach attempt to discern the 'core elements' of an 'ideology' (understood as a 'system of ideas'), or understand it as a tension between two extremes, such as libertarianism and collectivism?[24] But the fundamental assumption is that systems of ideas are to be studied in terms of their internal structures ('in their own right') and that, in order to do this adequately, it is necessary to focus on their most elaborate and demanding expressions.[25] As a consequence, those who study ideas as philosophical discourse generally pay very little attention to the processes of communication between producers and audiences.

Ideas as Public Political Discourse

Second, there are ideas communicated as what I shall term 'public political discourse'. At this level, ideas are articulated, debate and discussion takes place, but these debates are seen as supremely political interventions and as elements of particular political strategies. They may have been the product of quiet reflection, or they may have been written with the fierce heat of a polemic, but they are all politically motivated in the sense that they are primarily written for the times in which they are produced: they are public and are embedded within a political and historical context. Communication here occurs through a wide variety of channels, but especially regular, mass communications, whose main audience is seen as reasonably literate and educated, and has access to such media. Communication of this type usually (but not always) involves greater numbers of people than ideas as philosophical discourse. Public political discourse can thus be defined as a process centred on an intermediate level of the communication of ideas in political life, the analysis of which involves studying neither 'great works' of political theory, nor 'mass' opinion as it is expressed through opinion poll data, and which involves a focus on both the production and the reception of political ideas.

When it comes to the framework of analysis, it may often be assumed that ideas as public political discourse arise out of 'real' politics, that their success or failure is dependent upon the success or failure of particular institutions, groups, or classes, and that they rise and fall with the particular agent with which they are identified.[26] Yet this assumption is not strictly necessary. A different view, consistent with the historical postmodernist view of language as generative of human consciousness outlined above, argues that the distinction between 'real' politics and ideas is artificial. In this perspective, politics is a linguistic practice, and our understanding of any political practice is incomplete if it does not refer to the discourses that surround and construct it.[27]

Ideas as Symbolic Discourse

Third, there exist ideas communicated as 'symbolic discourse'. This is the sphere in which symbols, ranging from the spectacular to the relatively mundane (processions, the wearing of particular colours, the burning of flags, and other iconography), contribute towards shared beliefs. It may also include bodily movements, whether conscious or not, such as gesture, stance, facial expression. Most communication at this level is either direct, or mediated through unobtrusive forms. Like public political discourse, communication of this type usually (but not always) involves greater numbers than philosophical discourse. When it comes to the framework of analysis, the populist ethos of some approaches, such as 'history from below' or cultural anthropology, take pride in digging up ideas as expressed through symbolic discourse. As with public political discourse, those who study symbolic discourse devote much attention to the forms of communication in a way that those who study philosophical discourse generally do not.

These three types of expression: philosophical discourse, public political discourse and symbolic discourse, have different implications for the study of ideas. They involve different sets of assumptions about evidence and explanation, and yet it is precisely these assumptions which are rarely made explicit. In the rest of this essay I will explore the communication practice of 'public political discourse' in an attempt to indicate its usefulness for the study of how parties, groups and movements construct shared frameworks of understanding.

Desiderata for the Public Political Discourse Approach

The public political discourse approach involves several desiderata. First, it is desirable that in the historical period under investigation, the ideas were in the public domain. If not, there should be a sensitivity to the complex relationship between public and private utterances. This introduces an important, yet often overlooked, distinction. There are immense problems with treating evidence from private sources in the same way as published opinion. The latter, by their very nature, are written in the hope of consolidating or reconstituting the political beliefs of audiences. They differ from private views, which were never meant for immediate public consumption. To take one example, the research on early Labour Party ideas is peppered with references to the diary of Beatrice Webb, but if such a source is taken as evidence of the ideas of Fabian socialism, then this clearly involves an assumption that the distinction between ideas in the public domain, and those in the private, is one not worth making. The argument here, however, is that such a distinction is important, because ideas in this view must be communicated and disseminated during a particular time period in order to exert an influence during that period. Protagonists' private behaviour may differ substantially from that which is designed for public consumption, and the two should be highlighted through careful juxtaposition. An awareness of the effects of this divide on the production and consumption of political ideas is again helpful in establishing levels of influence.

It should be stated, however, that this distinction does not rest upon the classic liberal distinction between public and private spheres. It does not seek automatically to privilege what takes place in the 'public' sphere at the expense of the 'private' sphere. It simply states that there is a distinct mode of ideational communication – public political discourse – which is best captured by attention to publicly communicated political ideas. As the leading feminist historian, Joan Scott, has argued, the linkages between personal and political experiences need to be acknowledged, but not at the expense of seeing *some* identities as fundamentally shaped by processes in the public sphere.[28]

Second, the public political discourse framework requires prioritization of the media for the communication of ideas in any given historical period. The obvious notion that the media through which ideas are constructed and transmitted change dramatically over time is frequently overlooked. Communication at the beginning of the third millennium occurs through a wide variety of media, but it would be highly controversial to assume that print media are now the sole means for the expression of political ideas. A framework for the analysis of ideas in 2000 is bound to consider mass broadcast media as a major site of conflict, construction and transmission – a site which has little relevance for 1900. Analysis of public political discourse during the pre-broadcasting era involves special attention to the mediated printed word with specific political content: especially journals, newspapers, pamphlets, and leaflets. If analysis is focused at this level, and not solely upon ideas communicated as philosophical discourse, it encompasses a wider range of writers than small groups of intellectuals. It is regularized, accessible communication involving a community.

Third, although ideas communicated as philosophical discourse and as symbolic discourse are not the main focus, the concept of public political discourse does not preclude discussion of them. The aim might be to establish connections between the different communication practices, or it might involve a recognition that complex combinations of all three might characterize certain texts. Consider the textual form of the web page as a contemporary example, the illustrated novel as an older manifestation, or even the meaning constructed by the combination, in Hobbes' *Leviathan*, of the original engraved title page and the written words within.[29] It is therefore necessary to look at 'high' and 'low', 'elite' and 'mass', 'official' and 'unofficial', 'sophisticated' and 'simple', and the combinations of these in given texts. This conclusion has been reached, albeit via a different epistemological route, by Stedman Jones:

> [T]here is no reason why the meticulous techniques devoted to the analysis of texts embodying more explicit, self-consciously reflective forms of thought or specialized forms of knowledge and mediated through highly formalized forms of communication, should not be extended to other kinds of text dispersed across the socio-cultural spectrum ... Similarly, and in contrast to the traditional approach to 'social movements', there is no reason why the 'intellective' elements of popular politics should not be analysed as rigorously and scrupulously as is customary in studies of the history of ideas ... [Few] attempts have so far been made to identify and trace the presence and interactions of different political, religious and other languages in the utterances and activities of large movements, mass parties, churches, religious groups or newspapers and their readerships in the modern era.[30]

In widening the range of evidence, the public political discourse approach attempts to provide a panoramic view.

Fourth, the approach should make it explicit that ideas are deeply embedded in a context of political competition, rivalry, conflict, even struggle. Shared meanings are negotiated and constructed by elites and non-elites, engaged in dialogical, reciprocal relationships (a point to which I return below). Yet meaning is never wholly fixed. Although asymmetrical power relations may exist, constituted both by discursive and extra-discursive factors, meanings are to be seen as perpetually undergoing contestation and redefinition, and are seen as an important source of collective and individual identity. It does not privilege certain ideas simply because they were expressed elaborately, or were developed by 'intellectuals' as political philosophers. Instead, it assumes that focusing on these intermediary texts can bring us closer to those ideas that were more relevant to the everyday political experiences of those involved. It must be stressed, however, that the concept of 'intellectual' is one worth retaining in its broadest sense. But the ability of intellectuals to create new and distinct political communities through the communication of ideas requires sensitivity to the negotiated relations between intellectuals and non-intellectuals.

Fifth, the public political discourse approach should begin from an important strand in critical discourse analysis concerned with the construction of meaning: 'intertextuality'. This concept is used to encapsulate how the meaning of a given text cannot be understood outside of its relation with the countless other texts to which it explicitly or implicitly relates. Texts are therefore seen as 'intersecting' within an 'indefinitely expandable web' of other texts, all of which have their own genres. It is therefore misleading to see a text as a hermetically-sealed unit, since both the producer and the audience are themselves producers and audiences of other texts. In this perspective, all writing and reading, and the construction of meaning as a result of this process, is intertextual.[31] It follows that the validity of the meaning of a text is not something which can be 'read off' an external source of power, such as authorial intention, or economic structure, but is dependent upon the success with which it operates within a given 'framework of validation'. Given the intertextual conditions of their production and reception, texts may be seen (in a metaphorical sense) as 'authorless', and the production of meaning may become detached from any identifiable, conscious human agent. What has been termed a 'surplus of meaning' may arise.[32] For a text to be successful, and for shared meanings to be constructed, it negotiates with, and refers (directly or indirectly) to, other texts. Over time, it may be added, new genres may emerge from the processes of intertextual communication. Frameworks of understanding are therefore built up, not out of the passive and unproblematic acceptance of 'seminal' texts, but rather from the processes of intertextual construction which take place in fairly stable, regular spheres, such as, for example, newspapers. Intertextuality therefore requires the panoramic approach to ideas just outlined. If we are to understand how meaning is constructed, and how that meaning contributes to political identity, this requires attention to a broad range of mediated intertextual evidence.[33]

Multiple and Overlapping Public Spheres

The final desideratum is that the approach should involve an awareness of the communication infrastructures which parties, groups and movements employ. One highly influential approach to understanding the role of communication in democracies is Habermas's concept of the 'public sphere'. Although there has been a heavy normative emphasis in the literature, there have nevertheless been attempts to apply the framework to concrete instances of communication.[34] Habermas argued that the development of early modern capitalism heralded a new era of communication which fostered a culture of enlightened critical public debate among the propertied, middle class. This culture was based upon an independent press, the reading of novels, discussion in physical spaces such as coffee houses, and so on. According to Habermas, this 'public sphere' developed in western Europe during the eighteenth century, reached its high point during the mid-nineteenth century, and subsequently declined during the late-nineteenth and early-twentieth centuries, as it increasingly came to be policed by economic monopolies and the state. The model therefore locates the development of particular forms of communication, providing a dynamic, macro-level perspective indicating how the structures which facilitate public political discourse have changed over time.

But it is still a blunt instrument for conceptualizing the communication of ideas. The demise of a single, relatively undifferentiated sphere of communication is difficult to portray empirically. Habermas charts the collapse of the public sphere in late-nineteenth century Europe, but it is arguable that it was precisely this period which saw the proliferation of many new and different groups and discourses, in particular feminism and socialism. The dissemination of these was carried out vigorously through channels of public political discourse. It is difficult to imagine labour, radical, socialist and feminist movements in isolation from the various newspapers they sought to establish. The single public sphere as a framework is therefore too restrictive, because it misses the emergence of new political groups, each with their own distinctive infrastructures of communication.[35] Utilizing a panoramic perspective necessitates sensitivity towards such minority discourses. The clash of relatively marginal currents must be incorporated into the broader landscape.

Recently, Susan Herbst has developed an approach to public expression 'outside the mainstream' by adapting the metaphor of the public sphere.[36] While she is concerned primarily with marginalized groups, one of the implications of her work is that, in order to develop a multi-layered notion of conflict and consensus, it is necessary to explore how groups, movements and parties develop and make use of their own distinctive channels of communication. This can illuminate all forms of political communication in which a party or group seeking to influence public political discourse constructs its own network of communication. Herbst uses three main concepts: 'linguistic space', 'community-building' and 'communication environments' to describe the communication relationships which groups, movements and parties develop in order to advance their own ideas, and which lead to the emergence of multiple public spheres. A modified version of this approach provides an important component of the public political discourse framework.

'Linguistic space' specifies the channels set up by group leaderships in order to communicate to their supporters, for their supporters in turn to communicate back, and for both leaders and supporters to communicate to the wider public.[37] The opening up of linguistic space facilitates the development of shared ideas by providing stable, regular opportunities for communication. While it may refer to the organized output of an established institution such as a political party, linguistic space does not assume that ideas are always formally attached to such institutions.

In this view, many different participants contribute to debate: they need not be formal representatives of organized opinion. Herbst's second concept – community-building – specifies the functions of public spheres for providing cohesion between groups and their supporters. It is suggested that processes of communication serve to draw boundaries around the group, constituting insiders and outsiders, thereby defending the group's beliefs from external attack.[38] Finally, Herbst's concept of the 'communication environment' refers to the power groups have to shape the patterns of communication in a particular field.[39] The 'powerful' in this sense have the ability to determine the boundaries of the communication environment, to decide who is able or unable to communicate and to influence the content of political discourse.

I would argue that Herbst's second concept, 'community-building', requires some modification because it does not seem to allow for the possibility of cross-fertilization between groups and parties. If all groups simply provided their supporters with their *own* communication networks, there would be little chance of building alliances based on points of consensus with other groups. It is therefore necessary to amend Herbst's theory by adding the notion of *overlapping* public spheres, which refers to the process whereby groups seek to build consensus based on common preoccupations and shared meanings.

Herbst's approach is complementary to the concept of public political discourse outlined above. It suggests that there are reciprocal relationships between elites and supporters, and it points to the ways in which groups and parties, large and small, seek to disseminate their ideas. In pointing to the infrastructures of communication set in place by parties, groups and movements, the concept of multiple, overlapping public spheres is an important dimension of the approach. It is useful for making sense of the consensus built up between different groups over specific issues. The notion of multiple and overlapping public spheres encourages us to look beyond narrow institution-based approaches, towards a recognition that groups and movements seek to forge alliances and constituencies of support. It aids in encapsulating shared meanings that are intertextually constructed.

Authors, Texts, Audiences and Contexts

Having established the principal features of the approach in the broadest sense, it may be useful at this stage to explore further the importance of the relations between texts and contexts. To argue for placing ideas in context is not particularly novel. But neither is it straightforward. There are contexts for ideas as philosophical discourse just as there are contexts for ideas as public political discourse and symbolic discourse. There *is* a distinction, nevertheless, to be made on the basis of the levels of internal coherence to be found in philosophical discourse and those of my other two categories. To completely ignore this would be to make highly unrealistic assumptions about how ideas 'work'. If all forms of ideas were as internally coherent and elegantly structured as political philosophy, it would be possible to argue that they 'work' highly efficiently, 'in their own right'. But if, as I have argued, the category 'political ideas' is not exhausted by philosophical discourse, then we need to recognize that the vast bulk of political discourse is not particularly coherent, and, further, that its effectiveness is not based upon its elegance as a 'system' of ideas. As Hall puts it,

> *most* ideologies … are rag bags, replete with many options usable by different groups at will … It remains vital, in other words, to examine not just belief but the circumstances that make it seem plausible to particular actors at particular historical conjunctures … Religion, or ideology more generally, tends to be seen in highly intellectualist terms. To concentrate exclusively on ideas in this sense is, however, a mistake. *Community matters quite as much as doctrine to most believers.*[40]

Ideas are acceptable to certain groups in certain contexts, and it must not be assumed that a constituency of support will always exist for ideas simply because they are expressed with elegance.

How are we to conceptualize the interaction of authors, texts, audiences and contexts? Quite obviously there are many possible answers to this question, but here I want to proceed in two neglected, but particularly suggestive, directions. One involves transposing some of the ideas developed by the Bakhtin circle of Russian linguists, whose influence has primarily been felt in literary and cultural studies.[41] The other involves a reappraisal of the work of the North American political scientist, Murray Edelman.

The work of the Bakhtin circle[42] is oriented around the nature of linguistic expression and interaction. But its novelty lies in its rejection of the two competing approaches that have dominated critical linguistics during much of the twentieth century: Saussurean structuralism and Freudian subjectivism. Bakhtin and his followers criticized Saussure's seminal *Course on General Linguistics* for its view of language as an abstract, self-contained system, divorced from its position in a context of human agency, contradiction and struggle. Freudians, on the other hand, were criticized for an individualizing perspective, which naively saw language as the creation of the psyche. To divorce words from the context of their use was, for Bakhtin, an incomplete method of analysis. To study meanings in the Bakhtinian framework is to study discourse between individuals as members of social (and political) groups and classes. It is to avoid the extremes of Saussurean structuralism, Freudian subjectivism, and, it may be added, deterministic Marxism.

The central concept here is 'dialogism'. The Bakhtin circle argued that language inhabits the boundaries between separate human consciousnesses, and it is only through examining the reciprocal relationships between speakers and audiences that we are able to discern the meaning of discourse. This view was based upon a micro-level theory of communication. In essence, argued Volosinov, all utterances must produce a response, but, crucially, the act of utterance contains within it an anticipation of response from another. As he put it:

> … *word is a two-sided act.* It is determined equally by whose word it is and for whom it is meant. As word it is precisely *the product of the reciprocal relationship between speaker and listener, addresser and addressee.* Each and every word expresses the 'one' in relation to the 'other'. I give myself verbal shape from another's point of view, ultimately, from the point of view of the community to which I belong. A word is a bridge thrown

between myself and another. If one end of the bridge depends on me, then the other depends on my addressee.[43]

Discourse is 'dialogical', and it is within this dialogism that we must analyse the construction of shared meanings.

If we accept that political discourse is dialogical, we can add a number of other insights. The first of these is the concept of 'speech genres'. Bakhtin argued that discourse generates shared understandings mainly through speech genres. Communication through these creates an environment of familiarity which helps provide a bond between addresser and addressee. Genres create and manage readers' expectations, reducing the amount of 'work' the text has to perform. Speech genres, once established, can be said to provide all-important 'shortcuts' to the shared understandings which are crucial for ideas to gain a foothold, exert, and reinforce, their influence on public debate. As Bakhtin argued:

> Each separate utterance is individual, of course, but each sphere in which language is used develops its own *relatively stable types* of these utterances. These we may call *speech genres*...an essential (constitutive) marker of the utterance is its quality of being directed to someone, its *addressivity* ...the utterance has both an author and an addressee. This addressee can be an immediate participant-interlocutor in an everyday dialogue, a differentiated collective of specialists in some particular area of cultural communication, a more or less undifferentiated public, ethnic group, contemporaries, like-minded people, opponents and enemies, a subordinate, a superior, someone who is lower, higher, familiar, foreign, and so forth.... Both the composition and, particularly, the style of the utterance depend on those to whom the utterance is addressed, how the speaker (or writer) senses and imagines his addressees, and the force of their effect on the utterance. Each speech genre in each area of speech communication has its own typical conception of the addressee, and this defines it as a genre.[44]

As an illustration, consider the effectiveness of a cultural genre such as soap opera in managing television viewers' expectations. Or, consider the example of a Conservative leader's speech at the Party's annual conference. What binds speaker and audience together are the expectations, part consciously held, part unconscious, which have been built up, over long periods of time, about how a Conservative leader is *expected* to speak. Leaders and supporters are able to build ties of reciprocity based on these short-cuts to meaning. By the same token, consider the differences between the speech genres appropriate for platform speeches, and those for cabinet meetings. Each has its own conventions.

Although genres make the building of shared understandings easier to achieve, they are never final. Discourse is, for the Bakhtinians, necessarily conflictual, and it is precisely the creative process of construction and reconstruction, in which meaning is never wholly fixed – a struggle between a unifying or 'centripetal' force, and a fragmenting or 'centrifugal' force, which provides opportunities for discoursal change.[45] The forces of fragmentation create what Bakhtin terms 'heteroglossia', a state in which multiple voices coexist and challenge each other. It is in the working out of conflict between those who wish to impose their own, monologic perceptions and those who seek to challenge them that the creative work of discourse is played out.

In his much-cited work, *The Symbolic Uses of Politics*, Murray Edelman proceeded from the assumption that 'The realistic study of political language and its meanings is necessarily a probing not only of dictionaries, nor of word counts, but of the diverse responses to particular modes of expression of audiences in disparate social settings.' [46] The approach understandably owes much to the public sphere of American social science in the 1950s and 1960s. It makes free use of social psychology and functionalist sociology, two paradigms whose influence on political science has since declined.[47] However, what is certain is that Edelman attributes to language a power to shape politics. As with the dialogical approach, its effectiveness is to be found, not within language alone, but within the meanings that are generated by the process of 'role-taking' by individuals. It is *usage* which matters here, and if sufficient numbers of individuals use language in the same way in the same context, 'common political meanings and claims arise'.[48] Language acts to shape and 'catalyze' behaviour.[49]

It is not difficult to see the similarities between this view of language and that of the Bakhtin school's concept of speech genres. Edelman, too, explored how diverse forms of political expression convey meaning in themselves, regardless of their content. Distinguishing between four political 'language styles', which he termed 'hortatory', 'legal', 'administrative' and 'bargaining', Edelman effectively collapsed the conventional division between content and form, arguing that 'style ... convey[s] meaning', and that this phenomenon is dependent upon the 'settings' in which language is produced and received.[50] For example, usage of a hortatory language style conveys an acknowledgement that the public has the 'right' to an influence over decision-making. Political elites must make appeals to their public, and the characteristic discourse signifies this by virtue of its style. Legal language, to take another example, conveys to 'the public' an impersonal, objective 'definition of law', with its own regular procedures, while to the elite it signifies precisely the opposite: ambiguity and openness which can then be exploited by judges, lawyers, politicians and bureaucrats to serve their interests and facilitate peaceful conflict resolution. Edelman also argued that while situated political discourse usually involves a combination of various language styles, using a particular style in the 'wrong' context blunts its efficacy. Thus, the rhetorical flushes of hortatory language, designed as they are for a mass public, are unlikely to have much impact in a context where a 'bargaining' style would be more appropriate, and vice versa.

In Edelman's account, language, symbol and ritual serve to promote social and political conformity by facilitating the expression of commonality. They therefore 'fix' future behaviour. At the level of national politics, rituals which affirm national greatness serve to unify a society otherwise divided along class, ethnic or gender lines. But it is possible to expand this unifying function of language to cover the study of parties, pressure groups and movements, where hortatory language predominates. Such language incorporates audiences because it rests on the unspoken but intrinsic assumption that the audience must be appealed to and persuaded; it perceives itself as valued, as worthy of making a contribution, however indirect, to public debate. Even if the demands on which the appeal is based have little chance of being met, individuals are, in an important sense, 'consulted'. They therefore accord their leaders greater legitimacy, because they perceive them as behaving responsibly and not arbitrarily. As Edelman argues, 'The network of social alliances cemented by these meanings constitutes a framework upon which evanescent political alliances and interests are built and a rhetoric in which they are expressed and related to more enduring interests and myths'.[51] In groups with little chance of success, especially those seeking radical change, hortatory language assumes an important role in keeping the group together, in unifying an audience. Thus, to transpose White's insightful formulation, the *content* of the hortatory language *form* has the effect of creating and reproducing political identity.[52]

Conclusion

The Bakhtinian concepts of dialogism, speech genres and heteroglossia, combined with Edelman's view of language styles, serve to capture the reciprocity which is at the heart of how political movements construct shared frameworks of under-standing. While this certainly does not exhaust all of the potential ambiguities and pitfalls of the relationship between texts and contexts, it does go some way towards an argument in favour of retaining such a distinction. When combined with the key elements of the public political discourse approach – focusing on texts in the public domain; prioritizing political communications media in a given period; establishing connections between 'high' and 'low', 'elite' and 'mass', 'official' and 'unofficial', 'sophisticated' and 'simple'; placing ideas in a context of political con-flict; recognizing intertextuality; and mapping relationships using the metaphor of multiple and overlapping public spheres – they constitute an explicit and defensible set of assumptions and prescriptions for the study of political ideas. If political science is as much concerned with asking questions as it is with answering them, I will hopefully have succeeded in demonstrating how discussion of the manner in which we ask can be a helpful preliminary to how we answer.

About the author

Andrew Chadwick, School of Politics, University of the West of England, Bristol, Frenchay, Bristol BS16 1QY, UK; e-mail: *Andrew.Chadwick@uwe.ac.uk*

Notes

I would like to thank participants in The University of the West of England's School of Politics Special Research Seminar, held in Bristol, December 1998, and participants in the workshop on Political Ideas and Political Action held at the LSE, January 1999. I am grateful to the Centre for Social and Economic Research of The University of the West of England for granting the Fellowship which made the research upon which this chapter is based possible. Any errors or shortcomings, are, of course, my own.

1   The list of references in this note may have proved extremely long. By way of avoiding this, I refer readers to one article, which extracts 27 'definitional elements' from 85 sources on the concept of 'ideology'. M. B. Hamilton, 'The elements of the concept of ideology', *Political Studies*, 35 (1987), 18–38.

2   See, for example, D. Nunan, *Introducing Discourse Analysis*. London: Penguin, 1993.

3   N. Fairclough, *Discourse and Social Change*. Cambridge: Polity, 1992.

4   See, for example, M. Foucault, *The Archaeology of Knowledge*. London: Tavistock, 1972.

5   N. Fairclough, *Critical Discourse Analysis: the Critical Study of Language*. London: Longman, 1995, pp. 4–5.

6 Not only is this due to postmodernism's inherent objections to such methods, it is also a quirk of political science itself. Postmodernism has largely been confined to political theory because the rest of the field has been dominated by the mainstream institutionalist or behaviouralist approaches. If we examine the major developments in postmodernism's impact on the social sciences and humanities, it is difficult to escape the conclusion that the major events have been the publication of new theoretical texts by celebrated authors such as Foucault, Derrida, Lyotard and Baudrillard, rather than insights derived from empirical types of research practice. One could argue that all intellectual paradigms exhibit such characteristics, but this would be to miss the extreme to which postmodernism has swung. We do not usually look in the book review columns for the latest 'application' of a postmodernist approach to (for instance) political parties, pressure groups, public administration, public policy, constitutions. We look instead for the latest theoretical exposition of what, as an intellectual paradigm, postmodernism *is*. It has carved out a niche where theoretical research practice is the norm, and where engagements with the work of others in that field has proved more intellectually rewarding. Like all writers, postmodernist theorists have craved an audience, a community of the interested.

7 G. Stedman Jones, *Languages of Class: Studies in English Working Class History 1832–1982*. Cambridge: Cambridge University Press, 1983, especially the Introduction and ch. 3, 'Rethinking Chartism'. There were, of course, several 'linguistic turns' during the twentieth century, from Ludwig Wittgenstein through J. L. Austin to the emergence of J. G. A. Pocock's and Quentin Skinner's approaches to political thought in the early 1970s. Though they are inevitably related to the developments in the field of social history, in that field the linguistic turn is usually taken to indicate the influence of postmodernist approaches to language, the roots of which are usually traced back to the early twentieth century structuralist linguist, Ferdinand de Saussure.

8 D. Mayfield and S. Thorne, 'Social history and its discontents: Gareth Stedman Jones and the politics of language', *Social History*, 17 (1992), 165–188. See the defence by J. Lawrence and M. Taylor, 'The poverty of protest: Gareth Stedman Jones and the politics of language – a reply', *Social History*, 18 (1993), 1–15, and the counter-attack by Mayfield and Thorne, *Social History*, 18 (1993) 219–233. See also A. Marwick, 'Two approaches to historical study: the metaphysical (including 'postmodernism') and the historical', *Journal of Contemporary History*, 30 (1995), 5–35, especially pp. 28–30.

9 D. Thompson, 'The languages of class', *Bulletin of the Society for the Study of Labour History*, 52 (1987), 54–57.

10 B. D. Palmer, *Descent into Discourse: the Reification of Language and the Writing of Social History*. Philadelphia: Temple University Press, 1990; L. Stone, 'History and postmodernism', *Past & Present*, 131 (1991), 217–218; R. Price, 'Languages of revisionism: historians and popular politics in nineteenth-century Britain', *Journal of Social History*, 30 (1996), p. 246. See also D. Nicholls, 'The new liberalism – after Chartism?', *Social History*, 21 (1996), 330–342, p. 331. For a critique based on the US experience, see J. Appleby, L. Hunt and M. Jacob, *Telling the Truth About History*. London: Norton, 1994.

11 J. Epstein, 'The populist turn', *Journal of British Studies*, 32 (1993), 177–189.

12 P. Joyce, *Visions of the People: Industrial England and the Question of Class, 1848–1914*. Cambridge: Cambridge University Press, 1991, pp. 1, 12, 17–18.

13 J. Lawrence, 'Class and gender in the making of urban toryism 1880–1914', *English Historical Review*, 108 (1993), 629–652, especially pp. 630–632.

14 Lawrence and Taylor, 'The poverty of protest', p. 12.

15 F. de Saussure, *Course in General Linguistics*, translated by R. Harris. London: Duckworth, 1983. The original text was published in 1916.

16 Joyce, *Visions of the People*, pp. 17–18.

17 N. Kirk, 'The continuing relevance and engagements of class', *Labour History Review*, 60 (1995), 2–15.

18 S. S. Friedman, 'Making History: Feminism, Narrative and Desire', in D. Elam and R. Wiegman, eds, *Feminism Beside Itself*. London: Routledge, 1995, 11–53, p. 13.

19 R. Berkhofer, 'The challenge of poetics to (normal) historical practice', *Poetics Today*, 1988, extract reprinted in K. Jenkins, ed., *The Postmodern History Reader*. London: Routledge, 1997, p. 149.

20 H. Kellner, *Language and Historical Representation*. London: University of Wisconsin Press, 1989, pp. vii–viii, 9.

21 M. Bevir, 'Are there perennial problems in political theory?', *Political Studies*, 42 (1994), 662–675.

22 Aristotle, *Politics*, Book VII, translated by T. A. Sinclair. London; Penguin, 1962, ch. 3.

23 J. Rawls, *Political Liberalism*. New York; Columbia University Press, 1993, p. 45. I am grateful to Nick Buttle for alerting me to this and the preceding reference.

24 For a classic example of the 'core ideas' approach, see B. C. Parekh, *The Concept of Socialism*. London; Croom Helm, 1975. For a more nuanced version, see M. Freeden, *Ideologies and Political Theory: a Conceptual Approach*. Oxford; Clarendon, 1996. The classic 'tension between two extremes' approach may be found in W. H. Greenleaf, *The British Political Tradition: Volume II: the Ideological Heritage*. London: Methuen, 1983.

25 R. Barker, 'A Future for Liberalism or a Liberal Future?', in J. Meadowcroft, ed., *The Liberal Political Tradition: Contemporary Reappraisals*. London: Edward Elgar, 1996, pp. 177–197, p. 184.

26 For discussion of this approach see R. Barker, 'A Future for Liberalism or a Liberal Future?', p. 184.

27 A. W. Sparkes, *Talking Politics: a Wordbook*. London: Routledge, 1994. See also, J. Street, 'Political culture – from civic culture to mass culture', *British Journal of Political Science*, 24 (1993), 95–113, pp. 100–102.

28 For further discussion of this issue see J. Scott, 'Women in history II: the modern period', *Past & Present*, 101 (1983), p. 156. For an opposing view see J. Rendall, Introduction to J. Rendall, ed., *Equal or Different: Women's Politics, 1800–1914*. Oxford: Blackwell, 1987, pp.1–27.

29 A detail from the original title page of 1651, depicting the sovereign's body composed of thousands of tiny human figures, can be seen on the title page of the *Penguin Classics* edition of 1985. T. Hobbes, *Leviathan*. London; Penguin, 1985.

30 G. Stedman Jones, 'The determinist fix: some obstacles to the further development of the linguistic approach to history in the 1990s', *History Workshop Journal*, 42 (1996), 19–35, pp. 28–29.

31 This approach has been fruitfully applied to the long-standing debate over the 'post-war consensus' in British politics. See J. Marlow, 'Metaphor, intertextuality and the post-war consensus', *Politics*, 17 (1997), 127–133, pp. 131–132 and J. Marlow, *Questioning the Post-War Consensus Thesis*. Aldershot: Dartmouth, 1996. See also, M. Worton and J. Still, eds, *Intertextuality: Theories and Practices*. Manchester; Manchester University Press, 1990, and Fairclough, *Critical Discourse Analysis*, ch. 8, 'Discourse and Text: Linguistic and Intertextual Analysis Within Discourse Analysis'.

32 The phrase was used by Ricoeur. For an illuminating discussion see Michael Freeden's contribution to this volume, pp.301–321.

33 The importance of a text's relations with other texts is, of course, one of the general preoccupations of Quentin Skinner, J. G. A. Pocock and the 'Cambridge School' of political philosophy. A major implication of Skinner's work is that the problematic nature of the relative importance to be ascribed to different ideological utterances forces the historian to discover as precisely as possible which texts questioned, rather than reinforced the mentality of a period. But the Cambridge methodology differs from that presented here, in that it is still ultimately concerned with the 'great works' of political philosophy. See Q. Skinner, 'On Meaning and Understanding in the History of Ideas', reprinted in J. Tully, ed., *Meaning and Context: Quentin Skinner and his Critics*. Cambridge: Polity, 1988, pp.29–67.

34 J. Habermas, *The Structural Transformation of the Public Sphere: an Inquiry Into a Category of Bourgeois Society*. Cambridge: Polity, 1989; G. Eley, 'Edward Thompson, Social History and Political Culture: the Making of a Working-Class Public, 1780–1850', in H. J. Kaye and K. McLelland, eds, *E. P. Thompson: Critical Perspectives*. Cambridge: Polity, 1990, pp.12–49; G. Eley, 'Nations, Publics and Political Cultures: Placing Habermas in the Nineteenth Century', K. M. Baker, 'Defining the Public Sphere in Eighteenth Century France: Variations on a Theme by Habermas' and D. Zaret, 'Religion, Science and Printing in the Public Spheres in Seventeenth Century England', all in C. Calhoun, ed., *Habermas and the Public Sphere*. Cambridge MA: MIT Press, 1992, pp.289–339, 181–211, 212–235; J. Vernon, *Politics and the People: a Study in English Political Culture, 1815–1867*. Cambridge: Cambridge University Press, 1993; D. Zaret, 'Petitions and the 'invention' of public opinion in the English revolution', *American Journal of Sociology*, 101 (1996), 1497–1555. On the USA see M. P. Ryan, 'Gender and Public Access: Women's Politics in Nineteenth Century America' and M. Schudson, 'Was there ever a Public Sphere? If so, when? Reflections on the American Case', both in Calhoun, ed., *Habermas and the Public Sphere*; M. Schudson, 'Historical Approaches to Communications Studies', in K. B. Jensen and N. Jankowski, eds, *A Handbook for Qualitative Methodologies for Mass Communications Research*. London: Routledge, 1991, pp.175–189. The point that the Habermasian approach involves an empirical argument is very often overlooked. See, for example, R. Blaug, 'Between fear and disappointment: critical, empirical and political uses of Habermas', *Political Studies*, 45 (1997), 100–117, which, despite its title, does not consider this dimension. For a brief commentary, see A. Chadwick, 'A communication on R. Blaug's 'Between fear and disappointment: critical, empirical and political uses of Habermas', *Political Studies*, (1997), 661–662.

35 Ryan, 'Gender and Public Access'. See also Eley, 'Nations, Publics and Political Cultures'.

36 S. Herbst, *Politics at the Margin: Historical Studies of Public Expression Outside the Mainstream*. Cambridge: Cambridge University Press, 1994.

37 Herbst, *Politics at the Margin*, p. 2.

38 Herbst, *Politics at the Margin*, pp. 22–23.

39 Herbst, *Politics at the Margin*, p. 30.

40 J. A. Hall, 'Ideas and the Social Sciences' in J. Goldstein and R. O. Keohane, eds, *Ideas and Foreign Policy: Beliefs, Institutions and Political Change*. London: Cornell University Press, 1993, 31–54, pp. 41, 49. Original emphasis.

41 Social historians have been surprisingly reticent in this area. For use of Bakhtinian theory, see, however, M. W. Steinberg, '"A Way of Struggle": Reformations and Affirmations of E. P. Thompson's Class Analysis in Light of Postmodern Theories of Language', *British Journal of Sociology*, 48 (1997), 471–492. See also, R. Williams, *Marxism and Literature* Oxford; Oxford University Press, 1977, pp. 38–42.

42 There is some debate over the authorship of the Bakhtin circle essays. The controversy, which dates back to 1973, centres upon whether Medvedev and Volsinov signed works which were originally written by Bakhtin. The murky politics of the Stalin period have rendered the issue irresolvable in the eyes of Morris, the editor of a recent anthology, who argues that the strongest evidence supports the view that all three authors provided significant contributions. This essay conforms to this line by referring to each article by its original signatory. See P. Morris, ed., *The Bakhtin Reader: Selected Writings of Bakhtin, Medvedev and Volosinov*. London: Edward Arnold, 1994, pp. 1–5.

43 V. N. Volosinov, *Marxism and the Philosophy of Language* (1929), translated by L. Matejka and I. R. Titunik. Cambridge MA, Harvard University Press, 1973, p. 86. Original emphasis.

44 From M. M. Bakhtin, 'The Problem of Speech Genres' (1952–53) reprinted in *Speech Genres and Other Late Essays*, translated by V. W. McGee, edited by C. Emerson and M. Holquist. Austin, University of Texas Press, 1986; passage reprinted in Morris, ed., *The Bakhtin Reader*, pp. 81, 87.

45 M. M. Bakhtin, 'Discourse in the Novel' (1935), reprinted in *The Dialogic Imagination: Four Essays*, translated by M. Holquist and C. Emerson, edited by M. Holquist. Austin: University of Texas Press, 1981, pp. 291–292.

46 M. Edelman, *The Symbolic Uses of Politics*. London: University of Illinois Press, 1964, pp. 130–131. It should be stated that Edelman does not appear to have been influenced by the Bakhtin school. There are no references to their work in the text.

47 Politics emerges as a force for the emotional involvement of the mass, a site on which 'hopes and fears or 'psychological tensions' and 'inner problems' are projected, which presents only 'threats' or 'reassurances', but which results in 'a remarkably viable and functional political system.' Thus the meanings of political symbols are to be found deep within the psyche of individuals and simultaneously in the society where they function. Edelman, *Symbolic Uses of Politics*, pp. 8, 9, 13, 15.

48 Edelman, *Symbolic Uses of Politics*, p. 115.

49 Edelman, *Symbolic Uses of Politics* p. 123–24.

50 Edelman, *Symbolic Uses of Politics*, p. 133.

51 This contrasts with administrative and bargaining styles of language, which often provoke resentment among the mass audience, a sense that they are being excluded from the decision-making process, as, indeed, they are. Edelman, *Symbolic Uses of Politics*, pp. 138, 151.

52 H. White, *The Content of the Form: Narrative Discourse and Historical Representation*. Baltimore; Johns Hopkins University Press, 1987.

5

Practising Ideology and Ideological Practices

Michael Freeden

Although among the categories informing the study of politics there are few as fundamental as those demarcating theory and practice, that distinction is highly problematic when applied to the analysis of ideologies. Many traditional as well as current approaches regard political thought as the area in which issues of moral philosophy pertaining to political entities are aired, with the objective of setting defining ethical and validating criteria which are then to be applied to political practice. A grounding of this view may be found in Kant, for whom individuals were subjected to clear and unequivocal moral duties and were *therefore* also men of affairs concerned with political right. As Kant argued, '... experience cannot provide knowledge of what is right, and there is a *theory* of political right to which practice must conform before it can be valid'. Hence, 'not all activities are called *practice*, but only those realizations of a particular purpose which are considered to comply with certain generally conceived principles of procedure.' The value of such a practice depended 'entirely upon its appropriateness to the theory it is based on'.[1] This position has recently been restated thus: 'The major goal of a moral theory is to resolve conflicts arising in moral decision making giving clear guidance on how to act'.[2] Building on ancient Greek views, such approaches hold contemplation to be inextricably linked to practical wisdom and virtue.[3] As a consequence, politics – inasmuch as it contains conflict – is seemingly transcended, at least until it encounters a new moral dilemma for which further guidance will be available. More recent hermeneutic accounts are subtler in assessing the interaction between theory and practice, identifying a mutual relationship of interdependence, in which the contingencies of politics continuously batter against the walls of our pre-formed conceptions. Nonetheless, these accounts remain wedded to the eliciting of new truths or holisms from the multiplicity of time- and space-bound human experiences.[4]

In either case, it is frequently unclear where ideology stands in relation to theory or to practice. Ideology is sometimes conceived of as bad theory – i.e. not even 'true in theory' – in the sense of its utter separation, through abstraction or dogmatism, from the actual world of contingent conduct and events. It is therefore deemed incapable of guiding political practice that is portrayed as pragmatic, if not opportunist, by its very nature. Standard views of political science in the 1960s articulated such understandings, and they have continued to assert themselves since. One prominent example of that notion of ideology has been promoted by Sartori, for whom ideology is a particular type of political belief system that is closed to action on relevant information. Instead of relying on empirical evidence based on correspondence, it constructs an internally coherent, rational and deductive view of the political world.[5] More recently, Minogue has continued this line of argument by classifying ideology as distinguished by a specific and impractical monistic logic which is alienated from actual politics.[6]

At other times, conversely, ideology is defined as action-oriented, that is, as political theory especially designed to direct political conduct and practices. Far from presenting a disjuncture with the world of practice, ideologies are thought-phenomena believed to be primarily concerned with controlling and changing political practices. Though some American political scientists see this as a neutral, functional aspect of politics, other scholars, picking up the Marxist conception of ideology, insist that ideology reflects power as manipulation, or that at least it commonly betrays the moral expectations attached to political philosophy. Hence ideology is another kind of bad theory, one reviled as polluted by power relationships that undermine the emancipated reflection required for good practice. Ideology thus reduces the status of political thinking to the level of crass instrumentality, in the service of the interests of the groups who exercise social control. As Minogue, straddling both approaches, sees it, 'those who characterize ideologies as "action-oriented" are no doubt correct but one striking feature of ideologies is that, at their core, they do not advocate, exhort, propose or concern themselves with policy except tactically'.[7] None of these views is entirely wrong, for they do not correspond to unknown instances of ideological thinking. But if we are to adopt a broader interpretation, we cannot assess ideologies through singling out particular cases as representative of them all. The above perspectives offer unhelpfully restricted vantage points from which to understand the specific shared features of ideologies. Those features are definitely not limited to solving moral quandaries, to illuminating the path of correct conduct, to 'rising' above the particular, or to imposing and justifying unassailable élites.

To compound the complexities involved, there is a further sense in which the study of ideologies is torn between Marxist and non-Marxist approaches. The former see ideology as a distorting or illusory epiphenomenon, obfuscating material relations and practices. This elicits a critical assault entrusted with the dual role of unmasking that type of political thinking, and concurrently replacing it with true understandings that arise out of unalienated human practice and activity. As Lefort sees it, ideology entails a split between 'an order of practice and an order of representation' and occupies an artificially separate domain.[8] The impact of such views has been to perpetuate the aversion to regarding ideologies as deserving analysis in their own right. Instead, they are consigned to metaphysical digressions from, or interventions in, what actually happens in the world.

The non-Marxist approaches are often disparagingly believed to involve mere description, whose very essence is considered to be non-normative and therefore irrelevant to guiding practices. So whereas engaging in normative political theory has been labelled as creative, engaging in the study of ideologies has not. Here the difficulty has been a naive understanding of description, erroneously assuming it to entail a mere correspondence with or reproduction of facts, rather than their reconstitution and re-assembly in an act of interpretation and analysis. Whether such an act is simplistic or sophisticated in the hands of its diverse practitioners, it too is creative and imaginative. Indeed, inasmuch as Marx announced that 'philosophers have only interpreted the world, in various ways; the point is to change it', it could be counter-argued that 'students of ideologies change the world by interpreting it in various ways'.

Political Thought-practices

Three discrete, if supporting, issues require bearing in mind. First, ideologies are themselves political thought-practices and as such have distinct features. Second, ideologies as a group contain a specific category of thought-practice pertaining to understanding the relationship between theory and practice. Third, each of the major ideologies displays different interpretations of the relationship between theory and practice. The third issue is thus central to illuminating the second, and the second constitutes an important aspect of the first.

A practice is here understood to mean the performance of, and participation in, an identifiable regularity of action or thought, one replicated as well as shaped by other such practitioners. It is hence a communal activity taking place in social space and recurring over time. Practices and acts are not synonymous: many acts do not constitute practices, and some practices-cum-regularities of thinking do not constitute acts. On the macro-level, the phenomenon of ideology is itself a particular yet ubiquitous type of thinking about politics that conforms to the above definition. On the micro-level, ideologies are sets of specific thought-practices whose content and morphology differ from one ideological family to another. To analyse an ideology (as distinct from to participate in formulating one) is to categorize, elucidate and decode the ways in which collectivities in fact think about politics, the ways in which they intentionally practice the art of political thinking, and unintentionally express the social patterns which that kind of thinking has developed. That analysis encompasses a span ranging from what is done to what can be done. It includes an exploration of what *ideologies* claim should be done, but excludes any judgement concerning what ought to be done from an external, absolute or unitary moral viewpoint.

A major problem then arises: if moral and political theory are ordinarily entrusted to tell us how to act, can an ideology, in its dual role as both theory and practice, do the same? Of course, most ideologies *purport* to tell us how, or how not, to act. But can the status of their recommendations attain theoretical respectability among communities of theory-producing scholars? This points to a disjuncture between the ideologist and the student of ideologies that is absent within the field of political and moral philosophy. The moral philosopher as scholar is indistinguishable from the moral philosophers to which he or she refers. Moral philosophers aim to improve on or elucidate the arguments of their predecessors, but both present and past philosopher are engaged in the same activity of morally philosophizing; they are both therefore oriented to recommending certain kinds of practices. This rendition of the activity of moral and political theorists does not fundamentally deviate from the understandings and motives they impute to themselves. Those theorists are thus participant-observers in a joint discourse.

By contrast, there is a considerable difference between the formulators and the students of ideologies. The former focus – as do moral philosophers – on the politically desirable, but their justifications rest on widely differing bases of truth and validity. Their thought-practices do not necessarily occupy the same, or even a broadly common, discursive space. The latter, exploring as they do ideologies as a thought-practice, possess a different starting-point. They are neither concerned with advocacy nor with improving the practices and techniques of ideologists (although their knowledge of ideologies may give us insights into what is desirable). Their interpretations may vary from the functional to the contextual or the morphological. The consequence is the production of a different kind of theorizing about ideologies, which is not directly and deliberately practice-oriented. It does not participate in the same thought-practices it analyses.

If, then, ideologies are thought-*practices*, can we conversely extrapolate from them guidelines on how to theorize? What would prevent those guidelines from being, in the cumbersome language of German hermeneutics, 'always already' a conservative affirmation of what is? Alternatively, if description becomes an act of reconstitution, and this serves as the measure of the reflexive nature of scholarship, then scholarly findings have an aura of contingency about them. That does not imply indifferent scholarship but an acknowledgement that the architecture of political thinking is overwhelmingly multiform. Inasmuch as ideologies are particular configurations of the actual and attainable meanings of political concepts, the investigation of thought-practices provides an insight into the ways given ideational systems are staked out, into the consequences of the connections among arguments, and among conceptual decontestations. At the very least these perspectives open up to the scholar a world of choice emanating from an appreciation of the pluralism of political thought-practices. The analysis of ideologies as practices thus offers tools through which to enrich the conventional relationship between moral philosophy, in which judgmental choices play a vital part, and political action.

Sound political theory is hence informed by three ingredients. First, by the assertion that, whatever else it may be, political thought is a set of socially mediated ideational practices, with their own (multiple and differentiated) regularities. Second, by the claim that all political practices are a crystallization of norms, values, interpretations which at least partly account for action-choices, though they are not themselves coterminous with action. Third, by an understanding of the costs and benefits of chains of thought-practices, of what is possible and compossible, and how various semantic fields are defined by certain conceptual configurations. That is one central outcome of the study of ideologies, and may be harnessed by moral philosophers to the end of furthering good practice itself.

Ethics and Ideology: Misrecognitions and Differentiations

What are the particular thought-practices associated with ideologies? To talk about ideologies as action-oriented does not constitute a sufficient boundary line between them and other types of political thought. Ethical theory is clearly action-oriented as well. Let us examine some differences, evident or alleged. One supposed distinction is that ethical theory may be universalized, while ideologies are particular to time and space. Another is that ideologies may be partisan and favour a particular set of practices irrespective of the latter's ethical merit. A third is that ideology has to do with (allegedly unethical) power and control and is therefore essentially linked only to social practices of that nature. A fourth is that ethics in theory and practice must be intentional, whereas ideology can be embedded also in unintentional practices. A fifth is that ethical theory needs be authentic, in the sense of being a creative discovery, in dialogue with others, of the life design of an individual,[9] whereas ideologies mask real thoughts and relationships. These invite further examination.

The temporal and spatial attributes of ideologies become evident when they are explored as conceptual configurations, in which general concepts, often courting universal appeal, and shared by the preponderant membership of an ideological family, are fleshed out by adjacent and peripheral concepts whose main function is to construct a two-way link between the concrete and the abstract. While most ideologies (fascism and some narrow nationalisms are obvious exceptions) are couched in universal terms, on closer inspection most do not meet these aspirations. The particular fails intellectually to attain universal status, even when it seems to succeed in doing so politically – at least in the short term. The contract theory of liberalism proves to be associated with constitutive practices, models of individual will, and rational forms of promising that fall short of boundless acceptability. De-alienated man in the Marxist vision is hampered by an insistence on a liberation from custom which emanates from a world in which material relationships overrule all others. Even the particularisms of conservatives are elevated to a position which, on the one hand, assumes a general fear of inorganic change while evoking the constants of human nature yet, on the other, topples conservatism from this psychological pedestal by accepting uncritically the unique experience of particular nations. However, while ethical theory is typically couched in a universal discourse, on reflection this usually applies only to a few fundamental principles, such as the sanctity of life and the gruesomeness of torture – on their own insufficient to delineate a semantic field. Otherwise, ethical theories themselves do not overcome ideational barriers to universalism.

Like all practices, ideologies are not only located in cultural and social space but exist over time. As a consequence, ideologies tend to be seen both by their practitioners and by their observers as constituting a tradition, whether past or future oriented. To conceive of an ideology as a practice is both to embed it in an historical setting, and to internalize history as a necessary dimension of ideology.

It is however quite true that ideologies do not always promote ethical ends or – a rather different point – they do not always promote political ends ethically. An appeal to a unitary state may use ethical rhetoric, but have no moral value on its own, or no more than an appeal to a federal state. The enhancement of some forms of political power may utilize blatantly unethical concepts, as in the revolutionary extolling of terror. And many progressive ideologies have suffered internal rifts when aspects of human welfare have been brought about by coercive means.

To claim disapprovingly, however, that ideologies are about power may have strange consequences. If power is the ability to get things done, then to remove ideologies as power-frameworks would be to disable practice entirely. But if power is exploitative and manipulative, ideologies are not wholly about power, and not all ideologies are primarily about power. Ideologies need be no more oppressive than the moral edict 'thou shalt not steal' which, presented as a divine rule, is backed up by spiritual as well as secular sanctions. If language constricts the choice of meanings we employ, then ideologies are a normal aspect of political language.

As for intentionality, ideologies clearly are a mixture of deliberate and unconscious thought-practices. The latter have been aptly summed up by Ricoeur's phrase 'the surplus of meaning', allowing for an utterance to contain more than its author intended. Of course, moral philosophers may – indeed, will – be 'guilty' of a similar surplus, but that would be seen as a deficiency or, at best, irrelevant in appraising their stated maxims. In the analysis of ideologies, unintentional thought-practices deserve to be treated as seriously as purposive ones, precisely because human practices are frequently not the deliberate product of identifiable human will. To restrict the exploration of political thought to its intentional manifestations is to neglect some of its most interesting practices. Liberalism's former blindness to ethnic diversity and its endorsement of the nation-state are centrally shared thought-practices; as is Marxism's unawareness of its re-engagement of power through the control over nature.

Nor is authenticity what ideologies are about. Ideologies focus not on the individual, even as a dialogical entity, but on the group in which dialogue or, more appositely, multilogue takes place. Ideologies always are group practices. Their production and consumption occur in a social context and would be indecipherable were the individual to be the unit of analysis. Moreover, when group experience is transmitted in an on-going process of political socialization, the conscious self-understanding of the individual is peripheral both to the morphology and the function of ideologies. Besides, the topic of authenticity presumes a reality behind ideological practice which, when contingent understandings are the order of the day, begs the question. It is quite possible to grant that ideologies are less than perfect representations of human political values, while simultaneously querying whether beyond them there exists a world of true values. There is a wide gulf between the good, the useful and the true, but all may be worthy modes of assessment. Ideologies are occupied in constructing conceptual configurations of political values in ways that can be either more, or less, intellectually, emotionally, even morally, satisfying. Ideologies may well be all we have, though this does not entail that their content is therefore invariable.

Interpretative Pluralism and the Ideological Assimilation of Political Practices

As I have argued elsewhere,[10] ideologies share some of their thought-practices with other kinds of political thought. But from their particular viewpoint, ideologies are less interested in the clarification of those practices than in providing readily available, applicable and widely consumable solutions for groups. In that sense both philosophy and ideology engage in informing and reflecting practice, but with different ends in mind. However, an ideology is itself a distinctive type of political thought-practice. It effects a decontestation of the political concepts it employs by means of a combination of logical and cultural proximities among them, which prioritize certain concepts over others, and certain meanings of each concept over other meanings. The external manifestation of this thought-practice is a unique conceptual configuration that competes over its legitimacy with other conceptual configurations. This practice arises from and indicates the existence of a plural world of meaning, and that in turn provides a justification for influencing the exercise of choices among sets of meanings. The effecting of such choices is itself a practice within a practice, a form of conduct; after all, we describe it as *making* choices. In sum, the conceptual configurations which constitute the theoretical form of ideologies, and the way we handle them, invoke political competition-cum-action. But the *internal* logic of ideologies directs them to straddle the divide between theory and action in a peculiar fashion: by reducing the rational, reflective component linking the two; and by problematizing, occasionally eliminating, the choice that moral theory claims to offer.

The thought-practice referred to as ideology is a common and ubiquitous one. But ideologies are not simply action-oriented, in the specific sense of providing an agenda for political action. The competitive action may be between different groups of theorists, writing books and pamphlets intended to refute each other's viewpoint, a practice common to all producers of ideology. Often, then, ideologies contend with each other as systems of ideas, and it would be rash to deny these activities – these 'wars of words' disseminated through the press and the mass media – their central standing as the *political practice* of influencing the manner through which we impart meaning to our societies.

Ideologies as distinctive thought-practices also interrelate with the world of concrete practices, of practices as regularities of action, in a distinct manner. Political ideologies are hence action oriented in the far broader sense of constituting mapping frameworks through which we can imbue any particular action with political meaning. Here theory itself is simply the imparting of plausible meaning to a set of practices, rather than the determination of correct relationships among facts, or the uncovering of truths. The upshot of this is another central linkage between ideology and practice, observed from the practice → ideology direction of the feedback loop: ideologies identify socio-political practices and locate them at the perimeter of their semantic fields, permitting them to assist in decontesting core and adjacent concepts while simultaneously absorbing those practices into their interpretative domains. Crucially then, there is not a one-to-one relationship between an ideology and a practice. A practice may be equally comprehensible by superimposing on it different theoretical maps (which is the same as extrapolating such maps from the practices themselves). A street demonstration is, in liberal-democratic eyes, a legitimate expression of pluralist dissent, if accompanied by a licence to march arranged through accepted procedures. The same demonstration may be interpreted as a revolutionary act by a radical socialist, or as a threatening example of populism by a traditional conservative. The theory-cum-interpretation extrapolated from that practice may range from regarding politics as the arena of legitimate procedures, to regarding politics as the exercise of group power against constraining structures, to regarding politics as a controlled and directed field of authoritative knowledge. But a street demonstration has also to be *identified* as a practice, and as a practice which has political import to begin with. Because ideologies can be decoded through the analysis of political practices, there is a case for asserting a two-way flow between practice and ideology. Unlike Kant's view of theory versus practice, neither ideology nor practice has ontological priority over the other.

Those who divorce ideology from practice are guilty of the same fault in their own analysis. Sartori's closed ideology is simply not supported by empirical evidence. There is a world of difference between the 'closure' that ideologies effect when controlling the meaning of political language, and insulation from social practices. That sort of insulation is chimerical. Even totalitarian ideologies interact with the political world in which they are located, drawing on existing practices (the Nazis' use of prior anti-Semitism) or adapting them in accordance with vital extraneous needs (Stalin's industrialization projects); they do not conform to their 'formal' or doctrinaire features. Ideologies always contain perimeter concepts and practices which ensure a certain amount of ideational flexibility as these react back on the core concepts. In the cases of non-totalitarian ideologies, such flexibility may be encouraged; in any event, it will result in continuous changes to the core itself. The relationships among the conceptual components of an ideology cannot be contained in abstract logical structures. Such structures would anyhow be unintelligible to most political actors, even including political élites. Moreover, Minogue's proposition that ideologies are only tactically interested in policy neglects the alignment of all ideologies with the promotion and realization of what they conceive to be fundamental social values, however distasteful some of them may appear to others.

Practice and its Constraints

We now turn to a discussion of some of the different positions concerning theory and practice embraced by thinkers and scholars who represent a spectrum of ideological positions in the broad sense adopted here. The literature on practice has itself not always been conducive to the study of ideologies and some of it runs counter to the exploration of ideologies as practices with an easily recognizable and theorizable structure. Two illustrations, relating to Pierre Bourdieu and Michael Oakeshott, will point to problems and ways of confronting them. Bourdieu has focused on the sociological and anthropological study of practices. He detects what he terms the logic of practice, but it is not a logic that suggests the theorization of designed patterns within practices. Rather, it is a special kind of theorizing that practices evoke. Abandoning the harmonizing congruity that sociologists have frequently sought to attribute to practices, Bourdieu retorts that the coherence of models, while economical, hides the impossibility of mastering the logic of practice, which is positioned somewhere between the coherent and the incoherent. For Bourdieu, 'theory ... is a spectacle, which can only be understood from a viewpoint away from the stage on which the action is played out'.[11] The kind of legitimate theorizing about practices such as rites lies in their very identification as activities which have no logic beyond their existence. Hence the interpretation typical of hermeneutics results in misrecognition, for the logic of practice is pre-logical. If practices are understood not to be implementations of plans, a way beckons of overcoming the limits imposed on conventional political philosophy by those who insist on intentionality as a necessary component of both theory and practice. On the other hand, by identifying the 'habitus' as a system of dispositions produced over time, a system which 'is the basis of the perception and appreciation of all subsequent experiences', it is nevertheless possible to stipulate continuities and regularities in practices without being able to account for their schematic nature. Summing up, Bourdieu sees the habitus as 'an infinite capacity for generating products – thoughts, perceptions, expressions and actions – whose limits are set by the historically and socially situated conditions of its production'. It is 'a spontaneity without consciousness or will'. New practices are neither mechanically reproduced nor reflective and they contain no 'unpredictable novelty'.[12]

It is instructive to contrast this with Hannah Arendt's understanding of action as having the character of 'startling unexpectedness', because for her action means taking an initiative, beginning something new.[13] The ontological fissure between the two thinkers indicates a different decontestation of the relationship between individual and society. In Bourdieu's case, culture, time and society themselves are seen to supply the infinite variety of human practice which constrains the individual as an acting corporeal body, in specific situation after situation. In Arendt's case, it is human consciousness itself that operates at the level of the particular, of opinion rather than truth. Human beings are creative conditioners of their own, unique, lives and of those with whom they share lives. Freedom is far more central in this scheme, albeit a freedom forged in the public spaces that combine differentiated individuals. No wonder, then, that for Bourdieu ideology is the imposed control of a cultural good, language, the superimposition of an objectivist understanding in which practices are represented and fitted into planned schemes, the symbolic 'gentle violence' by which domination is misrecognized as legitimate.[14] And no wonder that for Arendt ideology is an all-inclusive logical consistency[15] in which the status of truth is separated from individual human judgment. Ideology loses out in either case. Both thinkers adopt a narrow conception of ideology as incompatible with proper practice and action.

Logical Arbitrariness, Intentionality and Change

How can a reading of Bourdieu apply to a more open view of ideologies? The great strength of Bourdieu's argument is to demystify practice and to show the limits or, alternatively, the arbitrariness of the ideological representation of practices. But arbitrary logic, rather than Arendt's logical consistency, is precisely one of the crucial features of ideology. The brute facts of ideological morphology are the infinite logical relations among political concepts and practices, and the limitless representations of those relations. It does not follow, however, that a particular decoding of logic, a particular logical path among political concepts, is devoid of significance. Even if we accept that practices simply exist, ideologies are precisely those devices that attribute meaning to certain practices. The process has two facets. First, through their identification by a political ideology, those practices have themselves already been recognized, or are newly recognized, as political. Second, the attribution of meaning occurs the moment societies enter a stage of reflexivity, however elementary, because it is then that such practices demand or attract cultural legitimization or delegitimization. So in one important sense it does not matter that practices may be unconscious and unwilled: once they exist, ideologies integrate them into patterns of significance or, to the contrary, ignore them. We are, of course, focusing exclusively on political practices. These are practices that are ideologically identified as public, that are harnessed to compete over collective decision-making processes, and that are pervaded by the justificatory and legitimating processes at the heart of ideological practice. When societies generate their own rules to govern these issues, they are arbitrary in the sense that no *specific* rule is dictated by logic, but necessary in the sense that these issues require cultural solutions for societies to function.

Does Bourdieu's account suggest an intractable conservatism? Not at all. Another merit of his approach is to detach the accentuation of tradition from aversion to human or social change. In that crucial sense all ideologies have a history and are formed by their past. Nineteenth century Marxism is consciously a product of the German metaphysics against which it reacts, and twentieth century liberalism has been closely wedded to ideas of evolutionary change, even regarding itself as a set of beliefs whose essence lies in its being subject to historical processes, processes that ensure the emergence of rational and energizing practices.[16] The thought-practice of advancing practices as the quintessence of politics need not signify a distaste for progress or for theorizing about progress. Nevertheless, Bourdieu cannot easily include the spatial permeability that is a feature of open ideologies. In complex societies, and with increasing intercultural communications, entire ideologies, as well as ideological fragments, interact across the traditional boundaries of family resemblances, forming new hybrids and displaying plastic morphologies.[17]

One final consideration respecting Bourdieu. In examining the relationship between theory and practice it is important to distinguish between a practice as a deliberate, and thought-out, attempt to change political conduct and processes, and a practice as a 'pre-theoretical' cultural pattern, which may then be raised to the level of consciousness. This impacts on two issues. The one concerns the question whether theory is ontologically prior to practice, in which case theory might also be accorded superior status in the conduct of research, giving rise to optimism about the possibility of human control over the political world; or whether practice is ontologically prior to theory, in which case we can only operate within the constraints of the existing, perhaps even the known. The other concerns the question whether theory is the product of individual minds, presumably of talent if not genius – in which case political theory would be an aspect of unique creativity awaiting more general acceptance; or whether it is the product of groups (whose collective consciousness is at the very least questionable) – in which case political theory would already have some of the features of an ideology and reflect the practices of complex interactions that take place between human beings at various levels of awareness.

Here what Bourdieu has to say on intentionality is acute. Much human practice is automatic and impersonal, for 'the habitus makes questions of intentionality superfluous'. Crucially, he claims to solve the 'paradoxes of objective meaning without subjective intention'.[18] The solution lies in the temporal dimension, which permits the emergence of 'a sequence of ordered and oriented actions that constitute objective strategies'. This insight is central to an appreciation of the workings of ideologies. Although they embody myriad variations, ideologies can be identified at least in part as distinct 'strategies' of thinking with patterns of argumentation, style and structure. Those strategies are social and cannot be traced back to any specific individual volition: in other words, they do not have a specific beginning.[19] They can only be discovered by tracking them over time and space, embedded as they are in particular cultural histories. In that sense ideologies have an 'objective' existence which Marx denied: objective not as transcendental, let alone impartial, but as a series of observable and discoverable practices in the world. Moreover, even revolutionary ideologies exhibit features parallel to the habitus. Both are a matrix 'generating responses adapted in advance to all objective conditions identical to or homologous with the (past) conditions of its production'.[20] Intentionality certainly cannot wholly account for action because, in Bourdieu's version of Ricoeur's 'surplus of meaning', 'it is because agents never know completely what they are doing that what they do has more sense than they know'.[21] And yet one cannot take the analogy between habitus and ideology too far. The more flexible the conceptual arrangements of an ideology are, and the more pluralist the political culture that nourishes it, the more it is capable of effecting change through an alertness to 'objective conditions' as well as through the volitional and conscious thought-processes of its more animated champions. Pluralism sensitizes a culture to the possibility of change, to the role of human will in the act of decontestation, in choosing the logical paths between ideas. Paradoxically, that role has been recognized even by Marxisant approaches, though mainly when attached to the ideology of exploitative bourgeois self-interest.

The Space between Theory and Practice: a Conservative View

If Bourdieu's examination of concrete practices does not inexorably lead to conservatism, the same cannot be said of Oakeshott. Oakeshott's early work began with an exploration of experience as the constituting unit of human understanding. Unlike Bourdieu, Oakeshott challenged the barrier between theory and practice from a different starting point, by postulating that experience was a thought or judgment, a 'world of ideas'. Precisely because experience was a totality of facts, it was a truth. Truth and experience were therefore inseparable. However, experience itself was apprehended as a continuously changing system, and the consciousness of it being a system was part of the world of ideas. Consequently, experience was not an interpretation of the world, because that would imply a world of ideas removed from and external to experience. There was simply no space between experience, and ideas about experience. The significance of an idea related to its necessary place in its world, and emerged from the coherence of that world – coherence in the sense that there was no other way of conceiving it. In sum, there was only one experience.[22]

Theory (or philosophy) and experience cannot consequently be seen as opposed. Philosophy is unreserved, self-critical and self-conscious experience, 'in which the determination to remain unsatisfied with anything short of a completely coherent world of ideas is absolute and unqualified'.[23] As for practice, it too was located in the world of ideas as a judgmental aspect of experience, yet as a vehicle for change it was concurrently to be understood as activity. Importantly, the change incurred through practice was not, as is often held, the realization of an idea in a world external to it, but 'always the co-ordination and completion of a given world of ideas'. Nor could practice be judged by its consequences, because that would involve an unattainable future-orientated truth instead of the truth of experience, which had to be not only given but holistically coherent.[24] Indeed, even practice fell short of that coherence, as it could not effect a final resolution of discrepancies in such a coherence, but only particular instances of such discrepancies. Hence practice could not supply an adequate assertion of experience and was irrelevant to the development of a critical philosophy.[25]

In *On Human Conduct* Oakeshott's notion of theorizing became far more tentative and conditional, a continual process of furthering understanding, but one always faced with a 'not-yet-understood'. The theorist is quite distinct from the theoretician. The latter intervenes in human conduct by formulating postulates, rather than exposing, attempting to understand, and rendering conditionally intelligible the contingent 'goings on', the postulates, performances and practices, in a society.[26] Indeed, the ideologist would be a particularly unwelcome version of the theoretician, as ideology was an abstract, superimposed abridgement of a concrete tradition.[27] Here also is an expanded version of Oakeshott's notion of practice. A practice is there to be understood, not directed. It is a more or less durable relationship among agents, involving observances, customs, principles and rules pertaining to human actions and utterances. It is also 'a prudential or a moral adverbial qualification of choices and performances ... in which conduct is understood in terms of a procedure'. It does not determine the substantive choices and performances of agents, but establishes the rules concerning how to make choices and how to perform. Importantly, no practice 'is capable of being participated in except by learning to do so.' It appears 'as various invitations to understand, to choose, and to respond'.[28] Every practice involves the exercise of intelligence, or learned response, however instantaneous; therefore there cannot be a 'thoughtless practice'. A practice 'is an instrument to be played upon', encompassing the understanding of a performer.[29]

Practices cannot be transmitted in the abstract but have to be engaged in by the would-be practitioner. And theory recognizes that understanding human conduct involves nothing more than making claims like the one made in the previous sentence. Theory can only generalize about the particular and the specific, through providing a map as an instrument of understanding. The relationship between theory and practice is such that 'performances may be theorized by being read in respect of their places upon this map or by being assigned a place upon it'. Identifying an action or a performance is a thought process that understands them as relating to practices, a reflective rather than directive relationship.[30] Intelligent thought cannot exist as distanciated from practices and other 'goings on': theory and practice intermesh. Practices also refer to human association – and that is why human conduct is social, not in any overriding and fundamental sense, but simply in the concrete free involvement of agents in practices – but they are not actions as such. They rather relate to speech and action, and include principles, rules, language, and morality, in terms of which to think as well as act. Crucially, Oakeshott sees practices as 'compositions of beliefs and sentiments' which are 'themselves historic occurrences whose intelligibility is contextual'.[31]

Oakeshott's version of the relationship between philosophy and practice remains deeply conservative in its portrayal of any attempt radically to change the world as futile, and in its non-pluralist holism, which lacks even the synthetic tension of opposing elements to be found in much Idealist thought. Despite a superficial

similarity with Bourdieu, whose notion of the habitus imposes constraints of continuity on time and space, as does Oakeshott's view of experience, and despite
the aversion of both scholars to planning, there are important differences. The
rough and incompatible edges of Bourdieu's practices, which may account for
innovation and variety but can be conceptualized only with difficulty, give way in
Oakeshott's writings to an aspiration to contain that rough variety of experience
within, and as, a total and coherent framework of thought: the very obverse of
Bourdieu's thoughtless spontaneity. As an example of conservative thinking,
Oakeshott's collapsing of the space between thought and experience and between
theory and practice fashions an ideology which allows little room for human choice
and diversity in the face of reality, or for differential experiencing of reality, let
alone for the designing of possible futures. Nor, conversely, does Oakeshott accord
unconscious patterns a role in understanding human conduct, inextricably linked
as it is to agency, though agency without an overall plan.[32] Oakeshott could not
entertain the possibility that some practices are discovered by the observer, and
that agents may be unaware of them. For even were all practices to be conscious
and intelligent, cannot different levels of consciousness and intelligibility offer a
possible ranking of practices? Ideologies operate both at the level of the conscious
willing of political ends and at the level of expressing unconscious accumulative
practices. Conservatism, as much as any other ideology, displays the two levels
because conservatives too choose to impose specific understandings of the past on
the political sphere and work to safeguard them in the present.

We may, however, wish to utilize Oakeshott's view of philosophy as the pursuit of
complete coherence by contrasting it with a view of ideologies as devices that
establish a *selective* coherence – though we may also doubt whether in that sense
philosophies ever surpass ideologies. On the macro-level, the scholarly study of
ideology provides the means to view the world from a range of alternative perspectives, precisely because ideologies are more selective mechanisms of coherence, less ambitious than Oakeshott's philosophy. Conversely, on the micro-level,
we may exploit Oakeshott's view of the contingency of occurrences to suggest that
different combinations of contingent occurrences may be intelligibly and reasonably offered by competing ideologies. While Oakeshott is suspended between an
unattainable totality and a limited contextual understanding, the flawed creativity
incumbent in the practice of ideologies offers the far superior tools.

Ideology and the Philosophy of Praxis: a Marxist Adaptation

Although early Marxism was replete with references to the distinction between
theory and praxis, later theorists within the Marxist tradition, of whom Gramsci is
a striking example, recognized political theory itself as a thought-practice. Through
Gramsci's extraordinarily perceptive discussion of the philosophy of practice one
can clearly appreciate how political thought is both illuminated and obfuscated by
its association with the critical thinking of the Marxist tradition. Western moral
philosophy may well fall short of the radical critique demanded by Marxism,
inasmuch at it fails to challenge some of its own categories or to internalize the
centrality of material and historical relationships. However, though ideology

undeniably includes uncritical because unconscious components, it is not therefore devoid of a critical dimension both in its practice in the world and in its practice in scholarship. In their practice in the world, some ideologies shape their conceptual configurations through disputing alternative existing ones. In an open society they also offer the experience of rivalry with its implications of choices between better and worse ideologies – a choice that is, after all, central to the rhetoric of ideology itself. In the practice of the study of ideology, as we have noted, the uncovering of ideological morphology offers a structured and explicable indeterminism that may be put to sceptical or creative uses but, either way, allows us to question any given conceptual arrangement.

Gramsci's contribution lay in the sociological and cultural exploration of the ways in which philosophy penetrates the world of social action, thus overturning the apparent denigration by Marx of (German) philosophy as metaphysics. Leaving aside the more common focus on Gramsci's notion of hegemony, it is of particular interest to explore the intricate way he grappled with the three-way relationship between ideology, philosophy, and practice, arriving eventually at a new understanding. His espousal of the unity of thought and practice is evident in the following passage: '… the majority of mankind are philosophers in so far as they engage in practical activity and in their practical activity (or in their guiding lines of conduct) there is implicitly contained a conception of the world, a philosophy'. In a signal departure from Marxism, philosophy is demystified and concretized by Gramsci, as well as reintegrated into the normal thought processes of individuals qua organic members of social groups. Studying 'the history and the logic of the various philosophers' philosophies is consequently not enough'.[33] Here then is a further gloss on Marx's final thesis on Feuerbach, which could now read: 'most philosophers change the world through their activity in it'.

Gramsci was particularly alert to the tension between philosophy as an expert activity, often pursued in transcendental and idealist forms, and as conceptions *of the world*, a term akin to *Weltanschauungen*, and emerging from real human activity. He did not entirely subordinate the first to the second, however. The disjointed and unformed thoughts of the masses could, and had to, be led by élites entrusted with imparting the dual attributes of coherence and critique. On the other hand, a comprehensive, total philosophy was both an historically concrete and a collective activity, a view which conformed to Marx's own notions.[34] At this point ideologies tentatively enter the interpretative field. For conceptions of the world exist in an embryonic and fragmentary manner in broader social groups, among the masses: 'a conception which manifests itself in action, but occasionally and in flashes'. The philosophy of praxis may be glimpsed crudely in mass understandings of political activity; indeed, that is so because of the historical and social nature of thought. In fact, the philosophy of an age exists on three, not two, levels: as individual philosophies (or philosophers' philosophies), as conceptions of leading groups (an articulated philosophical culture) and as popular 'religions' or faiths. And here Gramsci crucially informs us: 'at each of these levels, we are dealing with different forms of ideological "combination"'. The role of intellectual élites is to modify the 'ideological panorama' of the age, not to dispense with it.[35]

The divide between the philosophical and the ideological thus begins to evaporate on some dimensions. Gramsci was torn between the view, culturally inherited within the Marxist tradition, of ideology as doctrinaire and abstract, and a recognition of ideology as an historical phenomenon within the framework of the philosophy of practice, which needed to be freed from its negative connotations. Societies exhibited ideology-cum-common sense, which incorporated a healthy nucleus of good sense. Hence ideology 'in its highest sense' was 'a conception of the world that is implicitly manifest in art, in law, in economic activity and in all manifestations of individual and collective life.' Yet concurrently even the much-vaunted philosophy of praxis tends, when it is confused with vulgar materialism, 'to become an ideology in the worst sense of the word, that is to say a dogmatic system of eternal and absolute truths'. Ideology in Gramsci's hands is a slippery phenomenon which, as he put it, is situated between philosophy and day-to-day practice but which displays the attributes of both and neither; which sometimes goes unnamed, or by other names, and at other times is explicitly identified; which in some of its forms is relegated to the unacceptable margins of social thought and at other times retrieved as a fruitful political force for positive change, sharing features with the philosophy of praxis, and located at the very point where practice and theory merge. Once the starkness of the Marxist dichotomy between truth and illusion is alleviated, there emerges a provisional and historical status of truth and its practical origins which, according to Gramsci, 'is valid also for the philosophy of praxis itself'.[36]

In some important features of his thought, Gramsci's analysis of ideology remained well within the Marxist tradition. If human thought cannot be perfected, it can at least be improved considerably. Gramsci was still wedded to the belief that ideologies can be refined when their concepts become more universal, and that they can then become more effective weapons in the struggle to achieve an autonomous and superior culture. Specifically, ideological unity and coherence are attainable within a given social bloc. But the process does not stop there. Only a totally unified system of ideologies, attached to different structures and superstructures at a particular historical period, 'gives a rational reflection of the contradiction of the structure and represents the existence of the objective conditions for the revolutionizing of praxis. If a social group is formed which is one hundred percent homogeneous on the level of ideology, this means that the premisses exist one hundred percent for this revolutionizing: that is that the "rational" is actively and actually real'. When Gramsci argued that only mass adhesion to an ideology was the 'real critical test of the rationality and historicity of modes of thinking', he was conceiving of the mass in that special sense. That total ideological system would be 'true' specifically and historically, and would therefore constitute a fusion of theory and practice. This rather naïve Marxist reworking of Hegelian philosophy significantly – and unlike Hegel himself – disavows the values ideological pluralism might contain. Nor can one fail to be struck by a Mannheimian undertone in the possibility of objectivity arising out of the total juxtaposition of the prevalent ideologies of a society. Ultimately, then, this method not only locks theory and practice into a fused unity, but decrees that a sole and singular manifestation of this unity expresses the social world *in toto*.[37]

Notwithstanding, Gramsci's analysis takes us considerably further down the road towards understanding the complexity of ideology. First, because it refers to a structure combining continuously varying levels of political articulation, style and argument, the concept of ideology can be applied to arenas of commonplace as well as rarefied political thought, and be assigned to concrete rather than metaphysical and distanciated guides to action. Second, this approach begins to indicate that ideologies are not as monolithic as the promoters of 'ideology as illusion' or 'ideology as dogma' would have it, but display diverse features. Third, the notion of an ideology as a collective structure suggests that it is a product of social activity and requires to be analysed as a form of human interaction, as historically and socially concrete. Fourth, when Gramsci claimed that for the masses philosophy could only be experienced as a faith,[38] he had in fact recognized the important and perhaps necessary emotional appeal of ideological argument. Fifth, Gramsci paid tribute to the organizational function of an ideology, implying that a specific form of practice was forged. Ideologies were no longer allocated to the realm of fancy. Rather, they 'create the terrain on which men move, acquire consciousness of their position, struggle, etc'.[39] Ideologies were central to practice in delineating semantic fields, providing political and social maps and identifying points of ideational competition, all of which enabled action. Mapping, as with Oakeshott, becomes a central property of theorizing. We may take this further, by regarding mapping as a major interpretative, not representational, feature of ideologies.[40]

Liberalism's Descent from Olympus

Liberal theory and ideology are often thought to view the relationship between theory and practice as one of applying universal and abstract standards to concrete cases. In earlier centuries, that had much to do with the appeal to natural law, via a theory of natural rights, in order to determine rules of right conduct. By the nineteenth century, a more anthropocentric perspective encouraged the search for such standards in human proclivities, although with similar ends in mind. As J.S. Mill asserted, whether or not one subscribed to intuitive moral principles, 'for the remainder of the practice of life, some general principle, or standard, must still be sought'. For Mill that general principle, 'to which all rules of practice must conform, and the test by which they should be tried', was the promotion of happiness.[41]

Twentieth century liberalism has demonstrated a more convoluted connection between theory and practice. L.T. Hobhouse continued to subscribe to the postulate of decisive guidelines in the structuring of practice, but was emphatic in insisting that 'the philosophies that have driving force behind them are those which arise ... out of the practical demands of human feeling' and were not based on deduction from abstract truths. This took Mill's utilitarianism into more complex terrain. For Hobhouse, 'the impulse to establish harmony in the world of feeling and action ... is of the essence of the rational impulse in the world of practice'.[42] That assertion was explained in greater detail in his book *The Rational Good*, subtitled 'A Study in the Logic of Practice.' Here Hobhouse introduced two considerations. First, theory did not influence practice from an external fulcrum but was itself at least in part the product of human characteristics. The world of human practice was that of values supported by feelings; indeed, rational intelligence had its roots in pre-rational impulse. Second, human emotions were themselves a legitimate object of the study of social conduct. If reason as knowledge was divorced from experience, and reason as conduct was divorced from feeling, that would be 'fatal to a true understanding'. Nevertheless, Hobhouse did not deviate from a view of principles as the test of practice. Even if theories 'owe their ready acceptance to a favourable emotional prepossession' the choice among them was still rational, logical and evidential, and judgments about values and emotions could themselves be assessed in terms of truth and reality. Practical reason was 'in permanent operation within the emotional field'.[43] Coherence, compatibility, mutual adjustment – these were central to the harmonious meeting of theory and practice.

British liberalism in particular found itself confronted with the ubiquitous suspicion of ideas embraced by British political culture. Practical reformers, who swore by piecemeal, eclectic and improvized policies, were taken to task by advanced liberals. J.A. Hobson accused them of shedding theory and abandoning intellectual principles entirely. This 'revolt against ideas' encompassed the opinion that great national issues turned 'upon the arts of political management, the play of the adroit tactician and the complete canvasser'. By contrast, Hobson invoked the liberal faith in the 'conscious play of organized human intelligence'. Between a 'half-intellectual, half-emotional' utopianism and a 'crude empiricism', Hobson advocated the 'practical utility of "theory" and "principle"', middle principles that emerged from 'legitimate generalization out of past experience'.[44] Of course, such generalization was posited on the liberal belief in progress, a core concept that significantly underpinned the movement of theory and assisted in structuring practice. Reason combined with progress was itself a theory of social development, enhanced by the evolutionary ideas of the time. It ensured that human intelligence emerged through political practice to increase both individual welfare (which included the liberty necessary for flourishing) and the collective regulation of goods in the interests of social justice. In this new liberal interpretation, the role of theory was to accelerate progress by transforming it into the 'conscious expression of the trained and organized will of a people not despising theory as unpractical, but using it to furnish economy in action'.[45] An ideology in which change was endemic, and was furthermore inextricably linked to the augmenting of co-ordinated rational intelligence over time and space, had to subscribe to privileging conscious over unconscious thought, directive over reactive thought, and patterned and adjustable practice over timeless or mechanical practice. Indeed, one of the pivotal liberal practices is a continuous reassessment of one's own interpretative standpoint. It is the general practice of deciding whether a particular practice should be discontinued.

Many recent versions of liberalism remain linked to conventional views of the relationship between moral theory and political practice, according to which the general rules of the former instruct the latter in formulating correct solutions to concrete cases. Yet an alternative version has emanated from British and American liberal traditions in which collective social life is seen as the source of social wisdom, or at least understanding. British new liberalism was the more influential in providing an account of the social, even organic, base of society.[46] American liberalism, especially through Dewey, insisted on a pragmatism which searched for meaning in the concrete world of human practices.[47] For Dewey, liberalism had originally cultivated a belief in two spheres of action, that of the individual and that of political society; and those spheres only began to converge in the latter half of the nineteenth century. Utilitarianism was one factor in that process, Dewey argued, because 'it greatly weakened the notion that Reason is a remote majestic power that discloses ultimate truths. It tended to render it an agency in investigation of concrete situations and in projection of measures for their betterment.'[48] Liberalism began to be understood as a type of political practice, involving governmental action for the purposes of social justice, and defined 'in the concrete'. That practice arose out of a 'spirit of reasonableness, fostered by social organization and contributing to its development.' It was also a form of vitalism: the component of activity as the dynamic driving force of societies, a prevalent theme of twentieth century liberal thought.

All this demanded that 'the method of inquiry, ... of test by verifiable consequences, be naturalized in all the matters, of large and of detailed scope, that arise for judgment.' Thus liberals appraised actions by the results they brought about, in the light of the already existing capacities of individuals. But they also appraised actions as historically situated, as occupying temporal and spatial points. Liberalism in the concrete was seen as related to the particular, not the universal. The recognition of concrete social conditions is a recognition of the locus in which these conditions occur, a community of human relations, an arena in which external conditions penetrate 'the internal make-up and growth of individuals', and a field of a practically 'experimental and constructive intelligence' counterpoised both to intuition and to custom. And experiment in the social sphere always implies planning; it was no longer an individual prerogative, as past liberals had regarded it, but a social activity. Dewey insisted that co-operative social intelligence was clearly both thought and practice. Moreover, social and historical inquiry were themselves organized practices, 'a part of the social process itself, not something outside of it'. Thought in action involved the understanding and judgement of meanings and these entailed the 'conversion of past experience into knowledge and projection of that knowledge in ideas and purposes that anticipate what may come to be in the future and that indicate how to realize what is desired'.[49] The rational modification of habits and practices is yet another challenge to a simplistic dichotomous relationship between the 'ought' and the 'is'. Because ideologies tend to interweave the two, this indicates one of the main areas where ideologies have a salient role. They are not merely recommendatory devices but interpretative ones of a peculiar kind: a thought-practice which claims, through decontestation, to describe the world, yet does so through recommending that very description.

What implications and limitations does this pragmatic liberalism have for understanding the interplay between theory and practice? As Anderson has noted, on this interpretation liberal principles become contextual tests of product, techniques and performance, but they are also themselves discovered in the process of creative practice and deliberation. Hence they are unencumbered by the rigidity of formal liberal philosophy and unhampered by the classic rational search for a single answer to problems. The relevance of this method to studying ideologies lies in its celebration of the flexibility of the interaction between principle and context and in its recognition of the malleability of political architecture.[50] It therefore offers a bridge – from the observer's viewpoint – towards conceptualizing the internal morphology of all ideologies as configurations of temporally and spatially bound understandings into culturally contingent wholes. It also centres on individual initiative and the capacity of co-ordinated social conduct to make a political difference.

On the liberal understanding ideologies are, to borrow Bell's phrase, levers for action.[51]

However, while pragmatic liberalism offers insights into the nature of political thinking-cum-ideologies, it is unmistakably a *specific* ideological variant. Morphological flexibility happens also to be a conscious core component of most liberal practitioners. It reflects the readiness of liberals to organize their key concepts, employing a reflective common-sense which permits a modicum of pluralist adaptability, and is prepared to contain a variety of views within the family of liberalisms. In parallel, and quite expectedly, pragmatic liberalism displays the *general* characteristics of ideologies – their ultimate refusal to recognize their own decontestations as preferences rather than truths. Anderson mirrors this in his concern to render best practice commonplace in the social sphere: 'to make the exemplary case general and routine'.[52] True, pragmatic liberalism cannot disguise the ideological feature of best practice as metapolitical and universal, as do many philosophical schools, because it derives best practice from reflective understandings of particular contexts. Its decontestations do not seek refuge in 'unassailable' political language. Nevertheless Anderson rejects the ideological status of pragmatic liberalism in typically ideological terms. Liberalism is not a matter of choice to be offered alongside other systems of political belief, but 'the foundation of our system of political understanding' and should be taught as such.[53]

Conclusion

The juxtaposition of the concepts 'theory' and 'practice' is a compressed surrogate for a number of complex and disparate issues. The tightly assumed flow between given theory and advocated practice no longer obtains, and this view on the political world is bound to strengthen the status of ideologies vis-à-vis some forms of political philosophy. First, for those scholars who deny that theory can be solidly grounded in moral postulates, a major sustaining reason for considering ideologies to be inferior theory has been removed. Indeed, ideologies, too, are grounded in rationally meaningful ways of understanding the world, in that their features are now acknowledged to be central to the process of contextual thinking itself. Second, the aspiration of theorists from Marx to Habermas to overcome distorted communication may be queried by students of ideologies not because communication and dialogue are impervious to standards of assessment but because 'undistorted' communication is unknowable. The question revolves rather around the kinds of communication presumed to be inevitable or even functional in political thinking. Third, ideological morphology dictates the existence of multiple routes from a given theory to a range of given practices and from a given practice to a range of possible theories. The metaphor of an open grid rather than a one-way channel seems more apt. Fourth, it is at least as plausible to link ideology and practice as it is to link theory and practice, because practices, like ideologies, are the product of groups and social intercourse, whereas theory may be the speculative product of individuals and hence not directly connected to practices. Fifth, if one *is* inclined to employ the language of truth, even an imperfect political thought-practice contains its own truth in two different senses. On one dimension, it demonstrates that societies simply *have* such thought-practices, just as the particular practice of permitting and encouraging political philosophers to prescribe political norms exists, and is itself an ideological practice worth examining. On another dimension, even were we to accept that ideologies involve distortion, misrecognition or rhetoric, there are contextual reasons for those features, and they too evince ideational patterns that may be decoded. They therefore make sense in a particular society; indeed, they may be essential for the transitivity necessary for collective political action.

As for ideology as a distinct political thought-practice, we may borrow Oakeshott's understanding of a practice – without subscribing to his broader purview – in attempting to explore the properties of ideologies. For they too are not only substantive sets of beliefs but a particular set of conventions, of procedural, or adverbial, conditions for thinking about politics: the conscious and unconscious decontestation of language through statements held, or masquerading, as truths; the forceful and purposive assertion of the legitimacy of concrete practices; the bestowing of political recognition on some patterns of human conduct; the marshalling of emotional support for certain practices, among others through the simplification of the issues on which such support can focus; the choice of specific logical paths linking political concepts through which cultural interpretations are sanctioned; and the semantic competition over the high ground of politics. These are the distinct features constituting the thought-practices of ideologies.

About the author

Michael Freeden, Mansfield College, Oxford OX1 3TF, UK; email: *michael.freeden@mansfield.ox.ac.uk*

Notes

1 I. Kant, 'On the Common Saying: "This May be True in Theory, but it does not Apply in Practice"', in H. Reiss, ed., *Kant: Political Writings*, Cambridge: Cambridge University Press, 1991, pp. 61, 63, 71–2, 86.

2 'Introduction', I. Shapiro and J.W. DeCew, eds, *Theory and Practice: Nomos XXXVII*. New York: New York University Press, 1995, p. 2.

3 M.C. Nussbaum, '"Lawyer for Humanity": Theory and Practice in Ancient Political Thought', in Shapiro and DeCew, *Theory and Practice*, p. 193.

4 Cf. H-G. Gadamer, *Truth and Method*. London: Sheed and Ward, 1979; P. Ricoeur, *Lectures on Ideology and Utopia*. New York: Columbia University Press, 1986.

5 G. Sartori, 'Politics, ideology, and belief systems', *American Political Science Review*, 63 (1969), 398–411. These understandings of rationalism have long since been challenged. See e.g. R.J. Bernstein, *Beyond Objectivism and Relativism: Science, Hermeneutics, and Praxis*. Philadelphia: University of Pennsylvania Press, 1983.

6 K. Minogue, 'Ideology after the collapse of communism', *Political Studies*, 41 (1993), Special Issue, 7–11.

7 Minogue, 'Ideology after the collapse of communism', p.7.

8 C. Lefort, *The Political Forms of Modern Society*. Cambridge: Polity, 1986, pp. 183–5.

9 See C. Taylor, *The Ethics of Authenticity*. Cambridge MA: Harvard University Press, 1991, pp. 66–8.

10 M. Freeden, *Ideologies and Political Theory: a Conceptual Approach*. Oxford: Clarendon, 1996.

11 P. Bourdieu, *The Logic of Practice*. Cambridge: Polity, 1990, pp. 11–12, 14.

12 Bourdieu, *The Logic of Practice*, pp. 54–6.

13 H. Arendt, *The Human Condition*. Chicago: University of Chicago Press, 1998, pp. 177–8.

14 Cf. J.B. Thompson, *Studies in the Theory of Ideology*. Cambridge: Polity, 1984, pp. 58–9.

15 See M. Canovan, *Hannah Arendt: a Reinterpretation of her Political Thought.* Cambridge: Cambridge University Press, 1994, p. 26.

16 Cf. M. Freeden, 'Twentieth Century Liberal Thought: Development or Transformation?', in M. Evans, ed., *The Edinburgh Companion to Contemporary Liberalism.* Edinburgh: Edinburgh University Press, forthcoming.

17 As an example see M. Freeden, 'The ideology of New Labour', *Political Quarterly*, 70 (1999), 42–51.

18 Bourdieu, *The Logic of Practice*, pp. 58, 62.

19 On the question of the 'beginning' of ideologies see M. Freeden, 'Editorial: The "Beginning of Ideology" Thesis', *Journal of Political Ideologies*, 4 (1999), 5–10.

20 Bourdieu, *The Logic of Practice*, p. 64.

21 Bourdieu, *The Logic of Practice*, p. 69.

22 M. Oakeshott, *Experience and its Modes.* Cambridge: Cambridge University Press, 1933, pp. 27, 28–9, 31, 34, 81.

23 Oakeshott, *Experience and its Modes*, p. 82.

24 Oakeshott, *Experience and its Modes*, pp. 256–7, 259, 264–5, 287.

25 Oakeshott, *Experience and its Modes*, pp., 291, 303–4, 319.

26 M. Oakeshott, *On Human Conduct.* Oxford, Clarendon, 1975, pp. 1–10, 106.

27 M. Oakeshott, *Rationalism in Politics.* London: Methuen, 1967, pp. 123–5.

28 Oakeshott, *On Human Conduct.* pp. 23, 55–8.

29 Oakeshott, *On Human Conduct*, pp. 89, 91.

30 Oakeshott, *On Human Conduct*, p. 99.

31 Oakeshott, *On Human Conduct*, pp. 87–8, 78–9, 100.

32 Oakeshott, *On Human Conduct*, p. 72.

33 A. Gramsci, *Selections from Prison Notebooks.* London: Lawrence and Wishart, 1971, p. 344.

34 Gramsci, *Selections from Prison Notebooks*, pp. 329–30, 326, 324, 321.

35 Gramsci, *Selections from Prison Notebooks*, pp. 327, 345, 340.

36 Gramsci, *Selections from Prison Notebooks*, pp. 328, 406–7, 427.

37 Gramsci, *Selections from Prison Notebooks*, pp. 388, 328, 366, 340.

38 Gramsci, *Selections from Prison Notebooks*, p. 339.

39 Gramsci, *Selections from Prison Notebooks*, p. 377.

40 Cf. C. Geertz, 'Ideology as a Cultural System', in D.E. Apter, ed., *Ideology and Discontent.* New York, Free, 1964, pp. 47–76.

41 J.S. Mill, *A System of Logic.* London: Longmans, 1970, p. 621.

42 L.T. Hobhouse, *Liberalism.* London: Williams and Norgate, 1911, pp. 51, 130.

43 L.T. Hobhouse, *The Rational Good.* London: Allen and Unwin, 1921, pp. 27–9.

44 J.A. Hobson, *The Crisis of Liberalism: New Issues of Democracy.* London, P.S. King & Son, 1909, pp. 114–16.

45 Hobson, *The Crisis of Liberalism*, p. 132.

46 M. Freeden, *The New Liberalism: An Ideology of Social Reform.* Oxford: Clarendon, 1978.

47 A. Ryan, *John Dewey and the High Tide of American Liberalism.* New York: Norton, 1995, pp. 126–7.

48 J. Dewey, *Liberalism and Social Action.* New York: Putnam's Sons, 1935, pp. 5–6, 20.

49 Dewey, *Liberalism and Social Action*, pp. 31, 39, 43, 45, 50.

50 C. W. Anderson, *Pragmatic Liberalism.* Chicago: University of Chicago Press, 1994, pp. 19, 156–8, 184, 43, 46.

51 D. Bell, *The End of Ideology.* New York: Collier-Macmillan, 1962, p. 400.

52 Anderson, *Pragmatic Liberalism*, p. 26.

53 Anderson, *Pragmatic Liberalism*, p. 198.

6

Pluralism and Toleration in Contemporary Political Philosophy

John Gray

Liberal Toleration

Liberal toleration began as a project of peaceful coexistence among communities of Christians whose rival claims to truth and political power had ended in war. The genealogy of toleration in the religious conflicts of early modern Europe makes it a poor guide to modus vivendi in the highly heterogeneous societies of late modern times.

Liberal toleration arose from the divisions of monocultural societies. In the conditions in which it arose, the liberal project of toleration made a signal contribution to human well-being. It allowed individuals and communities who did not share religious beliefs nevertheless to have some kind of life together. There are no imaginable circumstances in which human society can dispense with that project of toleration. Yet it has a limited relevance to the circumstances of the contemporary world. Liberal toleration presupposed a cultural consensus on values even as it allowed for differences in beliefs. It is an inadequate ideal in societies in which deep moral diversity has become an established fact of life.

Some contemporary liberal philosophers have sought to supplant traditional liberal toleration by an ideal of neutrality. Others have recognized that liberal political morality is not neutral amongst conceptions of the good but rather promotes a particular way of life. Neither of these liberal responses – neutralist or perfectionist – takes the fact of pluralism in late modern contexts with sufficient seriousness. The natural successor of liberal toleration is not neutrality or perfectionist partisanship for the liberal form of life. It is a project of modus vivendi amongst different ways of life.

The early theorists of liberal toleration shared a common understanding of morality which was rooted in shared religious beliefs. As is well-known, John Locke's defence of toleration was not notably inclusive. It did not extend to Catholics and atheists. There are familiar reasons having to do with the character of political conflict in Locke's time for his exclusion of Catholics. More enduringly significant, however, is Locke's exclusion of unbelievers.

Old-fashioned liberal toleration of the sort theorized classically by Locke found it hard to cope with people who failed to share the categorical morality of Christianity. Locke was at a loss how people whose conception of morality was not that of sin and disobedience could lead any kind of ethical life. To be sure, there had long been Christian Stoics and Christian Epicureans who attempted a synthesis of the ethical outlook of the ancient world with that of Christianity. Even so, none of these thinkers theorized ethical life in terms solely of human well-being. Anyone who tried to do so stepped beyond the pale of Lockean toleration. The conception of morality that Locke and all the protagonists in the Wars of Religion held in common rendered the ethical life of people who lacked belief in a supreme being unworthy of trust. Indeed such a mode of ethical life was barely intelligible.

The European tradition from which liberal toleration arose took for granted that a single way of life was best for all humankind. The claim to have identified that way of life was made by all the protagonists in the Wars of Religion and had long been at the core of the Christian religion; but it was by no means exclusively Christian. The founders of Greek philosophy, above all Socrates, equally took for granted that there was one best human form of life.

Liberal toleration may be understood as an early modern adjustment of a Socratic-Christian faith to the historic realities of intractable rivalry about the content of the best human life. It is not a coherent project in circumstances, such as ours, in which the social fact of many ways of life coincides in the larger public culture with a growing conviction that no way of life is best for all.

The limitation of liberal toleration does not come chiefly from the fact that the substantive ethical beliefs that were shared in early modern Europe are so no longer. It comes from a cultural limitation in the categories in which liberal toleration was framed. Liberal toleration was a restraint on diversity of beliefs and practices among people who had a common understanding of morality and religion. It cannot promote coexistence among people who lack any such common understanding. It is ill-equipped to guide people who doubt, or deny, that one form of life could (even ideally) encompass the human good.

Liberal toleration was not a project of coexistence among different forms of life, mutually acknowledged to be legitimate and worthwhile. It was one of restraint in relation to beliefs and practices confidently judged to be false or wrong. Liberal toleration was of evils, and that fact is not accidental. As I noted in an early discussion of the subject: 'The objects of toleration are what we judge to be evils. When we tolerate a practice, a belief or a character trait, we let be something we judge to be undesirable, false or at least inferior; our toleration expresses the conviction that, *despite* its badness, the object of toleration should be left alone. This is in truth the very idea of toleration, as it is practised in things great and small ... As the Oxford analytical philosophers of yesteryear might have put it, it is the *logic* of toleration that it be practised in respect of evils'.[1]

As it was understood by thinkers in the liberal tradition, toleration expressed a common form of ethical life. It made moral disagreement possible for those within it while those who stood outside it were consigned to unintelligibility. In societies that honoured the liberal ideal of toleration, dialogue could be sustained among people who lacked common beliefs. At the same time, those who did not share the categories of thought presupposed by rival beliefs were shut out from the conversation.

Liberal toleration developed at a time when moral variety did not extend to diversity in the virtues that are given recognition in different ways of life. It is ill-suited to a time in which society contains ways of life that differ as to what is a virtue and what is not. In late modern societies, value-pluralism has ceased to be a theory of ethics whose credentials come chiefly from historical examples or traveller's tales of remote cultures. It has become common knowledge. Among us, value-pluralism is not a stance in ethical theory that is defended by invoking strange and remote cultures. It is a phenomenological commonplace.

Liberal toleration embodied an acceptance of reasonable disagreement; but it was an agreement to disagree in a common language. Wittgenstein noted: 'If language is to be a means of communication, there must be agreement not only in definitions but also (queer as it sounds) in judgements'.[2] The implication of Wittgenstein's observation is that disagreement in opinions presupposes agreement in forms of life. Whether or not this is necessarily true, it is a necessary truth in the practice of liberal toleration. Within that practice, the character of the virtues and the nature of morality is taken as given. It is only moral beliefs that are at odds. For that very reason, liberal toleration cannot guide us in advancing modus vivendi amongst ways of life honouring different goods and virtues.

Pluralism, Neutrality and Perfectionism in Contemporary Liberal Political Philosophy

Recent liberal political philosophers have not reflected deeply enough on what is implied by the fact that the liberal conception of the human subject that the ideal of autonomy articulates is not generally shared. Or, to express the same point in different words, recent liberal thought has not appreciated the full implications of multiculturalism.

When I refer to multiculturalism I do not mean the trifling local debate on American national identity that has occupied many in the USA. I mean the fact that many contemporary societies contain different ways of life, embodying differing understandings of the human subject. This is far from being a uniquely, or even a distinctively modern state of affairs. In this respect, late modern societies may resemble ancient societies more than they do those of early modern times. Now, as in some times in the ancient world, value-pluralism is not so much an ethical theory as an established social fact.

Most contemporary political philosophers, especially those within the lately dominant Kantian school, understand value-pluralism as a theory of the conflicting imperatives that arise within liberal morality. Less superficial and impoverished understandings of value-pluralism can be found, however, within the broader tradition of analytical philosophy. As it was understood by Isaiah Berlin, value-pluralism referred to moral conflicts arising within particular forms of ethical life *and* to differences between forms of ethical life.[3]

In much of Berlin's work, the former type of conflict is taken to be an experiential reality in the lives of individuals, while the latter kind is a result of historical and anthropological inquiry. In many of his writings on value-pluralism Berlin reproduced its proto-version in Herder, in which it is a thesis about conflicts among the ideals espoused in different cultures and epochs. In other writings, such as his magnificent essay on Machiavelli,[4] Berlin recognized that European morality contains conflicting elements deriving from different religious and ethical sources – Christian, Jewish, Roman and Greek, among others. Berlin was not swayed by Nietzsche's thoughts on morality; but like Nietzsche he understood the hybrid character of European ethical life.

Berlin's insight into the hybridity of modern European morality seems to me one of his most important legacies. It suggests an alternative agenda for contemporary moral and political philosophy, in which modus vivendi is adopted as the successor of the liberal project of toleration. Such an alternative agenda would abandon as a dead end the currently fashionable ideal of neutrality and the project of a rights-based liberal theory with which it is associated. As in early modern times, liberal thinkers today seek to formulate a minimal morality that commands universal assent. They imagine they have found such a minimum morality in principles of justice which adopt a stance of neutrality towards rival conceptions of the good life.

The displacement of toleration by neutrality represents a fundamental shift in liberal thinking. Yet it has not usually been acknowledged – or, for that matter, understood – as such. The explanation for this oversight is to be found partly in the historical illiteracy of most contemporary political philosophers. Few philosophers have any grounding, or for that matter any interest, in the history of ideas. Lacking in historical memory, they are apt to treat the local and ephemeral conventions of debate of the past generation as if they were immemorial. As a result, the absurdity of attributing an idea of moral neutrality to any thinker before about 1970 has gone unnoticed.

Recent accounts by philosophers of the central 'concepts' of liberal thought are not only breathtakingly parochial in their narrow cultural assumptions. They are often sadly anachronistic in the claims they make about European intellectual and political traditions. Most recent political philosophers make an unhistorical assumption of continuity in the basic categories and problematic of liberal theorizing. Few have taken the trouble to read Quentin Skinner on neo-Roman ideas of freedom or John Dunn on Locke's political thought.[5]

Philosophers who are deficient in historical knowledge and understanding find it possible to assume that liberal thought deploys the same 'concepts' and addresses the same 'problems' over the past three hundred years. They are able to do so because they are ignorant of the major conceptual and political discontinuities that have occurred within that tradition. As an unavoidable consequence, they have not noticed the occasions on which their own work marks just such a discontinuity.

The shift from toleration of evils to neutrality regarding the good is such a shift. It has gone with an ambitious programme of reconstructing liberalism as a project in the philosophy of right. It is not by accident that the notion of neutrality has been associated with deontic liberalism. Neutrality *requires* the priority of the right over the good. If the good can be shown to come before the right neutrality is an impossibility. That such a deontic reconstruction of liberal political morality cannot be carried through is – in my opinion – one of the few truly demonstrative reasonings in political philosophy.

The proposal that principles of neutrality or equality are constitutive or foundational in liberal morality, rather than any conception of the good, breaks down on the demonstration that such principles acquire a content only by way of substantive judgements about human well-being. We do not know what are the demands of rights unless we know what different structures of rights imply for human well-being. We cannot resolve conflicts between the demands of different rights unless we can give weights to the interests they protect and promote. When conceptions of human interests differ intractably, or exponents of the same conception of human interests rank them differently, arguments about rights become inherently inconclusive. Claims about rights are intermediary or conclusionary moves in moral and political reasoning, never its bottom line. That the good is prior to the right is not a substantive objection to any specific liberal theory of rights. It is a necessary truth regarding all discourse about rights.[6]

The breakdown of the deontic project in political philosophy carries with it that of the project of supplanting toleration by neutrality. One response to this breakdown has been to accept that liberal political morality is not neutral between specific conceptions of the human good but instead encapsulates a particular ideal of life in which personal autonomy is central. This perfectionist successor to neutralist liberalism has been most powerfully developed in the work of Joseph Raz. In Raz's work an attempt has been made to reconcile the traditional liberal ideal of toleration with the social realities of value-pluralism. It is a fascinating enterprise of reconciliation.[7]

Yet I cannot but think it was bound to fail. The reason lies chiefly in the limitations of Raz's contextual argument for the value of autonomy. That argument is two-fold – part functional, part cultural. Raz's functional argument is that people without the skills in choice-making of an autonomous agent will be unable to advance their well-being in a mobile, changeable society. His cultural argument is that the majority of people in contemporary societies have a conception of themselves as part-author of their lives. Neither of these arguments supports the claim that personal autonomy is a necessary condition of well-being, still less a necessary ingredient in it, for all or most people in late modern societies. The functional argument is a version of the long-familiar liberal claim that labour mobility, technical change, and scientific advance entail or presuppose liberal values. Time-honoured as this argument may be, I know of no evidence that shows it to be a law, or even a generalization, which applies in all modern societies.

There are many counter-examples of societies that have modernized without coming to honour personal autonomy as a central good. Japan, Singapore and Malaysia have achieved rapid and far-reaching economic modernization without embracing liberal values. Indeed in the USA – the society that is commonly perceived, particularly by Americans themselves, as the very paradigm of modernity – ideals of personal autonomy have evoked powerful resistance from fundamentalist movements. If, very improbably, the USA were to become a thoroughly fundamentalist society, it would cease to be one that either liberals or pluralists could reasonably admire; but it would not thereby necessarily fall behind in the technical and economic achievements of modernity. Even this paradigm case, then, fails to show conclusively that a modern society requires personal autonomy for its citizens.

Stuart Hampshire is closer to historical realities when he comments on the claim that the growth of scientific knowledge and the authority of science as a cultural institution go together with the spread of liberal values that it is 'a positivist theory of modernization, a theory that is traceable to the French Enlightenment. The positivists believed that all societies across the globe will gradually discard their traditional attachments to supernatural forces because of the need for rational, scientific and experimental methods of thought which a modern industrial economy involves. This is the old faith, widespread in the nineteenth century, that there must be a step-by-step convergence on liberal values, on "our values". We know now that there is no "must" about it and that all such theories of human history have a predictive value of zero.'[8] In the sense in which positivists, Marxists and many liberals have understood it, modernity is merely an Enlightenment myth.

Raz's cultural argument fares no better. It is, in effect, an argument for assimilation to liberal individualist practices as a precondition of thriving in modern society. Yet, as Bhikhu Parekh has noted, there is little empirical evidence that supports it in respect of Asian immigrants in European countries.[9] In fact, unless well-being is defined (question-beggingly) in terms that require personal autonomy as an ingredient, the evidence points the other way. Immigrant groups in which personal autonomy is not an honoured value do better on many of the indices of well-being that are accepted in the wider society. Further, Raz's cultural argument to the value of autonomy makes a crucial empirical assumption – that there exists a majority liberal culture. Yet this is doubtful in many countries, and it is necessarily untrue of all societies that are deeply multicultural.

The expectation that immigrants living in predominantly liberal societies will assimilate to liberal values rests in part on the belief that such assimilation is necessary if they are to advance their well-being. If the latter belief is ill-founded a crucial support for the expectation of assimilation to liberal values collapses. The force of Parekh's argument is that *even in multicultural societies that have a liberal majority* there is no consistent correlation of personal autonomy with socially accepted measures of well-being. If so, it follows that Raz's cultural argument must fail in one of the key tasks he requires of it, which is to ground the liberal value of autonomy in late modern, multicultural societies.

Raz rejects the claim that personal autonomy is a necessary feature of the good life for humans. Rightly, he notes that unnumbered millions of human beings, now and in the past, have lived good lives in which personal autonomy does not figure. At the same time, he insists that personal autonomy is a central requirement of human well-being in most, perhaps all contemporary societies. He combines the pluralist recognition that there are many types of human flourishing, some of them not containing personal autonomy as a necessary ingredient with the claim that in modern contexts personal autonomy is nevertheless a necessary condition of human well-being. Raz's perfectionist liberalism is disabled by the social fact of value-pluralism.

Taking value-pluralism seriously does not support autonomy-based liberalism. For one who rejects the project of a deontic reconstruction of political morality on the ground that the good is prior to the right, and who accepts that there are many varieties of the human good, autonomy can have no overriding value. If, as value-pluralists hold, there are irreducibly many varieties of good lives among humans; if, contrary to positivist, Marxist and liberal philosophies of history, there is no overall, consistent connection between liberal values such as personal autonomy and what is needed for individual well-being in a modern society; and if, in many modern societies, the liberal virtues of autonomous choice belong to one way of life amongst others, then there can be no general argument from value-pluralism to liberal morality.[10] What follows from value-pluralism is not liberalism but an ideal of modus vivendi, which is the natural successor of liberal toleration.

Value-pluralism

Liberal toleration made for a conversation among diverse moral idioms and dialects, but not among different languages of ethical life. That is not an incidental feature of liberal toleration but rather its most fundamental presupposition. So long as ethical life in liberal societies reflected that built-in limitation, toleration worked to advance modus vivendi. In our circumstances it is not sufficient for that purpose. Multicultural societies harbour variety not only in moral beliefs but in understandings of ethical life. In nearly all late modern countries there are distinct ways of life, overlapping with each other in important respects but differing from one another no less fundamentally.

The complex character of late modern value-pluralism has not been reflected in the standard varieties of liberal or communitarian thinking, nor is it well addressed in analytical moral and political philosophy. Philosophers who have considered value-pluralism as a species of ethical theory have been at pains to distinguish the different ways, more or less contingent or constitutive, in which goods may be uncombinable; they have considered whether there are incommensurable goods, whether they are incomparable, and if so in what respects; they have made the point that uncombinability and incommensurability are different relational properties of goods; they have anxiously debated whether value-pluralism is a species of objective pluralism or merely a variation on subjectivism or relativism; and they have noted correctly that even if goods are in some sense incommensurable there may still be better and worse settlements of conflicts among them.[11]

No doubt these are useful discussions. Yet they do little to clarify the types of moral conflict that properly concern political philosophy today. The kind of ethical diversity that is most distinctive of late modern, multicultural societies is not the pluralism of personal ideals and life-plans of which liberal individualism has spoken so much. Even before large-scale immigration and mass media enriched ethical life in most late modern societies such a view of value-pluralism was shallow and narrow. It is notably anachronistic at a time when the ethical conflicts that have most bearing on human well-being are not divergences in personal value-judgements but rivalries between ways of life. In countries as different as Sweden, Israel, France, Turkey, Russia, Holland, India, Algeria, the UK and the USA, pluralism of lifestyles and personal ideals is found alongside a deeper diversity of communities having different kinds of ethical life. In some of these countries there is a liberal majority adhering to individualist values in which personal autonomy is central; in others there is a nonliberal majority, honouring values in which personal choices and individual well-being are not constitutively connected; in yet others there is no majority ethical culture, liberal or otherwise.

Among the many interconnected varieties of ethical conflict which occur in societies exhibiting ethical pluralism of this deep and complex kind, conflicts among communities have the largest implications for human well-being. Such conflicts can weaken the cohesion of the larger societies in which they occur, in some cases producing a breakdown of civil order. In Algeria this has taken the form of civil war between Islamists and secularists, in India of sporadic Hindu-Muslim clashes, in the US of bombings of abortion clinics.

To say that in present circumstances conflicts between communities should be the principal object of philosophical reflection is *not* to say that late modern ethical conflict occurs between well-defined forms of common life exhibiting a seamless consensus in their respective ethical beliefs. In our time, even more than in earlier periods of history, ways of life are rarely strongly individuated; many people belong, by choice, chance, or fate, to more than one; and all ways of life contain conflicting movements. When talking of ways of life it is well to recall that they are complicated things.

Communitarian theorists have criticized the unreal abstraction of the liberal subject. They have rightly argued that a conception of the subject in which it is disembedded from all social situations and detached from its ends and goals is at too great a remove from any imaginable human reality to be serviceable even as a theoretical or ideal-typical construction. Unfortunately, these communitarian thinkers have not noticed that the idea of community that they invoke is no less abstract, unreal and unserviceable than the Kantian and Benthamite conceptions they attack.

A modest advance might be made if discourse on community were conducted always in the plural. Adopting such a convention might make it more difficult to disregard the centrally important late modern phenomena of hybrid and multiple identities. Throughout history there have been people who stood, or found themselves caught, between communities. Pre-modern forms of pluralism in which the basic right-holders were not individuals but communities often made provision for conversion, intermarriage and other movements across community boundaries. Such provisions were possible, partly because people of hybrid identity were rare.

Pre-modern pluralism of this kind is not, however, a recognition of multiple identity. Rather, it is a set of procedures for altering a univocal identity. Among the Romans, the Ottomans and the Moors, it was possible to classify individuals by their membership of one among a small number of ways of life that could be clearly individuated. In modern societies, the individuation of communities that was normal in ancient pluralism is a sign that modus vivendi has broken down.

In pre-modern societies, hybrid identity was a marginal phenomenon; today it is common, and signifies a vitally important aspect of human well-being. In late modern societies, many people practice variations on the several traditions in which they are situated. The interpenetration of divergent, sometimes rival ethical perspectives is one of the most distinctive features of ethical life today. In few late modern societies is it sensible to count forms of ethical life. In our world interactions between different traditions have become constitutive parts of many of them.

Among us, ways of life are not – if they have ever been – windowless Leibnizian monads, mirroring one another blankly. They are prisms, whose shifting colours cannot be separated.

This interaction of ways of life is still far from being the norm. In all contemporary societies there are well-defined cultural enclaves. In much of the world, communities that seek to defend themselves by exclusion are predominant. As we move towards the close of the twentieth century, many societies contain at least three kinds of ethical life – that of such exclusionary communities, that of liberal individuals and that of people of hybrid identity. No political philosophy that neglects any of these forms of ethical life, or takes any one of them to be definitive of the human subject, can hope to capture the conditions of human well-being in our time.

Modus Vivendi

A shift in thinking is needed if the complex social facts of value-pluralism as an historical condition are to be well understood. Liberal individualist and communitarian conceptions of the human subject have in common a resistance to moral conflict. Pluralism in ethics and political philosophy begins with the recognition that, in the soul as in the city, conflicts among values are permanent and constitutive. The question is not how they are to be stilled into harmony, but how they are to be made less injurious to human well-being.

No shift in thinking can make all conflicts among ways of life negotiable. Peaceful coexistence is not an a priori value that all human beings are bound to honour. Some social and political conflicts are insoluble by reason. The terms of modus vivendi amongst ways of life cannot be deduced from universal truths about human beings. There is nothing in the human circumstance or in the nature of human agency in virtue of which peaceful coexistence is always an overriding good. That this is so follows from the central claim of value-pluralist ethical theory, which denies that the rivalrous goods honoured in different ways of life – or, for that matter, in any one way of life, or by all human beings everywhere – can be ranked in an overall hierarchy of value.

Even so, there are good reasons for pursuing modus vivendi. Value-pluralism does not deny the existence of pan-cultural goods and evils. It affirms that some goods, some evils, some virtues, some vices, are anthropological universals; but, in opposition to Aristotle and his natural-law disciples, it denies that these generically human ethical attributes can be ranked in an order that is compelling, or even acceptable, to all reasonable people. Peaceful coexistence among ways of life is a good in virtue of the humanly universal evils that it prevents and because of the generically human goods which it promotes. Also, it may be a good that is recognized in the ways of life which it regulates. Even when a single way of life is prescribed for all humankind, as in fundamentalist religions and liberal universalist political philosophies, humanly universal goods may give reason for practitioners of that way of life to seek modus vivendi with others.

The core of value-pluralism considered as an ethical theory is the claim that the human good harbours rival perfections. Its consequence is that no single way of life exhausts the possibilities of human flourishing. A diversity of ways of life is good because there are many kinds of life – many, no doubt, yet to be invented – that human beings find worth living. Modus vivendi is good because it embodies that diversity.

It is worth noting that, from a value-pluralist standpoint, the goodness of modus vivendi among different ways of life does not come from the fact (if it is a fact) that it maximizes individual choice. That is an obscure and disputable claim I will not defend. Nor, as I have already intimated, is it that such a society advances personal autonomy. For autonomy is a good in some but by no means all the ways of life that late modern societies harbour. Rather, the good of modus vivendi derives from what it does to promote the interests of the practitioners of those ways of life. A society containing several ways of life is good because no one way of life can contain the many kinds of life that human beings find worth living.

Nothing follows from value-pluralism for the desirability of modus vivendi as a matter of strict entailment. Modus vivendi cannot be deduced from the fact that the human world contains many ways of life. It stands in relation to that truth as liberal toleration did to the Socratic-Christian faith that there is one way of life that is best for all humankind. An ideal of modus vivendi may be understood as an adaptation of the liberal project of toleration to an historical context – our own – in which the belief that there is one right or best form of life for humans has ceased to be credible.

I have said nothing as to the terms of modus vivendi. That is partly because they cannot be specified universally. If value-pluralism is true there can be no such thing as an ideal regime. Totalitarian and fundamentalist regimes make modus vivendi impossible because they identify the human good with a single way of life; but that does not mean that liberal regimes alone are left in the field. Different institutions will advance modus vivendi in different circumstances. Both liberal and nonliberal regimes may advance peaceful coexistence; equally, both may make it unrealizable.

In some contexts, federal or consociational institutions may promote modus vivendi; in others, something more like a unitary state may be best. Aside from making the crucial point that there can be no such thing as a regime that is best or ideal for all times and all places, a value-pluralist political philosophy has little to say on these questions. It can suggest some normative constraints on the range of acceptable modi vivendi; but I cannot address here what those might be.[12]

I have said nothing to show that value-pluralism is a true theory of the human good. My aim has not been to demonstrate the truth of value-pluralism, still less to argue that an ideal of modus vivendi is entailed by it. More modestly, I have tried to suggest that the account of value-pluralism that is given in recent philosophy is an inadequate reflection of its complex reality as an established social fact. It is partly because the account of ethical life they contain has been so thin that the contributions made to political practice by the political philosophies that have been dominant over the past thirty years or so have been so slight and unprofitable. It is a commonplace of contemporary political philosophy that liberal morality is a solution to a problem of pluralism. My argument has been that contemporary political philosophy has not taken pluralism seriously enough.

About the author

John Gray, London School of Economics, Houghton Street, London WC2A 2AE, UK; email: *J.Gray@lse.ac.uk*

Notes

1 'Toleration: a Post-liberal Perspective', in my book, *Enlightenment's Wake: Politics and Culture at the Close of the Modern Age*. London: Routledge, 1995, pp.18–19.

2 L. Wittgenstein, *Philosophical Investigations*. Oxford, Basil Blackwell, 1958, Part 1, Section 242.

3 I have examined Berlin's value-pluralism in my book, *Isaiah Berlin*. London and Princeton NJ: Harper/Collins and Princeton University Press, 1995, ch. 2. I have considered value-pluralism more extensively in ch. 2 of my book, *The Posterity of Liberalism*. Cambridge: Polity, 2000.

4 See Isaiah Berlin, ' The Originality of Machiavelli' in Henry Hardy and Roger Hausheer, eds, *The Proper Study of Mankind: an Anthology of Essays*. London: Chatto and Windus, 1997, pp.269–325.

5 See Quentin Skinner, *Liberty Before Liberalism*. Cambridge, Cambridge University Press, 1998; John Dunn, *The Political Thought of John Locke: an Historical Account of the Argument of the 'Two Treatises of Government'*. Cambridge: Cambridge University Press, 1969.

6 I have set out this argument in my paper, ' Where pluralists and liberals part company', *International Journal of Philosophical Studies*, 6, 1 (1998), 17–36.

7 See especially J. Raz, *The Morality of Freedom*. Oxford: Clarendon, 1986 and *Ethics in the Public Domain*. Oxford, Clarendon, 1994.

8 Stuart Hampshire, ' Justice is Strife', Presidential Address, American Philsophical Association, Pacific Division Meeting, *Proceedings and Addresses of the American Philosophical Association*, 65, 3, (November 1991), pp. 24–5.

9 B. Parekh, 'Superior people: the narrowness of liberalism from Mill to Rawls', *Times Literary Supplement*, 25 February 1994.

10 Isaiah Berlin argued that liberal political morality is supported by the truth of value-pluralism. I have considered this argument in my book, *Isaiah Berlin*, most particularly in ch. 6.

11 See Ruth Chang, ed., *Incommensurability, Incomparability, and Practical Reason*. Cambridge MA, Harvard University Press, 1997.

12 For a more extended discusssion of some of these points, see Gray, 'Where pluralists and liberals part company', pp. 25–27.

7

Philosophic Tramps

W. H. Greenleaf

I

While the relation between the theory and practice of politics no doubt takes many forms, the focus here will be on themes which in Britain have influenced the exercise of (what Locke called) the federative power, the conduct of relations with the world outside. And one immediately obvious feature of the attitude of those concerned with this task is that they are notably indifferent to reflection of an abstract kind as well as to speculative surveys or long-term projections, regarding these as lying quite apart from their particular business. In this sense they may be said to share the motto of Maitland's 'philosophic tramp', that problems are best solved *ambulando*.

It is a characteristic which has long been recognized as when the fifteenth Earl of Derby remarked that it was not possible 'to lay down any formula or any general rule which shall bind us in our foreign policy for all time and on all occasions. We must deal with the circumstances of each case as it arises.'[1] Similarly Viscount Grey described how the plans of a British Foreign Secretary were more likely to be guided by current perceptions of national interest than by 'far-sighted views or large conceptions or great schemes'. Ministers do not, he declared, look beyond the moment and the direct consequences of policy: the indirect results are incalculable anyway.[2] In the same fashion a memorandum on international arbitration drew a clear contrast between discussion which is of 'a theoretical and abstract character' and that based on 'actual experience'; and the judgement was made that reliance on the former leads to conclusions not warranted by the facts.[3] Naturally there has been the same constrained response to any proposal deemed visionary in character: and it is hardly fanciful to link the British reaction in 1815 to the Tsar's suggestion of a Holy Alliance and that of the Thatcher government in 1985 to the idea of European monetary and economic union. The first was seen as a 'piece of Sublime mysticism and nonsense', the latter as based on 'cloudy and unrealistic aspirations'.[4] In the event, and despite the British reservations, both conceptions were pushed ahead determinedly by their advocates. But the point is the response itself: that such projects, being merely chimerical, could not be proper objects of policy. In the conduct of affairs it is vital to remain firmly in touch with reality and (as with Antæus) disaster follows if this foundation is lost. The touch of federative business is death to dreams; and the idealist will hardly be at home in Downing Street or Whitehall. Of course there is a role for vague rhetoric or sweeping dogma but this is as public justification. When Pitt was at last driven into war with France in 1793 it was for strategic and diplomatic not ideological reasons; but once hostilities had opened Burke's philosophy immediately became of use as government propaganda.[5]

The stance is clear enough. Yet two observations need to be made about it.

One is that the attitude must not be attributed to a fear of abstract inquiry or to wide-ranging review as such for when occasion demands either will be ventured. Thus in the official papers there are analyses of such ideas as sovereignty, human rights, self-determination, suzerainty, contraband and the power of search, paramountcy, dominion, protectorate, prerogative, trusteeship, and guarantee (among many others). About the precise meaning and implications of such notions the diligent clerks of the federative departments will, if necessary, logomachize at length. Of course these terms merit attention not through any unengaged conceptual interest but as they arise for consideration in some practical context such as writing a constitution, drawing up a treaty, responding to a resolution at an international assembly, justifying a blockade, framing a law, conducting a negotiation, dealing with protests from foreign Powers, and the like. Similarly, because official action must be taken with as much forethought as possible, it is usual to produce background material to aid the process of decision: abstracts of previous correspondence, summaries of past proceedings, lists of precedents, historical synopses, reports ranging over an entire subject, reviews of policy options, and so forth. And again such surveys are undertaken with a particular purpose in view: hard-pressed ministers and their advisers are naturally loath to spend time on extensive memorials that have no immediate bearing on current problems.[6] Perhaps one of the most celebrated such *tours d'horizon* may stand as example. The Eyre Crowe memorandum of 1907 is a splendid general essay on relations between the Great Powers of Europe and the recent course of German policy towards Britain. However it was written not for its own sake but with specific practical intent, to heighten official awareness of the growing menace of an aggressive German nationalism.

The second comment is that, although officialdom is dubious about abstract or extensive speculation, its attitudes are not merely arbitrary: policy-making is not a series of *ad hoc* responses to events, a matter of 'waking up each morning and considering, "What would I like to do?"…, and doing it'.[7] For, while there are no ineluctable principles by which the conduct of affairs may be directed, there are certain broad categories of concern which suggest (or limit) possible courses of action; and these are derived from a long experience and an understanding of Britain's changing position in the world and of the character of that world. Because circumstances must always come in, the make-up of these rule-like considerations varies over time (as does what might be called their 'mix'). As well any of them may become obsolete or irrelevant: clearly the business of Britain as a world power, the possessor of a global empire, cannot be the same as that of today's relatively weak offshore island. Yet this manifold of categories, relating to various key aspects of the national interest as this is conceived from time to time, makes up the framework of maxims within and by reference to which the external policy of the state is formed and carried on: the 'theory', so to say, which moulds federative 'practice'.

II

(a) First there are the factors relating to diplomatic policy, strategy, and defence.

The condition of international affairs is one of anarchy tempered by arrangements and ranges from rampant violence to peaceful co-operation. There is always rivalry between states and each pursues its national interest, the objective being to gain by negotiation or threat that form of accommodation which offers the greatest benefit; or, where this is not possible, to secure the best outcome from any conflict. Given this condition of things the disposition deemed most suitable to Britain's purposes has varied. It might be sustaining a concert of the Great Powers to resolve major issues and disputes; or maintaining an international balance to prevent the emergence of some hegemon. And both such aims imply a shifting pattern of engagements and also interference should the consensual determination need to be enforced or the equilibrium restored. In contrast the object has sometimes been isolation, the avoidance (except for some definite and immediate object such as a war or the protection of a specific advantage) of the obligations involved in standing alliances and other such commitments, so as to preserve the greatest freedom in making federative decisions and in maintaining world-wide the posture of an imperial power. Latterly there has been support for means of international amelioration, for participation in world organizations and regional groupings, a course which, if it might have once seemed idealistic or unnecessarily restrictive, has become more attractive as Britain's relative strength waned. Naturally other states had their own vital resolves which it was necessary to respect and which constituted limits on what British policy might attempt. One obvious example of this was the Monroe Doctrine which, declared as a central principle of American foreign policy, restricted (or at least affected) the activity of European Powers in the New World.

But this is all rather general in form; and these broad diplomatic projects are always related to, or construed as, a series of considerations of a more specific and concrete kind. And the particular nature of the demands involved may be exemplified by reference to the special position occupied in the British scheme of things by India and to the not unrelated Eastern Question: both matters which for so long dominated British external policy.

After the loss of the American colonies the received view saw Britain and India as twin centres of imperial wealth and strength. Not only was the sub-continent a major element in the working of the British economy (in terms of both the investment located there and the value of the goods exchanged) it was also the focus of an important regional system of trade. As well there was the Indian Army, a force crucial to the structure of British influence throughout the great land arch which stretches from the East African seaboard to South-East Asia, and a vital supplement to British sea power: 'Between them', it has been said, 'the sepoys and the Royal Navy guarded the commercial empire throughout the eastern seas and the Pacific'.[8] The tie with India was strong, too, because so many British people spent much of their lives there. Whether the facts really sustained a favourable view of 'English merchant-mastership in Ind' is another question: but the pervasiveness of the belief itself is undoubted.[9] So it was deemed imperative to make safe the lines of communication between Britain and the East via both the Cape and Egypt; and during the entire nineteenth century and after, 'the protection, development, and control of the approaches to India and other possessions in the East' ranked 'among the leading enterprises of the British people'.[10] Equally it was seen as crucial that the states on the northern frontier and adjacent regions of Central Asia should not be allowed to fall under hostile (which largely meant Russian) political influence or military control. Hence, for instance, the Afghan Wars, the Great Game, the Penjdeh incident, the military missions to Turkistan in 1918, and (between the Wars) the concern about the unrest and anti-British activity in the Middle East and India being systematically fomented by the Soviets. Russia had, then, to be prevented from enlarging its boundaries and sphere of influence towards, on the one hand, the Straits and the Mediterranean and, on the other, Asia Minor and beyond. So the position of the Ottoman Empire was recognized as crucial: as Prince Albert once wrote, 'The overthrow of Turkey by Russia no English statesman could view with equanimity'.[11] This was a factor which notably affected British policy in respect of, say, the Greek revolution of the 1820s, the situation leading to the Crimean War, and the crisis of 1875. The Russian 'power of menace' (as Curzon called it) exercised indeed a long and wide spell; and it is no wonder that early in the last century (especially when the German threat began to loom close to home) an accommodation with Russia became the primary goal of British foreign policy.[12] Just as after 1945, once it became apparent that co-operation with the USSR was hardly possible, that power was regarded as 'potentially hostile', a threat to the 'strategic security' of the United Kingdom.[13] Hence the need to contain Communist power in Europe by the establishment of a counter-balancing *bloc* under the leadership and with the economic and military aid of the USA; and in addition to oppose its manifestations in other parts of the world.

In all this the armed forces had a pivotal role, their functions being to defend the home islands and the Empire; command the seas; provide an oversea attack force; support diplomacy; protect trade; and fulfil a further array of tasks such as aiding the civil power in cases of unrest, undertaking punitive and rescue operations, and securing intelligence. So it was always important to ensure that the services were adequate to the purposes in view though what was required differed according to the arm concerned. If the Royal Navy embodied the preponderant sea power that was for so long regarded as vital, no attempt was made to match, let alone surpass, the military strength of other nations. Moreover British regiments were widely scattered as an imperial police which meant that the army was ill-suited for its other main task of providing an expeditionary field force to support government policy: it was certainly not capable by itself of intervening effectively on the Continent (which was one reason for avoiding major commitments). In this regard the army later came to be seen rather as a nucleus to be supplemented in a major war by conscription. A factor of the greatest significance in this context has been technological change. The pace of innovation and overcoming the obsolescence to which it led were decisive elements in the loss of maritime supremacy; military *matériel* increased greatly in complexity; while the aeroplane and the nuclear missile are in themselves symbols of this sort of development and all it implies. Not least the increasing financial burden imposed is apparent from the fact that, as a proportion of a growing GNP, defence costs rose from 2.4 per cent in 1890 to 5.5 per cent in 1979.[14] At a time when Britain's economic strength was in relative decline as compared with her rivals, it was obvious on the ground of cost alone that her strategic posture was bound to change and her role on the international scene diminish accordingly.

(b) A second category of business relates to the imperial affairs which for so long exercised a determining influence on British oversea policy.

The reasons which led to official interest in the acquisition of colonies in the first place were numerous and ranged widely in nature: from the protection and development of trade and control over raw materials to the abolition of slavery; from the establishment of penal settlements to the forestalling of claims by imperial rivals. Sometimes annexation arose out of crisis as when the East India Company was superseded or Egypt invaded; or it was the result of war (Hong Kong and the Sudan, for instance, or the League of Nation's mandates). Acquisition for strategic purposes was frequent: the Cape, Aden, Mauritius, the Somaliland coast. And so on. Then, once a direct responsibility had been assumed, there was the need to maintain authority and civil order. To this end Britain would if necessary undertake a war or use whatever lesser degree of force was required to sustain its control over a colonial territory or to restore security of life and property there. Over the past couple of centuries there have been numerous occasions which illustrate this from, at one extreme, the wars to suppress the Sepoy Mutiny or the Boer republics, through the quelling of a rebellion (as in Jamaica in 1865 or Kenya in the 1950s), to the repression of mere street violence or agitation at the other. This is largely a military or police problem and the principles and means of action involved are well established: for instance there is (or was) a regularly updated official booklet on 'internal security duties' which exhaustively reviews these matters.[15] In fact official preparation in this regard was meticulous: throughout the Empire each colony was required to formulate (and to update every year) a defence scheme to cope with an internal rising or riot.[16] And to this end all the many forms of regulation and suppression were employed from simple surveillance and censorship to deportation, imprisonment, and execution.

As well once a territory was taken over it was necessary to aid its political advance. Self-governing status had been granted quite early to the 'white' colonies but elsewhere in the Empire the guiding principle was one of protective trusteeship to safeguard the interests of the native population. And, while it was supposed that all colonies would progress in constitutional terms, it was equally anticipated that in most places the process would be long drawn-out and dependent, too, on previous economic development. Yet government did relatively little in this latter respect:

> Until the second World War it was not normally considered incumbent on a colonial Power to finance development in its colonies from its own metropolitan budget. The major contribution to [their] economic transformation ... was therefore made by private enterprise, which exploited ... natural resources ... , especially minerals and land, and stimulated trade and commerce. The traditional role of government was first to establish the rule of law and to constitute an efficient administration, where possible making use of indigenous institutions; then to lay the foundations for education, health and other social

services; and at the proper moment to introduce the machinery of representative government.

Consequently much of the wealth needed to support government services 'was produced by external enterprise, skill and capital' and the task of developing the local economy was – and remained – costly, difficult, and protracted.[17] But after 1945 the situation was transformed. Colonial economic development was given a greater priority and the pace of constitutional change accelerated considerably. The truth was that Britain no longer possessed the strength and resources of an imperial nation and, though its colonial pretensions died very hard, they had to give way before the growing demand for self-determination and the strong international pressure to hasten the transfer of power.

(c) The third group of considerations has to do with the protection and development of Britain's commerce and investment abroad: her 'greatness, even her existence, depends upon her foreign trade; and to place that trade upon sound foundations must be one of the most important of her interests'.[18] Even in the days when a limited view of the state's domestic role was usual it was none the less believed that it was the business of government 'to open and to secure the roads for the merchant', that one of its 'first duties' was 'to obtain for our Foreign Trade that security which is essential to its success'.[19] And over the years these matters became a substantial area of official concern: during the Great War one report noted that Britain was 'now committed to a national trade policy which will enter largely into the conduct of our foreign relations and may dominate them'.[20] Perhaps too little was actually accomplished in this respect; all the same by the early 1950s a third of the work of the Foreign Office was economic in nature.[21]

There have been various aspects to this duty. First there is the formulation of commercial policy which could range from the pursuit of free trade (requiring the removal of restrictions) to some degree of protectionism by which parts of the British (and the imperial) economy might be especially advantaged (which could involve considerable, and continuing, intervention). Secondly general aid could be offered to British oversea trade as by the collection of commercial data, looking for new markets or sources of raw material, making trade contacts and securing concessions, obtaining contracts from foreign governments, and the like. In this context the embassies, their growing commercial staffs, and the network of consular offices were crucial, the last being particularly important as it exercised a wide range of functions from responsibilities for British shipping to the promotion of exports. Then there is the specific protection and aid offered to British subjects and firms actually trading abroad as by helping businessmen who found themselves in local difficulties of some kind, for instance when trying to secure redress for grievances suffered. It was often argued that, if such official aid and protection were not forthcoming, the confidence and sense of security of British traders would diminish and thus affect their willingness to work in foreign countries. In consequence industry would be less able to export its products; the funds for investment abroad (at one time a very considerable amount indeed) and so the interest earned, would probably fall; and the spread of British commercial interests would thereby be inhibited or halted. The sort of assistance offered ranged from the negotiation of extra-territorial rights and the establishment of capitulatory régimes in such places as China and the Ottoman Empire to diplomatic support and, beyond all this, the use of 'all the enginry of Force', armed intervention, of which there are numerous cases from, say, the first Opium War (1840–2) to the Venezuela blockade of 1902. Finally there were the occasions when government was substantively involved in matters directly or indirectly to do with foreign trade as for instance by: recognizing the South American republics; the acquisition of the Suez Canal Company shares; helping to develop colonial infrastructure as with the construction of the Uganda railway; supporting exploration (an early example is the Euphrates expedition of 1835 to survey a route from the Mediterranean to the Persian Gulf); participating in the search for and control of oil resources (as through the Anglo-Persian Oil Company); developing imperial communications (Cable and Wireless and Imperial Airways for instance); the establishment of import boards for bulk purchase; the introduction of such schemes as that for growing ground nuts in East Africa; the creation and support over a long period of chartered companies (like the East India and Levant Companies); and so on. Under this head might be considered, too, the role government played in aiding the movement of people abroad as by supporting schemes for assisted passage and settlement to help open up 'waste lands' in the oversea possessions. Lately there has also been the increasingly substantial amount of foreign aid given to Third World countries, especially British ex-colonies, some of which is returned as increased demand for British goods and services.

(d) Fourthly there is the attention that has to be paid to the requirements of constitutional principle and certain aspects of the domestic political scene. Thus the supremacy of Parliament and the importance of public opinion make it difficult (it has sometimes been said impossible) for a British government to make a treaty or other agreement entailing the *casus belli*. Lord Salisbury once wrote (in a dispatch of 1897) that

> The institutions under which we lived entirely prevented H[er] M[ajesty's] Gov[ernmen]t from making any engagement with respect to the military or naval action of England upon contingencies which had not yet arisen. When these contingencies arose, they would be fully considered by the Parliament and public opinion of this country, and no influence of any Government, and probably no promise into which any Government might have entered, would in such a case avail to prevent the country from acting upon its own views of what was right and expedient in such a matter.[22]

All the same, governments gave such guarantees when the national interest required (the Anglo-Japanese Alliance of 1902 is a case in point).[23] But the dictum continued to be asserted as by Grey during the military conversations with France before the Great War.

Ministers are answerable to the Legislature so opinion expressed there (and especially in the House of Commons, its committees, and party groups) can never be neglected even though it is the case that (in contrast to consideration of domestic affairs) the role of Parliament is limited in various ways. There is for instance relatively little legislation; secrecy often surrounds federative business and the realm of executive discretion is greater; opportunities for debate and inquiry may be relatively restricted and procedural difficulties can arise (as over the scrutiny of treaties). None the less Parliamentary views sometimes have a significant impact. They may, for instance, affect the attitude of other states and so the conduct of any negotiations under way. The influence of even one MP may be considerable as in the controversy in 1959 about deaths at the Hola Camp in Kenya. In some circumstances a debate on federative affairs may even lead to a ministerial resignation or the fall of a government as in 1855 or 1940. Much depends, of course, on whether there is a front-bench consensus on major issues, the size of the government's majority, the degree of pressure within the party, and so forth. Especially significant is any division over a major question of policy. Palmerston and Russell found that because of opposition within the Cabinet (and outside it) they could do nothing to save Denmark from being crushed by Austria and Prussia. An even more crucial illustration is the dilemma faced by the Liberal administration in August 1914. If it decided against war there would be a political crisis and the likelihood was the government would fall through the resignation of the Foreign Secretary and other senior ministers; the Conservatives would then come in either alone or as part of a coalition. In any event the Liberal Party would be split with disastrous consequences for its future. On the other hand if the Cabinet decided for war the result would be much less traumatic, probably the loss only of a few radicals (even though this might lead to the formation of an anti-war party). To professional politicians the choice was obvious. The march of events – the German invasion of Belgium – 'may have helped to *confirm* a decision already made on political grounds, but it did not *determine* that decision'.[24]

Disparate attitudes within a federative department also may have their effect as with the divergence over German policy in the Foreign Office before the Great War. So may disagreements between departments like that between the Foreign Office and the government's service advisers in 1936 over the area to be kept occupied in Egypt and, after the war, over the prospect of co-operation with the Soviet Union; or as between the Foreign Office and the Colonial Office in the early 1950s about how to approach the problem of nationalism.[25]

The press, too, has long been a factor of importance not least since the staff of the most important London papers began to include people who were in effect foreign editors or diplomatic correspondents and since foreign news services developed thus providing an alternative to the presentation of events given by official sources. Of course the papers might be influenced in what they said. It was not (as in some places) that they could be controlled or that they depended on government subsidy; but they could be fed news and estimates of its significance. Yet for many years the use made of the press varied considerably. If Castlereagh ignored the newspapers Palmerston did not and gave inside information to friendly journalists both at home and abroad and (though he never admitted it) actually wrote articles for publication.[26] The modern tendency is obvious: the public derives its information about oversea affairs from the media of mass communication while ministers make considerable use of them to present policy and attempt to influence public views; and there is the paraphernalia of news departments, briefings, and all the rest of it. Of course this requires a great deal of time and energy; but the effort is essential. Certainly the pressure popular opinion can exert may be significant as numerous instances suggest: from agitation to end the slave trade or stop the Bulgarian atrocities to votes in the Oxford Union and the mass meetings of pro-Boers or CND. However on the whole organized pressure-group activity tends to be less marked in the sphere of oversea affairs; though in the usual way some bodies may for special reasons be consulted or listened to.

Economic considerations may have an important effect as with the way in which the need for financial retrenchment became an increasingly significant factor as Britain's relative economic position weakened at the same time that defence costs were rising. Before 1914 the growing cost of maintaining command of the sea and of defending India caused the government great concern because the level of taxation involved (not least in a context of costly social reform) was likely to reach a level beyond that which Parliament and the public would accept and, as well, would probably exacerbate the already disturbing array of industrial and other troubles: when, in the end, war came and the BEF went to France, two divisions had to be retained at home to be used if necessary in aid of the civil power.[27]

(e) Finally there is (what might be called) the moral dimension to federative affairs, the imperative being one either accepted by the policy-makers themselves or resulting from the pressure of others. It arises in some form or other in a whole range of questions. Where possible regard is paid to international law, precepts such as the duty to keep pledges formally made, and to acknowledge limitations in the way force is used in the settlement of disputes. Sympathy for a people struggling to be free and support for the cause of constitutional government have long been regarded as proper attitudes for a British government to adopt. Similarly there are the manifestly humanitarian issues in which Britain played an active part such as the abolition of the slave trade or the prevention of genocide.

Of course in matters of diplomacy moral pressure alone is likely to be ineffective. In negotiation for example however virtuous some end might be a guarantee of force hovering in the background always carries weight: as Lord Salisbury once said, it is no good, and may even be dangerous, to be 'optimistic' and have 'an undue belief in the effect of amiable acts not supported by requisite strength'.[28] As well any ethical consideration is never unalloyed: the extent to which it is compelling will vary according to the circumstances and it may be largely or entirely ignored where questions of national interest are seen to be involved: the conduct of federative policy is not the prosecution of a crusade.[29] As one official paper put it: 'it was the duty of a Government to guard against future contingencies, and to provide for the permanent interests of their country, and in the performance of this duty they must not be guided by their sympathies'.[30] There is (to say the least) always likely to be some ambivalence about the role of ethical concerns in this respect. For example in 1787, when considering British policy towards the warring factions in Prussia, Fox declared that he 'deprecated any discussion of the justice of the cause of either party' for that 'was not the question a British Minister was bound to look to', his concern being simply which group 'was most likely to promote the interests of Great Britain'.[31] And, while Britain's considerable diplomatic and naval activity to suppress the slave trade was undoubtedly undertaken on humanitarian grounds, there was also the intention to ensure that other countries did not enjoy advantages denied to British commerce; just as the acceptance of complete emancipation, morally desirable in itself, was delayed by a series of political considerations (concerning among other influences the West India interest). In the same manner Canning's Latin America policy was governed much more by power politics and commercial considerations than by dislike of Spanish colonial rule or by a philanthropic interest in the new states. Again at the time of the Greek revolution in 1821 there was much Philhellenic support for those resisting the evils of Turkish rule: but this was not allowed to determine British policy which was guided rather by major diplomatic and strategic issues concerning the Russian threat to the Porte and the passage to, and stability of, India coupled with the wish to avoid a general war arising out of the turmoil in the Morea. Given the importance attached to sustaining the Ottoman Empire sympathy for the Greeks was a strange aberration and, when publicly expressed, a cause of embarrassment to the government which pursued a policy of strict neutrality.[32] Similarly Belgian claims to independence from Holland, while in general regarded with favour in Britain as morally right, were always judged in the context of how they might affect relations between the Powers and subordinated to such matters as barrier fortresses and the security of the Scheldt: what Britain needed was a safety zone and an independent Belgium was supported because it was the best way to secure this end. And when for instance the question of frontiers was under review, ethnic and linguistic affinities or the wishes of the inhabitants of a particular area were, if the key considerations demanded it, likely to receive very short shrift. Egypt is another case in point. Whatever the justice of the original invasion Britain became ensconced there, and in the region generally, for a whole range of reasons mainly related to strategy and trade. But the position was difficult because of the need to try to

> reconcile two inherently irreconcilable principles of traditional British foreign policy, namely, (a) the principle of self-determination and non-intervention in the internal affairs of another country, Egypt; and (b) the vital necessity of self-preservation, e.g., Imperial communications.[33]

And of course the intrusion of moral fervour into the realm of policy may be highly embarrassing, not to say dangerous if it leads to war. Salisbury told Curzon he was loath to interfere in the Congo to prevent the cruelty going on there, believing that the tyranny might thereby only be driven underground; and 'I have', he said, 'no belief in a policy of scold'.[34] And where ethical considerations stand in the way of national survival they are equally likely to receive short shrift: clearly the deliberate attack on a civilian population involved in a policy of sustained area bombing may be regarded as immoral and contrary to international law; but few resisted it during the Hitler War when it was generally accepted as a legitimate and, given the military situation, an essential weapon of offence.[35]

Such considerations, then, have been among the parameters of federative thinking. Of course none has been exclusive or absolute; and it is manifest that changing circumstances could render any particular factor irrelevant. Equally conflicts of purpose were always possible: as for instance when the rigid application of free trade principles (which demanded the reduction of all duties) could not easily be reconciled with Britain's position as leader of the movement to abolish slavery (an aim suggesting a preferential tariff to disadvantage slave-grown sugar).[36] Indeed the ever-shifting kaleidoscope of federative affairs makes it difficult, as Lord John Russell once said (about an awkward situation in foreign policy), 'to lay down any principles from which deviations may not frequently be made'.[37] So it is very true that to 'learn the grammar of the policy-makers' and to 'construe their texts' is likely to be a matter of some complexity.[38] What is involved, what sort of weight might be attributed to each element, the kind of guidance these categories provided, can really only be indicated by reference to individual acts of decision-making. Space permits only one somewhat abbreviated exercise of this kind; but it may suggest what are the springs of official action, the relation between the general objectives already described and specific federative practice. The instance chosen (for no better reason than that the material was to hand) concerns the matters taken into account before Harold Macmillan visited Africa in 1960 to make his speech about 'the wind of change' blowing through that continent.

III

Although some concern had been expressed about the colour bar when the Union of South Africa was created in 1910, it was only later that there was any widespread condemnation of the political settlement and its consequences for race relations. Indeed the issue only took stage centre after 1948 when the electoral victory of the Nationalist and Afrikaner Parties meant that racial legislation would come to the fore. Ten years on the accession to power of Dr Verwoerd made it apparent that the policy of apartheid would be pursued even more persistently. The British government had to decide how to react to these developments not least given the unprecedented pace of political adjustment occurring in Africa as a whole (and Asia too) and the intense hostility to the Union's racial policy that existed world-wide. And, when he became Prime Minister in January 1957, Macmillan determined that, if confirmed in office by a general election, he would go to Africa at the earliest opportunity to express the United Kingdom's position in an uncompromising form. Consequently, after his success at the polls in October 1959, a tour was planned in detail with the visit to South Africa and the address to the Union Parliament as the real purpose and climax of the journey.[39]

It is the particular considerations which determined the adoption of this course that are now relevant (though so far as I know they were nowhere presented, or indeed ever brought together, in the bald summary form used here).

Foremost was concern about the future course of the cold war. It was assumed that, given the power of modern weapons, 'neither side dare face global war'. This meant that the continuing struggle with the Communist Powers was 'likely to be largely political and economic' and would be waged in 'the newer and uncommitted countries' not least those of Africa in which the Soviet *bloc* was 'taking an increasingly direct and positive interest':

> The strategic objective of the Soviet Union is to remove Western influence from Africa and ultimately to bring the peoples of the continent within the Communist system. In February 1958, Mr. Khrushchev told the Soviet Communist Party Congress that support of the struggle for African liberation was a principal aim of Soviet policy.

Consequently 'Whether we like it or not, opinion in these countries is something that we simply must take into account, else we shall surely lose this battle in the long run', that is, 'the battle against Communism for men's minds in black Africa'.[40]

Further it was believed the Soviets had decided that penetration on orthodox lines through Communist Parties would probably not be successful so they intended

> to ingratiate themselves with African 'nationalist' movements, in particular by supporting demands for the ending of colonial rule. Their exploitation of 'anti-colonialism' and racialism serves both to weaken the Western hold on Africa and to provide a respectable approach to the peoples of Africa behind which the ultimate objectives of extension of the Communist system and world domination can be concealed.

To this end the Russians were 'now making use of all the conventional techniques of diplomacy, trade, economic assistance and cultural relations in order to become accepted by Africans as a powerful, respectable and sympathetic friend'. And in the attack on colonialism, Soviet propaganda and subversion will concentrate on racial conflict and 'seek to identify all United Kingdom policy with that of the Union of South Africa'. Association with the Union was thus 'an anomaly and a source of weakness' and becoming 'a heavy liability to the West'.[41] It was likely therefore that Britain would quite soon be unable any more 'to go along' with the South African government's racial policies.[42] So apartheid had to be repudiated as part of the broad defence of the free world and of the attempt to win the new non-aligned nations for the West. It was indeed one of the great issues facing the second half of the twentieth century.[43] After the speech had been delivered the South African government itself was in no doubt that it basically reflected 'an opportunistic decision motivated by cold war considerations': 'It therefore amounts to this, that because of Britain's foreign policy and her prominent position in the NATO Powers, she is prepared to see South Africa – and also the Federation and Kenya – subjected to eventual Black control'.[44]

In addition to this general consideration relating to the strategy of the cold war, there were also particular naval issues arising. For while it might be necessary, for all sorts of good political reasons, that Britain should distance itself from the Union, specific defence requirements had always to be borne in mind:

> From the defence viewpoint, Africa as a whole is of course of consider-able strategic importance to the West. Hostility or even neutrality in the strategic parts of Africa would expose the southern flank of NATO and imperil our sea communications in the Atlantic and our air routes to the Far East.[45]

The problem was that, if relations with Britain deteriorated, the Union might 'with-draw the use of Simonstown, Cape Town and Durban which they have agreed to give us for our military purposes should we be engaged in a war with a Communist power'. And, while 'the value to us of these arrangements may not now be so great as it was', if 'the Suez Canal were closed again, the goodwill of South Africa could be very valuable' in keeping open the sea routes round the Cape which would be vital 'in the "broken-backed" period of a major war'.[46]

Next there were the economic aspects of the question in regard to which the sig-nificance of Africa lay 'mainly in the number of raw materials which the continent produces, many of which are essential in the sense that they could not easily be replaced from elsewhere'. For example 'Africa produces 50 per cent. or more of the world's supplies of gold, diamonds, sisal, lithium, cocoa and palm oil' as well as sizeable quantities of other important commodities such as manganese, chrome, asbestos, copper, iron ore, and much else. And, assuming the world economy is not violently disturbed, future 'opportunities for economic development in Africa should be very considerable'. All this 'may mark the beginning of a wholly new era in the life of large parts of Africa, in which profound political and economic changes will be effected by this new source of wealth and power'.[47] Naturally there were limitations to the rate of economic growth which might be anticipated but Britain ought to sustain its vital economic interest in Africa and maintain and develop its trade and investment there.[48] On these grounds alone bad relations with the emerging African states could have untoward consequences so that it would be advantageous to improve the connection by a gesture critical of apartheid. Of course any such step would be badly received in the Union but its government could be reminded of the strong economic bonds with Britain that it would be wise not to diminish: 'We should emphasise that the Union was our third best customer and that we were easily their best customer. We should also press the capacity of the U.K. for investment overseas and its good history in this regard.'[49] These considerations were indeed stressed by Macmillan in his speech.[50]

Another issue was the importance of keeping the Empire and Commonwealth together at a time when its character was undergoing radical change and when relations were in any case likely to be strained, even suffer considerable damage, as a result of the perceived need to tighten immigration controls, an issue reaching a critical point in the late 1950s. Macmillan once held firmly colonialist views: in 1942, as Parliamentary Under-Secretary of State for the Colonies, he invoked 'a spirit of stern defiance to all those who would wish either to give away our Empire for us or to take it away from us'.[51] But latterly he had become keenly aware of the tide of national consciousness in Africa (and elsewhere) and wanted, if he could, to moderate the dangers this might cause; and his becoming Prime Minister signalled a change in the pace of colonial policy arising from recognition of the need to transfer power to Britain's remaining dependencies as quickly as possible simply because there was no practical alternative.[52] So naturally South Africa was bound to appear as 'the ugly duckling of the Commonwealth', her racial policies being 'badly out of tune' with the ideas and practice of the association as a whole and 'a source of weakness' to it.[53] Such a situation faced Britain with 'numerous and growing embarrassments' which would be bound to get worse so long as it failed to be openly critical of the Union's racial policies.[54] This it had been difficult for Britain to do hitherto as (apart from anything else) it would lead to problems in connection with the High Commission Territories for the Union could, if it wished, 'make life very unpleasant' for them.[55] On the other hand if Britain did nothing to condemn apartheid openly there would be bitter resentment on the part of the African and Asian members of the Commonwealth. Looming over all this was the question whether, in the end, South Africa would leave the Commonwealth if it were criticized or be forced out if it were not. Either way the association might break up and this was something to be avoided at all costs.[56] So the government saw its task as one of buying time in the face of the probably irresistible force represented by the newly independent countries of the Commonwealth. It was necessary to dissociate Britain from South African racial policy without at the same time condoning any attitude adopted by black leaders or conceding their every demand. The Colonial Office welcomed the firmness of tone adopted in the Cape Town speech. After seeing the draft one official wrote that it was a relief to know the Prime Minister proposed:

> to admit publicly that the South Africans are some embarrassment to us. I have been asked to say … that if the Prime Minister had not felt able to take this sort of line when he was in South Africa, we think the repercussions in many colonial territories might have been serious.[57]

The Commonwealth Relations Office also commented in favourable terms that the proposed speech brought 'into the open the fact that we and the Union are at variance' on the question of race; indeed that it stated in 'pretty explicit terms that we consider <u>apartheid</u> wrong'. It should therefore have a good reception from all those, in Britain and elsewhere, who were opposed to racial discrimination.[58] And after the tour was over Sir John Maud thought the address had 'done much to re-establish the faith of the African and coloured population of the Union in Britain and the Commonwealth'.[59] The departure of South Africa from the Common-wealth could not be prevented though at least the association did not disintegrate over the racial issue. The worst possible case that Macmillan had hoped to head off by his Cape Town speech had not occurred and the Commonwealth had been saved even though a major rift had appeared and a sacrifice had been necessary.[60]

Meeting political criticism at home and abroad was another aspect of the decision to make the Cape Town speech. It was recognized that 'the increasing moral detestation of apartheid' in 'the world at large' had 'reached the proportion of a serious political force'. And, to the extent that it appeared to condone racial discrimination in South Africa, Britain was caused 'very grave embarrassment' in its international relations:

> Our attitude is now sharply in question and we are faced with an acute dilemma. Continued support of South Africa is going to cost us more and more; the sincerity of our professions and purposes in all other directions is going to be suspect. The damage to our prestige and influence is great....[61]

There was, first of all, the need to appease opinion in the USA with which there had been serious differences over the pace at which power should be transferred in colonial territories. These difficulties had emerged during the war over the pro-posal for a joint declaration on decolonization and the discussion about how to apply the principles of the Atlantic Charter.[62] And, even though by the mid-1950s independence had been granted to a number of places, the Suez War simply reinforced traditional American views about British imperialism.[63] In its aftermath it seemed all the more necessary to mitigate US criticism which was reflected in the policy of voting at the UN for resolutions opposing apartheid and by the expression in official discussions of increasing 'disquiet over our attitude on the South African items and the consequent damage they apprehend to relations between the African States and the West.'[64] As part of the process of attempted conciliation officials used regularly to visit Washington for discussions about cur-rent problems in Africa.[65] Similarly an important official survey of the likely course of events there was quickly sent for comment to the USA (and Canada); and a meeting was held to sound American opinion before the Prime Minister started on his tour.[66] In this context the positive response of the President to the 'masterful address in Cape Town' was particularly gratifying.[67]

It was necessary, too, to meet critical opinion expressed at the UN for 'the position and influence of the United Kingdom in the world depend to a large extent on what other countries think of us' and their 'reactions are liable to be brought into particularly sharp focus at the United Nations'.[68] From the outset British representatives at the UN had (like their predecessors in earlier such contexts) fought a rearguard action against proposals for the rapid and more or less indiscriminate application of the principle of the 'self-determination of peoples'.[69] This had been recognized in the UN Charter and was regarded by some observers as a rule of international law. Certainly it was continually being urged in the Assembly (and elsewhere) by the anti-colonial forces which were led, in a sort of unholy alliance, by the USA and the Soviet Union. The British government was diffident to say the least, its position being expressed in one place in these characteristic terms:

> in recent years the anti-colonials have been trying to use the 'right' of self-determination as a means to justify interference in non-self-governing territories. Our attitude in the U.K. is that self-determination is not a human right at all and is not exercisable by the individual e.g. like the right of freedom of religious conscience. It is a political principle whose application depends on the facts of each case and which has to have regard to the economic, political and social development of the people concerned.

It depended also on the needs of security and the requirements of world peace.[70] But it was all to no avail: the tide had set strongly against the British view and the UK, as the main colonial power, invariably bore the brunt of the hostile feeling expressed at the General Assembly and its committees. An additional consideration in this regard was the rapidly growing number of African delegations at the UN which materially affected the balance of power there. These African states 'were naturally somewhat anti-colonial or neutralist and their vote on East/West matters could be of great importance'. Clearly it was necessary to do everything possible 'to strengthen the hands of the moderates among them' and this meant dealing with the South African question which was particularly embarrassing as it was continually being raised.[71] The British view was that the UN Charter clearly forbade intervention in the domestic affairs of member states so that discussion of South Africa's racial policy was *ultra vires* and Britain had, as a matter of principle, always opposed attempts to raise the matter. The trouble was that this position, undoubtedly formally correct, was taken to involve a defence of apartheid as such with the result that Britain was inevitably made to appear as the defender of 'racial discrimination and white supremacy'. As the situation was becoming increasingly uncomfortable Britain's attitude needed to be reconsidered not least in the context

> of the struggle against Communism which will increasingly be fought on political and ideological grounds where our record on <u>apartheid</u> is already a heavy liability. The case for reviewing our policy towards South Africa, and in particular over the South African items in the United Nations, is therefore stronger than it has ever been.[72]

'The longer', wrote Lord Home, that 'we stick to our present policy, the worse the situation in the U.N. is likely to become and the greater the odium we shall incur there and elsewhere'.[73] So far, then, as that body was concerned the recommendation was that we should retreat from the exposed position there in which we were placed by our attitude hitherto and be more openly critical of apartheid itself.[74]

Then there was the state of opinion in Britain to consider.[75] Some months before the general election of October 1959, one Cabinet colleague (soon to become Colonial Secretary) wrote to the Prime Minister about this:

> 'Black Africa' remains perhaps our most difficult problem as far as our relationships with the vital middle voters is [sic] concerned. It is the only one in which our policies are under severe criticism and for example the only one on which we are regularly defeated at the universities. Indeed the universities feel more strongly on this issue than on any other single matter...I see in a recent issue of the Spectator that they say that this issue is the only one on which the Socialists can reasonably still hope to turn the tide for them and although I think this is rather special pleading unquestionably we are in a difficult position.

The whole subject was 'potentially so explosive' that something had to be done.[76] Indeed the Parliament of 1955–9 ended with some 'bitter colonial debates'; and during the election campaign Labour made the most of these issues though, in the outcome, it seems that the government's difficulties in Africa had 'little impact upon the electorate'.[77] All the same Macmillan himself was acutely conscious of deficiencies in the Conservative record in this respect. At the beginning of November 1959 he wrote a minute to the Cabinet Secretary in which he commented *inter alia* that Africa

> seems to be the biggest problem looming up for us here at home. We just succeeded at the General Election in 'getting by' on this. But young people of all Parties are uneasy and uncertain of our moral basis. Something must be done to lift Africa on to a more national plane as a problem to the solution of which we must all contribute, not out of spite – like the Observer and the New Statesman – and not out of complacency – but by some really imaginative effort.[78]

And Macmillan hoped that by a personal visit to South Africa 'he might help to focus public opinion at home on this problem' and perhaps 'lift it to a plane above that of narrow party politics'.[79] Over the years the climate of opinion in Britain had indeed been changing quite radically about the question of granting independence to colonial territories; and the record since 1947 showed how much had been achieved in this regard though there remained the difficult question of the colonies in which there was significant white settlement.[80] In preparing his speech the Prime Minister was fully aware of the significance of this public view. Certainly the South African government itself believed that the speech was in part a response to criticism of the Macmillan administration in the British press and Parliament.[81]

Clearly, then, there were considerations of a strategic, diplomatic, and political kind, not to mention the morality of the matter, which strongly invited a condemnation of the Union's racial policies. At the same time there were substantial British interests relating to defence, trade, and the commonwealth which had also to be protected. Something of the mix of considerations borne in mind is suggested by a memorandum written in 1963 by Edward Heath, then Lord Privy Seal, about a UN resolution on apartheid that proposed total sanctions on South Africa:

> There can clearly be no question of our agreeing to the imposition of economic sanctions. It would seriously damage our economic interests and the position of the High Commission Territories. We must also take account of our defence arrangements, the Simonstown Agreement and their communications: we may need this route to the Gulf and the Far East.

If necessary therefore Britain should veto the resolution. The Cabinet agreed.[82] It is all rather like a nineteenth-century government deciding how to sustain British interests in the East against the threat of Russian interference. *Plus ça change...?*

IV

Federative policy is thus a kind of resultant emerging from the interaction of the diverse considerabilities that have been described. Of course the review may not have got the pattern of thinking right or be correct about its elements and their mix. And fairly obviously such general guidelines, as a collective, hardly constitute a theory in the traditional sense; equally they are not much like a conventional ideology, being too limited in scope and too little coherent to be so designated. Perhaps this array of aims and arguments is simply best referred to as an official doctrine: a sort of summary of the themes involved in the making of federative policy, not separated from practice but part of it. After all there are different kinds of political thinking each in its own way capable of considerable sophistication; but to expect them all to aspire to the highest level of reflective thought is to misconstrue their varied natures and purposes.

In any case the relation between practice and certain forms of theory is easily misconceived. Just because someone subscribes to a given philosophy, ethic, or ideology does not mean that it is what causes him to act. If, say, a philosopher concerns himself with current issues (and he often does) his views about them do not depend on or derive from his metaphysical or other such ideas. For one thing the speculative themes may be cast in such broad or abstract terms that they do not imply anything definite in the way of action. As it used to be put (in the positivist heyday of the fifties) the concepts involved are so general that they can mean anything or nothing; and unless they are defined to entail something specific, nothing in particular follows from them. For instance exactly how do T. H. Green's ethical theory or his principles of political obligation entail his ardent opposition to Disraeli's Eastern policy and no other opinion about this aspect of the federative business of his day? Equally just because a politician, diplomat, or soldier acts in a certain way does not mean that a general theory lies somewhere at the back of what he does. Indeed theoretical or ideological principles are not a prior cause at all. They do not so much move people to act as constitute a means to rationalize, justify, or embellish what is determined on other grounds. Particular political prejudices (the term is not used pejoratively) are, so to say, biographically established and emerge independently of any general principles (or broad abstract themes) which lie, more or less compatibly, at their side. Green was a Liberal of the radical school first and his philosophical paraphernalia are logical and chronological subsequents either irrelevant to the foundation of the practical views or subordinate to them. I recall listening (some 40 or so years ago) to a lecture by A. J. P. Taylor on John Bright's attitude to the Crimean War: first, he said, Bright decided he was against it; then he worked out the arguments to justify his opposition. Quite so. Leslie Stephen hit the nail on the head when he confided that what people call their 'principles' are really their pretexts for acting in the obviously convenient way.[83]

It would seem to follow that, in studying the relation between political ideas and action, more analysis of theory, ideology, or concepts, however sophisticated, is likely to be redundant and that, instead, more attention should be paid to the other side of the equation, to ask what considerations actually determine the practice of federative politics. That is, we could do with more history of divers kinds and a lot less theorizing. And, as one of the most important aspects of this enterprise concerns the way in which governments determine policy, this chapter has attempted to give an example of this process and to review the formative factors involved.

There are other ways, too, in which the practical side of the equation can be emphasized. For instance it would be interesting to take some of the writers usually studied in the history of political thought to see exactly how their general ideas are related to the range of their specific political views (or if they are related at all). I imagine that, in this respect, it would be found that the work of even the most profound or abstruse philosopher is touched with the bar sinister of preconceived opinion. Similar (and perhaps more useful still) would be an examination of outstanding political or official figures with the same sort of question in mind. The ideas of, say, a Palmerston or Salisbury are as much worthy of study as those of a Green or Hobhouse: and, having attempted both sorts of exercise, I can say that (in academic terms) each can be as testing as the other.

It is part of the strength of those who have exercised the federative power that they have invariably understood a good deal of all this. Of course differences of opinion about the conduct of policy can easily arise as when varying judgements are made about either the priority to be attached to the diverse objectives in view or the means appropriate to their achievement. It may not be too difficult (in the light of later events) to observe errors which have been made in the way these criteria have been interpreted and applied: there is no mistake-proof procedure to be followed. But at least the statesmen and their agents rarely give themselves false intellectual airs and have wisely and sceptically concentrated on the sorts of consideration which are relevant to their office in the world (and which have been reviewed here). Not exquisite reason perhaps; but reason good enough.

About the author

W. H. Greenleaf, 57 Westport Avenue, Mayals, Swansea SA3 5EQ, Wales

Notes

A substantial part of the present text has been culled from material originally used for a much longer paper on 'The official British view of nationalism' presented to a conference on 'European Nationalisms Revisited' held at Tulane University, New Orleans, in March 1994. So far as I am aware these proceedings remain unpublished.

1 224 Parl. Deb. 3s., 31 May 1875, col. 1099.

2 Viscount Grey of Fallodon, *Twenty-Five Years 1892–1916*. London: Hodder & Stoughton, 1925, i.6, 16, 25.

3 Sir J. Headlam-Morley, 'The British Government and Arbitration' (1928), reprinted in *Studies in Diplomatic History*. London: Methuen, 1930, pp. 10, 13–15.

4 Castlereagh to Liverpool (28 September [1815]) in C. R. Middleton, *The Administration of British Foreign Policy 1782–1846*. Durham NC: Duke University Press, 1977, p. 32; M. Thatcher, *The Downing Street Years*. London: HarperCollins, 1995, p. 552.

5 J. S. Watson, *The Reign of George III 1760–1815* Oxford: Clarendon, 1960, p. 325. That astute observer of the British character Emile Boutmy commented on the tendency to subordinate metaphysics and ideology to practical purposes such as justification: see *The English People: a Study of their Political Psychology*. London: T. Fisher Unwin, 1904, pp. 17–20, 42, 142, 298.

6 Lord Strang, *Home and Abroad*. London: Deutsch, 1956, pp. 16 n.1, 280.

7 M. Oakeshott, *Political Education*. Cambridge: Bowes & Bowes, 1951, p. 10.

8 R. Robinson and J. Gallagher (with A. Denny), *Africa and the Victorians: the Official Mind of Imperialism*. London: Macmillan, 1983, p. 13.

9 For a critical analysis of the conventional idea about India's value to Britain, see e.g. John Bright's speech (16 April 1879), in J. E. T. Rogers (ed.), *Public Addresses of the Rt. Hon. John Bright*. London: Macmillan, 1879, pp. 498–503; and for a similar, modern view, C. Barnett, *The Collapse of British Power*. Gloucester: Sutton, 1987, pp. 76–80, 133–66.

10 H. L. Hoskins, *British Routes to India*. London: Longmans, 1928, p. 79.

11 Prince Albert to Baron Stockmar (18 April 1854) in Sir T. Martin, *The Life of His Royal Highness the Prince Consort*. London: Smith, Elder, 1875–80, iii.55–6.

12 K. M. Wilson, *The Policy of the Entente: Essays on the Determinants of British Foreign Policy 1904–1914*. Cambridge: Cambridge University Press, 1985, p. 71.

13 An official review of the world strategic situation (17 November 1947) cited in S. Croft, *The End of Superpower: British Foreign Office Conceptions of a Changing World, 1945–51*. Aldershot: Dartmouth, 1994, p. 187.

14 See Table 2 in my *The Rise of Collectivism*. London: Methuen, 1983, p. 34. It ought to be added that, over the same period, the proportion of GNP spent on social, economic, and environmental services rose from 3.2 per cent to 41.8 per cent, ibid.

15 A copy is to be found in CO 537/971, 'Civil disturbances in the colonies...' (1946–7). All references in this form are to Crown Copyright material at the Public Record Office.

16 See, for example, the heads of consideration established in 1947 in CO 537/2531, 'Defence schemes – revision...'; also, for an instance of the considerable planning detail required, consult CAB 11/75–6 for the Cairo Defence Schemes elaborated before the Great War.

17 CAB 134/1355, Africa (Official) Committee, 'Africa: the Next Ten Years' (30 October 1959), p. 2 §§7–8. For the key case of India and the role of private initiative in economic development there, cf. W. Woodruff, *Impact of Western Man: a Study of Europe's Role in the World Economy 1750–1980*. London: University Press of America, 1982, pp. 33–4.

18 CAB 1/1, L[ouis] M[allet], memorandum on 'Commercial Treaty with Austria' [1866], p. 3.

19 Palmerston to Lord Auckland (22 January 1841), in Sir C. Webster, *The Foreign Policy of Palmerston 1830–1841: Britain, the Liberal Movement and the Eastern Question*. London: Bell, 1951, ii.750–1; Granville to Russell (12 January 1852), in H. Temperley and L. A. Penson (eds), *Foundations of British Foreign Policy from Pitt (1792) to Salisbury (1902)....* Cambridge: Cambridge University Press, 1938, p. 184.

20 Memorandum by the Board of Trade and the Foreign Office with respect to the Future Organisation of Commercial Intelligence, 1917–18 (vol. xxix), Cd. 8715, Appendix, Report of the Foreign Office Committee, p. 19 §16.

21 FO 366/3178, Foreign Service Review, (10 November 1960), 'The Rôle of the Foreign Service', p. [2] §7.

22 Cited in Temperley and Penson, *Foundations of British Foreign Policy*, p. 497.

23 See the discussion in C. Howard, *Splendid Isolation: a study of ideas concerning Britain's international position and foreign policy during the later years of the third Marquis of Salisbury*. London, Macmillan, 1967, ch. 9.

24 See Wilson, *The Policy of the Entente*, ch. 8: the sentence cited is at p. 147 (italics in original).

25 For the differences over the Egyptian treaty, see the papers in CAB 16/107; and for the divergence on nationalism, those in CO 936/217. The dissident view of the service chiefs about co-operation with Russia is discussed in Croft, *The End of Superpower*, ch. 2 esp. p. 35.

26 Webster, *The Foreign Policy of Palmerston*, i.50–3.

27 Wilson, *The Policy of the Entente*, ch. 1 esp. pp. 10–16.

28 75 Parl. Deb. 4s., 28 July 1899, col. 662 (during a debate on Transvaal affairs).

29 Cf. M. Oakeshott, *The Politics of Faith and the Politics of Scepticism*. New Haven CT: Yale University Press, 1996, p. 82.

30 FO 881/842, 'Memorandum of Correspondence respecting the Suez Canal projected by M. de Lesseps' (28 December 1859), p. 13.

31 Cited in E. Halévy, *A History of the English People in the Nineteenth Century*. London: Benn, 1961, ii.245 n.2.

32 For the embarrassment, see the dispatches in FO 78/120 and 133.

33 CAB 16/107, Sir M. Lampson to Sir J. Simon (7 July 1934), p. [1] §§5, 6.

34 K. Rose, *Curzon: a Most Superior Person*. London: Macmillan, 1985, p. 309. For other examples of Salisbury's attitude, *ibid.*, pp. 310–11.

35 Cf. Churchill's proposal to destroy one German town each night; also his remark that it was absurd to consider morality when contemplating the use of poison gas; what was needed was 'a cold-blooded calculation' whether it would be advantageous or not: see R. Lamb, *Churchill as War Leader – Right or Wrong?* London: Bloomsbury, 1993, pp. 308–9 citing PREM 3/89 and DEF 2/1252.

36 Cf. Sir H. Maxwell, *The Life and Letters of George William Frederick Fourth Earl of Clarendon*. London: E. Arnold, 1913, i.268.

37 Lord J. Russell to the Queen (29 December 1851), in A. C. Benson and Visc. Esher (eds), *The Letters of Queen Victoria…Between the Years 1837 and 1861*. London: Murray, 1911, ii.353.

38 Robinson and Gallagher, *Africa and the Victorians*, p. 25.

39 For the more general context of decolonization, see P. E. Hemming, 'Macmillan and the End of the British Empire in Africa', in R. Aldous and S. Lee (eds), *Harold Macmillan and Britain's World Role*. Basingstoke: Macmillan, 1996, ch. 5.

40 CAB 134/1355, Africa (Official) Committee, 'Africa: the Next Ten Years' (May 1959), p. 5 §18; CAB 21/3156, CRO, 'Policy Towards South Africa: the United Nations Items. Detailed brief for Prime Minister's Party' (18 December 1959), §§14–16.

41 CAB 134/1355, Africa (Official) Committee, 'Africa: the Next Ten Years', pp. 5–6 §§19–21; CAB 21/3156, CRO, 'Policy Towards South Africa: the United Nations Items. Detailed brief for Prime Minister's Party', §2. In addition, see e.g. FO 371/118676–7, 'Africa: Soviet influence and penetration' (1956) and DO 119/1227, 'Soviet Penetration in Africa 1960–61'.

42 CAB 134/1353, CRO note on 'The Next Ten Years in Africa', (9 January 1959), §4(b).

43 CAB 134/1353, 6th meeting of the Africa (Official) Committee (2 March 1959), p. 1 §1(a); and the Chairman's summary, ibid., p. 3. Macmillan later recapitulated the issues in the same terms: see his *Pointing the Way 1959–1961*. London: Macmillan, 1972, pp. 157, 476–7 (citing the South Africa speech).

44 CAB 129/101, 'The Prime Minister's South African Tour', No. 2 Despatch from the United Kingdom High Commissioner in the Union of South Africa (18 February 1960), p. 163 §17 citing *Die Burger*, the organ of the Cape Nationalists; DO 35/10570, statement by the Union Minister of External Affairs reported in the *Cape Times* (9 February 1960). Cf. DO 35/10570, High Commission to CRO (no. 89, 16 February 1960), 'Reactions to Prime Minister's Visit', §3(A).

45 CAB 134/1353, CRO note on 'The Next Ten Years in Africa', §1 *ad fin*.

46 CAB 21/3156, CRO, 'Policy Towards South Africa: the United Nations Items. Detailed brief for Prime Minister's Party', §11(c); Lord Home, 'Policy Towards South Africa: the United Nations Items' (no.111/59, 17 December 1959). §4(5).

47 CAB 134/1355, Africa (Official) Committee, 'Africa: the Next Ten Years', p. 9 §33.

48 Ibid., pp. 10–12 §§35–41; p. 19 §68; p. 20 §71(b); and pp. 26–30 §§ 94–101, 102(c). Also PREM 11/2587, D. Heathcoat Amory (Chancellor of the Exchequer) to Prime Minister (30 July 1959).

49 CAB 21/3157, 'Note for the Record' of a meeting between the Prime Minister, the Commonwealth Secretary (Lord Home), and the High Commissioner (Sir J. Maud) (14 December 1959), p. 3.

50 Macmillan, *Pointing the Way*, p. 474.

51 CO 968/67/1, 'Post War Reconstruction: Policy with regard to the Colonial Empire (1942)', Macmillan minute (13 August 1942).

52 Macmillan, *Pointing the Way*, pp. 118–19; DO 35/7896, Notes of Prime Minister's discussions with Dr Verwoerd (2–4 February 1960), p. 7. For an earlier acknowledgement by Macmillan of the power of the 'tidal wave' of colonial nationalism, see the 1957 speech cited in D. Horowitz, 'Attitudes of British Conservatives towards decolonisation in Africa', *African Affairs*, lxix (1970), p. 16.

53 CAB 21/3156, CRO, 'Policy Towards South Africa: the United Nations Items. Detailed brief for Prime Minister's Party', §§[1]–2.

54 CO 936/217, Sir T. Lloyd to Sir W. Strang (9 September 1952), §3.

55 For this concern, see e.g. CAB 21/3156, CRO, 'Policy Towards South Africa: the United Nations Items. Detailed brief for Prime Minister's Party', §11(a)(iii); and Lord Home, 'Policy Towards South Africa: the United Nations Items' (no. 111/59, 17 December 1959), §§[1], 4(5).

56 CAB 21/3156, CRO, 'Policy Towards South Africa: the United Nations Items. Detailed brief for Prime Minister's Party', §3. Cf. Macmillan, *Pointing the Way*, p. 481.

57 CAB 21/3157, J. H. Robertson to T. J. Bligh (1 January 1960).

58 CAB 21/3157, D. W. S. Hunt to T. J. Bligh (30 December 1959) (underlining in original).

59 CAB 129/101, 'The Prime Minister's African Tour', No. 2 Despatch from the United Kingdom High Commissioner, p. 165 §22(iii).

60 For Macmillan's reaction, see his letter to Sir J. Maud (21 March 1961), in *Pointing the Way*, p. 302.

61 CAB 21/3156, CRO, 'Policy Towards South Africa: the United Nations Items. Detailed brief for Prime Minister's Party', §12; Lord Home, 'Policy Towards South Africa: the United Nations Items', §§1–2, 4(1).

62 See J. E. Williams, 'The Joint Declaration on the colonies: an issue in Anglo-American relations, 1942–1944', *British Journal of International Studies*, ii (1976), pp. 267–92.

63 For these views, see e.g. W. R. Louis, 'American Anti-Colonialism and the Dissolution of the British Empire', in W. R. Louis and H. Bull (eds), *The Special Relationship: Anglo-American Relations since 1945*. Oxford: Clarendon, 1986), ch. 16; also the useful brief summary in CO 885/123, J. Thompson, 'America's Attitude to Nationalist Developments in British Colonial Territories', part of a Colonial Office symposium on *Nationalism and the Commonwealth* (1954), pp. 31–7. There are particularly trenchant analyses of the difficulties arising in CO 537/4589, Sir O. Franks to Foreign Office (no. 5896, 21 December 1949) and CO 537/5698, Franks to Bevin (no. 32, 14 January 1950).

64 CAB 21/3156, CRO, 'Policy Towards South Africa: the United Nations Items. Detailed brief for the Prime Minister's Party', §5.

65 Sir D. Hunt, *On the Spot: an Ambassador Remembers*. London: Peter Davies, 1975, p. 23.

66 The relevant papers are in CAB 134/1355.

67 Eisenhower to Macmillan (15 February 1960), in Macmillan, *Pointing the Way*, pp. 163–4.

68 CAB 134/1355, Africa (Official) Committee, 'Africa: the Next Ten Years', p. 30 §103.

69 The papers in DO 35/10604–5 on 'Human rights: self-determination of peoples', covering the period 1954–8, are representative.

70 DO 35/10605, 'Human rights: self-determination of peoples (1957–8)', minute (17 July 1958), §2; DO 35/10604, memorandum on 'Self-Determination: Note on Legal Aspects...' (3 October 1955).

71 CAB 134/1355, report of a meeting with the Americans and Canadians to discuss the report on 'Africa: the Next Ten Years' (November 1959), pp. 9–10 §§36, 39.

72 CAB 21/3156, CRO, 'Policy Towards South Africa: the United Nations Items. Detailed brief for Prime Minister's Party', §§4, 5 (underlining in original).

73 CAB 21/3156, Lord Home, 'Policy Towards South Africa: the United Nations Items', §4(6).

74 CAB 21/3156, CRO, 'Policy Towards South Africa: the United Nations Items. Detailed brief for Prime Minister's Party', §§12, 16.

75 Cf. PREM 11/2588, Home to Macmillan (serial no. 38/59, 29 May 1959), p. 1.

76 PREM 11/2583, I. Macleod to H. Macmillan (25 May 1959). Certainly notice was taken of expressions of opinion in the press: see e.g. CAB 21/3157, T. J. Bligh to J. Hunt (29 December 1959), on a letter

in *The Observer* newspaper from four prominent South Africans asking the Prime Minister to be critical of apartheid in his speech.

77 D. E. Butler and R. Rose, *The British General Election of 1959*. London: Macmillan, 1960, pp. 41, 198.

78 CAB 21/3155, Macmillan to Brook (1 November 1959), §3.

79 CAB 129/101, 'The Prime Minister's African Tour' (12 April 1960), p. 3 §[1]. Cf. Macmillan, *Pointing the Way*, p. 119 (which is clearly based on the Cabinet document cited).

80 CAB 21/3157, 'Suggested speaking notes for the Prime Minister in discussion with Dr. Nkrumah on Africa' (5 January 1960), §§1–3. Cf. DO 35/7896, Notes of Prime Minister's discussions with Dr Verwoerd (2–4 February 1960), p. 7.

81 CAB 129/101, 'The Prime Minister's African Tour', p. 152; DO 35/10570, Statement by Mr. E. Louw reported in the *Cape Times* (9 February 1960).

82 CAB 129/113, memorandum on 'South Africa and the U.N.' (29 March 1963), §2; CAB 128/37, meeting of 4 April 1963 §6. Cf. CAB 129/114, instructions to the new British ambassador, Home to Stephenson (no. 55, 12 June 1963), summarizing the continuing British interests in South Africa.

83 In a letter to C. F. Adams (2 February 1899) in F. W. Maitland, *The Life and Letters of Leslie Stephen*. London: Duckworth, 1906, p. 451. Cf. The view of one professional diplomat, Sir David Kelly, 'I have many times seen purely personal likes or dislikes, personal health, vanity, prejudice, or just lack of time for proper consideration, decide important issues. The men who take the decisions usually rationalize them later': see *The Ruling Few or the Human Background to Diplomacy*. London: Hollis & Carter, 1952, pp. 1–2.

8

Disposing of Dicey: from Legal Autonomy to Constitutional Discourse?

Carol Harlow

1. Authorized Version: True or False?

The authorized version of the relationship of law and politics in England presents us with two autonomous worlds where, to cite Barker, law is 'neutrally detached from the contests of political ideas and argument', 'legal ideas [are] invisible in the elaboration of political argument', and 'the general assumptions of law have been little considered in debates about the political character and goals of the nation'.[1]

Writing of the cusp of the nineteenth century, Barker is here discussing the failure of the great legal historian, F.W. Maitland, to impress his views on the public consciousness. Although passing mention is made of Maitland's contemporary and rival, A.V. Dicey, his influence is also downplayed as largely confined to the purely legal sphere of 'administrative law and of delegated legislation'.[2]

Barker's assessment is certainly unfair to Dicey, whose views undeniably inserted themselves into the national consciousness. Laski – a political scientist whose work is infused with legal vocabulary and concepts[3] – wrote on Dicey's death that: 'Few Oxford teachers since T.H. Green have exercised an influence so wide as he'.[4] Dicey's ideas supply the 'background theory' of the British constitution,[5] and still influence political debate today. His views have shaped debates about the most fundamental political goals of the nation, including all the issues (European Union, devolution of government to Scotland and Wales and human rights), discussed in later sections of this chapter. And Dicey was no mere lawyer. It has been said that, 'despite his strong commitment to academic law, politics remained his secular vocation'.[6] He was the author of a highly original treatise whose central thesis is the relationship of law with politics and public opinion.[7] Perhaps this is the real reason why Dicey, like Bagehot, succeeded where Maitland failed.

Yet Maitland's gently evolutionary picture of the constitution was in some ways more faithful than that of Dicey. The society portrayed in Maitland's constitutional writings[8] is one in which law and politics have always been deeply intertwined.[9] For centuries, administrative and judicial systems met in the single person of the justice of the peace. Knowledge of the law and system of government was considered part of every gentleman's education. It was diffused in the shape of Blackstone's *Commentaries*, through which the precepts of the common law were carried to the New World with the settlers who claimed its rights. Judges were (and remain) generalists, who often describe themselves as representing the community and public opinion.[10] The common law originated in 'custom and practice' and was seen to embody common sense; it is not coincidental that its central metaphor of 'the reasonable man' is also the common man 'on the Clapham omnibus'. The jury system dictated (and still dictates) the way in which legal argument can be presented and the general principles of the common law – though not of statute – remain strikingly accessible.

If then, as Barker suggests,[11] legal ideas are 'invisible in the elaboration of political argument', they are nonetheless present. Law has always been a traditional path to a parliamentary career and legal language permeates parliamentary debates. Legal concepts are intrinsic to political debate and Dicey's central doctrine of parliamentary sovereignty is constantly cited by politicians and political actors who may not even recognise his name. It would be more accurate to see such ideas as rendered invisible by the fact that the two activities employ a common language based on common understandings of the unwritten, common law constitution. This aspect of our constitutional heritage was clear to Oakeshott, for whom the common law was a central cultural and political artifact.[12]

The idea of law as 'a world neutrally detached from the contests of political ideas and argument'[13] was largely a theoretical construct and, paradoxically, one which owes everything to Dicey.[14] It is Dicey's depiction of law as apolitical, scientific and technical which infuses the authorized version. This portrayal was not 'invented' by Dicey but rather by Bentham and Austin, fathers of legal positivism, a school of jurisprudence which defines law as a discrete and autonomous discipline founded on distinctive legal concepts and possessing its own distinguishing method of legal reasoning.[15] Towards the end of the nineteenth century, positivism established itself as the dominant school of legal theory, outstripping the historical school of jurisprudence which formed its main rival.[16] Dicey's contribution to its spread was to make scientific rationalism an essential component of British constitutional theory, an area of law to which it was arguably least appropriate. Thus Dicey left an enduring and, it has been argued,[17] a disabling legacy for English constitutional law. His application of the positivist or 'scientific' method to public law was to obscure the close relationship between law and politics which he himself had always recognized. This is the paradox concealed within the 'authorized version'.

The influence of positivist doctrine, which formed an essential component of the authorized version of apolitical law, lasted well into the second half of the twentieth century. To the astonishment of an American visitor in 1961, English judges were still denying their policy-making function, the task of the judge being described as 'wholly analytical – to discover the previously existing law, and to apply it logically to the case before the court'.[18] As late as 1978, Lord Hailsham presented adjudication as dependent 'upon the strict application of a clearly formulated rule of law, and not dependent on the subjective opinion of the individual judge'.[19] By then realist theories of jurisprudence, which now dominated the American scene,[20] had begun to take root here. The denial of judicial discretion was questionable and the era 'when law could be perceived and taught as a self-sufficient and self-referential set of rules, elucidated where necessary by textual scrutiny and judicial precedent',[21] nearly over. Inside the legal profession, realism is today tacitly accepted, while academics find rival theories – functionalist, sociological, post-modern – more seductive.[22] Outside the world of law, however, positivist doctrine may be more tenacious.[23]

This chapter adopts the position that legal and political worlds never have been, and never can be, discrete. The relationship is close; in Loughlin's compelling phrase: 'Public law is simply a sophisticated form of political discourse'.[24] Part 2 explores the myth of law's autonomy and considers its contribution to constitutional legitimacy. Part 3 describes the gradual emergence of a more explicit and transparent relationship, designed to legitimate law in the present context of political pluralism and a growing mood of populism. Part 4 records the skilful use of legal formalism by the contemporary judiciary to legitimate the incursion of law from Europe, masking innovations which might have been seen as a shift to judicial policy-making. Finally, Part 5 argues for a different relationship in the context of constitutional changes introduced by New Labour, and the installation of a regime in which the judiciary can find a new legitimacy and new functions.

2. Law's Autonomy

The fiction that the judiciary does not form part of the state[25] has been crucial to maintaining a tacit separation of powers in the English constitution. Indeed, the eminent legal historian, Sir William Holdsworth, once called the guarantee of judicial independence in the 1701 Act of Settlement the 'best of all securities for the stability of a state'.[26] Thus judicial independence is an essential component of legal autonomy. A new generation of lawyers would question the need for judicial autonomy in the sense of an isolated judiciary, divorced from public affairs and political debate (the 'Who are the Beatles?' syndrome) but this is not the same as querying judicial independence. The present climate indeed veers towards setting in place more, not fewer, guarantees.

The autonomy of law, however, stretches well beyond the concept of judicial independence. The close link between Bench and Bar, from which the judiciary has always been appointed, dictated or seemed to dictate the need for an autonomous legal profession. Local government, powerful professions, boards and independent agencies, universities and the judiciary, all formed part of a pattern of independent power blocks. Self-governance, a power and privilege possessed by the two professional associations (Law Society and Bar Council) in common with other professional bodies, came to be seen as an element in the doctrine of legal autonomy, though conversely, judicial independence could be used as justification for a self-governing profession. Thus the legal profession came to occupy in its own eyes, 'an invisible status in the body politic'.[27]

A formal conception of the rule of law locked these various facets of legal autonomy into a coherent whole. Echoing Barker, Craig justifies a formalist interpretation of the rule of law – by no means the only possible position – in terms of legal autonomy:

> There is a wealth of literature devoted to the discussion of the meaning of a just society, the nature of the rights which should subsist therein, and the appropriate boundaries of governmental action. Political theory has tackled questions like these from time immemorial. To bring these issues within the rubric of the rule of law would therefore have the effect of robbing this concept of any function *independent* of such political theories.[28]

Once again the version of this guiding principle familiar to British lawyers is that of Dicey. Dicey used the principle to shore up the unentrenched position of the 'ordinary' courts[29] and common law. In Dicey's 'balanced constitution', the courts ensured responsibility of state officials through personal legal liability but the concept of law's autonomy limited the rule of law courts, by debarring them from the consideration of 'policy'.[30] In a complex junction, the concept of law as neutral and autonomous legitimated the rule of law, while invocation of the rule of law legitimated law's detached, autonomous position.

In a virtual paraphrase of the formalist rule of law position, Dunleavy and O'Leary crucially link the rule of law with concepts of the liberal state. The state is described as:

> a recognizably separate institution or set of institutions [whose] sovereignty extends to all the individuals within a given territory, and applies equally, even to those in formal positions of government or rule-making. Thus sovereignty is distinct from the personnel who at any given time occupy a particular role within the state.[31]

The view of law as the primary instrument of state power thus creates a need for the impartiality that forms an important element of the liberal rule of law principle and doctrine of legal autonomy.

Dicey's exploration of the notion of sovereignty is essentially positivist in character.[32] He strives to separate the legal and political, focussing on the concept of law as a hierarchy of legal norms with statute law at its apex. Confusion is however introduced when Dicey describes 'external' limits to sovereignty in the shape of 'serious or insuperable resistance to the commands of the ruler'. In a classic fudge, he says:

> Where a Parliament truly represents the people, the divergence between the external and the internal limit to the exercise of sovereign power can hardly arise, or if it arises, must soon disappear. Speaking roughly, the permanent wishes of the representative portion of Parliament can hardly in the long run differ from wishes of the English people, or at any rate of the electors; that which the majority of the House of Commons command, the majority of the English people usually desire.[33]

Thus Dicey's doctrine of legal sovereignty is actually premised on the legitimacy of the political order and Dicey makes no better provision for the 'unthinkable' situation in which the legislator loses legitimacy through illegitimate commands than to recommend resistance:

> If a legislature decided that all blue-eyed babies should be murdered, the preservation of blue-eyed babies would be illegal; but legislators must go mad before they could pass such a law, and subjects be idiotic before they could submit to it.[34]

Politics thus underpins a model of legal sovereignty drawn from a positivist vision of law as a science and Dicey's illustration, borrowed from Stephen's *Science of Ethics*,[35] sets positivism inside the wider nineteenth-century movement to bring the study of society within the boundaries of science with its supposedly 'objective' standards. The positivist definition of sovereignty would thus be fed back into a political science receptive to it.

If, as has been suggested, the concept of an autonomous legal system and profession was largely a fiction, then the myth has served the unwritten constitution well. Legal sociologists recognize[36] the technique of 'legal closure' whereby legitimacy is provided for decisions and actions by shifting them from the political to legal terrain. The aura of strict neutrality associated with law, which provides law's distinctive contribution to dispute-resolution[37] comes into operation to neutralize disputes. The demand for legal closure provides the primary rationale for legal autonomy, legal autonomy provides the machinery for legal closure. Similarly, law provides an essential part of the legitimation of the constitutional order from which at the same time it receives legitimation.

3. Responsive Law

It is, then, hardly surprising if Griffith's *Politics of the Judiciary*[38] met with a predominantly hostile reaction from the profession. It uncovered the mechanics of legal closure. By describing the judicial function as innately political, it disclosed legal autonomy as a myth and did this in a popular and accessible book. The aloof and uncommunicative judiciary was exposed to public controversy over its political role described by a future Lord Chancellor as 'highly unedifying'.[39] Some response was necessary.

The Griffith attack could be brushed off simply as a further instance of a long-standing left wing antipathy to the judiciary and legal profession. Helped by more liberal leaders, notably Lord Chief Justice Parker and Lord Chancellor Mackay, who revoked the 'Kilmuir rules' requiring the Lord Chancellor's approval for public appearances by the judiciary,[40] judges learned to promulgate their views more openly. The terms of reference of the Benson Commission posed a more serious threat. Appointed by Mr Callaghan to review legal services, the Commission was required to consider whether 'any, and if so what, changes are desirable in the public interest in the structure, organization [and] regulations' of the legal profession.[41] Again the warning was warded off too easily; the Commission fudged vital issues of accountability[42] and, by the time it reported, the Callaghan Government which appointed it had fallen.

Perhaps in consequence the profession was ill-prepared to meet Mrs Thatcher's bid to tame it by rendering it more accountable to government, at least for its management of the legal aid fund.[43] The profession mistakenly took for granted public sympathy for their viewpoint that:

> lawyers' authority lay not in a grant of powers from the Crown or Parliament, but in civil society itself. The autonomy of law and the 'sovereignty' of the professions, therefore, counterbalanced state power, not on the sufferance of state largesse, but with the time-honoured ballast of civil authority.[44]

The Government was able to draw on public dislike of lawyers to present a case for economy in public spending. The case for government intervention and regulation gained credence from the failure of the self-regulatory system in handling complaints. Transmuted by Lord Chancellor Irvine into an attack on legal 'fat cats', the case for reform was winning popular sympathy while the profession was being successfully presented as motivated solely by self-interest. Autonomy and self-governance were under serious attack. The legislative programme announced by the Blair Government in November 1998 contained proposals for a criminal legal aid system based on franchising, a serious incursion on professional autonomy, the rights of the defence and independence of both Bar and Bench. Fight as it might, the profession was powerless to stop legislation.

Yet in the same period the judiciary was paradoxically building itself a position as a political force. Judicial review of administrative action had become increasingly penetrative and was establishing itself in the public consciousness. The Civil Justice Review of 1988 made the significant assumption that 'public law cases' would remain the prerogative of the High Court,[45] an important assumption twice confirmed tacitly.[46]

A serious debate among the judges about the legitimacy of their public law functions opened up in which leading members of the judiciary began to participate publicly.[47] Legal autonomy and implicit separation of powers were the basis on which Lord Browne-Wilkinson had sought to justify extensions of judicial review in 1992.[48] The decline of Parliament's power to call the executive to account had, he suggested, forced the judiciary to step in to fill the gap. But separation of powers, it could be argued, had never formed part of a constitution rooted in parliamentary sovereignty.[49] An alternative vindication lay in the classic conception of judges as representative of the public and public opinion. But popular support might be transient and was there really, as Sir Stephen Sedley intimated, 'considerable public support for judicial control of an otherwise unaccountable executive, or of unresponsive public authorities?' Did popular consciousness really cast administration 'in the role of dragons and the judiciary in the role of St Georges'?[50]

As rights-talk became the universal language of politics, the judiciary were exploring this new and less slippery footing for legitimacy. The gathering influence of the European Convention on Human Rights (ECHR) was evident and the judiciary began publicly to advocate incorporation.[51] In a demonstration of obedience to the will of Parliament, the House of Lords ruled against judicial, or 'backdoor', incorporation of the Convention,[52] leaving it in the position of an interpretative aid. But this could not defeat judicial ingenuity, and a rights-based case law of judicial review began to evolve fashioned with only the indirect help of the ECHR.[53] In *R v Lord Chancellor ex p. Witham*,[54] for example, a judge ruled that only express words in an Act of Parliament would be sufficient to abrogate the 'constitutional' right of access to the court. Some judges might be prepared to go further. Testing the water extra-judicially, Lord Woolf asserted that legislation which sought to undermine the rule of law might be beyond the competence of Parliament.[55] A process had started which would find its logical culmination in the Human Rights Bill introduced in 1997 by the Blair Government 'to bring rights home'.[56]

As courts increasingly came under pressure from litigants and pressure groups versed in the techniques of the international human rights movement, they began to move towards a more open model of public law litigation.[57] Traditional judicial review was available only to individuals 'directly affected' by, or possessing some 'special interest' in, a contested decision. Gradually this rule was chipped away until it was conceded that pressure groups could initiate actions where the court considered that it was in the public interest to permit this.[58] Hotly political issues – such as the contentious subsidy to the Malaysian Government for the construction of the Pergau Dam, with its undertones of arms deals and financial impropriety – which previously fell within the exclusive competence of the House of Commons – were now contested also in the Royal Courts of Justice at the suit of a pressure group.[59] Argumentation of a style associated with the political process was cautiously admitted and the rule which had barred courts from considering the parliamentary history of statutes as an aid to their construction was finally abrogated.[60] A distinctively political contribution now infused legal argument. Pressure groups demanded and began to obtain a right to intervene in lawsuits between third parties. Step by step, courts were beginning to set themselves up as an alternative political forum[61] and the utility of legal process as a bargaining card began to be recognized.

Then, in ill-fated proceedings surrounding the extradition of General Pinochet,[62] the House of Lords demonstrated its new leniency to third party interventions by agreeing to hear argument from Amnesty International in support of extradition. This brought Lord Hoffmann's neutrality into question when he was shown after the decision to be a director of Amnesty International Trading. Uniquely, and with justifiable embarrassment, the House agreed to set aside its own decision on grounds of possible bias. The logical culmination of the flirtation with legal politics was spelled out conclusively.

4. Europe, The Great Houdini

In parallel, judges were finding a prop for judicial legitimacy in a very different European order. Even before UK accession to the European Community, legal discourse had shaped and permeated a debate in which the Diceyan confusion of legal and political sovereignty was turned to good account. Formulaic legal assurances were used to mask the real political implications of accession.[63] Government advisers rushed to assure the public that the Diceyan doctrine of Parliamentary sovereignty was not in issue; nothing would change.[64] Community law would derive its force from an exercise of parliamentary sovereignty in the shape of United Kingdom legislation. In every later parliamentary debate over accession, Treaty amendment and ratification, this pattern was to be repeated. The legal concept of parliamentary sovereignty formed a central ingredient of the political debate to the point where debates on the ratification of the Maastricht Treaty have been described as 'a tournament of lawyers'.[65]

Not surprisingly the implications for the judicial process of Community membership were not central to the accession debate. Yet s. 3 of the European Communities Act 1972 instructs our courts to interpret any point of EC law in accordance with the jurisprudence of the Court of Justice and provides for reference to be made in case of doubt to the Court for a preliminary ruling. Although the section could be read as altering the domestic hierarchy of legal norms, its implications were not at first obvious. Yet, the section was to prove crucial when a direct clash of legal norms finally arose.

In a strategy designed for the protection of UK fishing quotas, the UK Government moved to restrict registration to boats with UK connections. When Spanish owners of fishing boats challenged refusal to allow registration, the question of the validity of an Act of Parliament in case of incompatibility with EC law was for the first time raised in the English courts.[66] The applicants asked for an interim injunction to protect their position during the litigation, raising an ancillary question of availability of remedies. s. 21 of the Crown Proceedings Act 1947 prohibits injunctions against the Crown in civil proceedings. The House of Lords ruled[67] that courts were barred from offering injunctive relief against the Crown but referred to the Court of Justice the question whether this restriction was compatible with EC law. The reply came back from Luxembourg that, if the only barrier between the applicants and adequate judicial protection lay in an Act of Parliament, this had to be 'disapplied'. At a bound Houdini had been unfettered!

As a brilliant example of 'legal closure', Lord Bridge's formalist speech is worth quoting:

> Some public comments on the decision of the Court of Justice, affirming the jurisdiction of the courts of member states to override national legislation if necessary to enable interim relief to be granted in protection of rights under Community law, have suggested that this was a novel and dangerous invasion by a Community institution of the sovereignty of the UK Parliament. But such comments are based on a misconception. If the supremacy within the European Community of Community law over the national law of member states was not always inherent in the EEC Treaty it was certainly well established in the jurisprudence of the Court of Justice long before the United Kingdom joined the Community. *Thus whatever limitation of its sovereignty Parliament accepted when it enacted the European Communities Act 1972 was entirely voluntary.* Under the terms of the Act of 1972 it has always been clear that it was the duty of a United Kingdom court, when delivering final judgment, to override any rule of law found to be in conflict with any directly enforceable rule of Community law. Similarly, when decisions of the European Court of Justice have exposed areas of United Kingdom statute law which failed to implement Council directives, Parliament has always loyally accepted the obligation to make amends. Thus there is nothing in any way novel in according supremacy to rules of Community law in those areas to which they apply and to insist that, in the protection of rights under Community law, national courts must not be inhibited by rules of national law from granting interim relief in appropriate cases is no more than a logical recognition of that supremacy.[68]

This passage neutralizes the decision, bringing it within the bounds of the classic constitution and rendering it apparently uncontroversial. Divesting the courts of all responsibility for an outcome presented as inevitable, the speech firmly allocates responsibility to Parliament, which should have perceived the implications of the legislation it was passing on accession.[69]

But was Lord Bridge's conclusion really so inevitable? It contains at least one non sequitur: to accord supremacy to EC law within its area of competence does not necessarily imply changes to the law of domestic remedies. Indeed, the House of Lords might have stood on an established principle of the procedural autonomy of national legal systems without troubling the Court of Justice.[70] Again, the questions for the Court of Justice could have been formulated in a way which invited a rather different response.[71] Without any real discussion, the House of Lords had effectively conceded to the Court of Justice not only jurisdiction to determine its own jurisdiction,[72] but also the power to abrogate a primary rule of the national constitution, namely that courts cannot review the legality of statute law.[73] The enormity of what they had done was masked by a veil of formalism.

5. A New Start

The Blair Government's constitutional reforms have been conceived in strictly Diceyan terms. The lawmaking powers of the Welsh Assembly are confined to secondary legislation and hence present no challenge to parliamentary sovereignty. The Scotland Act too is conceived in terms of parliamentary sovereignty. It delegates broad legislative competence across the gamut of home affairs, subject to reservation of matters 'effectively and beneficially handled on a United Kingdom basis'.[74] These include the constitution, the Crown and – significantly – the UK Parliament and questions of human rights.

However well they are drafted, these arrangements will inevitably generate disputes for which the envisaged pre-legislative checks – convention and concordats – are unlikely to prove sufficient. The demarcation lines between local, regional and central tiers of government will be fought out through formal adjudication.[75] Courts, previously accustomed to deal with a subordinate local government and a sovereign Parliament, will now have to tackle questions of competence more familiar in the European Court of Justice. A significant legalization of political relationships is clearly foreseeable.

The Human Rights Act 1998 also falls well within traditional constitutional boundaries. The lesson of *Factortame* has been learned and there is to be no extensive transfer of powers from the legislature. This Act does not permit our courts to 'disapply' legislation; they will be restricted to a 'declaration of incompatibility', without legal effect. It will be left to government to decide whether or not to amend statute law to conform with the Convention, using a novel 'fast-track' parliamentary procedure if appropriate. The case law of the Court of Human Rights must be 'taken into account' but will remain in principle less binding than that of the Court of Justice.

The present Lord Chancellor champions this Diceyan solution, seeing a proper balance of power between Parliament and courts.[76] Dicey, however, wrote in the nineteenth-century, while Lord Irvine is supposed to be planning for the twenty-first. It has to be said that the judicial architecture which he is handing down to future generations leaves much to be desired. No change in the existing judicial structure is envisaged other than the use of the Judicial Committee of the Privy Council to give rulings on disputed questions of competence.

The consequence of having an unwritten constitution is that the idea of constitutional adjudication is alien to our society. True, parliamentary systems of government in general find more difficulty in accommodating constitutional adjudication than presidential systems and those with an inbuilt constitutional bias to separation of powers.[77] But the absence of proper machinery for constitutional adjudication began to seem a weakness when the UK ratified the ECHR and later signed up to its adjudicative machinery and the weakness emerged more strongly after accession to the European Community. *Factortame* demonstrated the unwillingness of our courts to entertain open and forthright argument about political problems. Their reticence contrasts unfavourably with the performance of the Irish Supreme Court[78] or the German Constitutional Court in its celebrated Maastricht decision.[79] The latter flatly refused to cede to the Court of Justice jurisdiction over the German constitution and its long and complex judgement was remarkable for the depth of the argument. The constitutional courts of our European neighbours properly see it as their function to protect the authority of the national constitution. They also see it as their function to develop a meaningful constitutional discourse with government and legislature. The constitutional changes we are on the verge of making cry out for constitutional adjudication of this kind.[80]

A central argument of this chapter has been that the metaphor of legal autonomy, the ideology of positivism and the methodology of formalism, have served the unwritten constitution well, helping the judges, in a famous metaphor, 'to keep their heads below the parapet' and facilitating dispute-resolution in highly charged political cases. But formalism in constitutional adjudication is largely incompatible with popular desire for transparency, while the march of populist democracy makes it hard to see sovereignty as indivisible and vested solely in Parliament.

Griffith once denigrated rights-talk as the substitution of a closed, legal discourse for the open political debate of 'claims' fought out in Parliament and the political process.[81] This is, of course, a presentation strongly influenced by our formalist and positivist legal tradition. Feldman neatly encapsulates the difference between legal and political discourse when he describes constitutional courts as having 'as their first duty constitutional rather than political legitimacy'.[82] Unlike Griffith, who sees rights-talk as an appropriation of political power and impoverishment of political argument, Feldman sees it as adding a valuable dimension to constitutional debate. Loughlin too sees public law as offering 'a fluid language which may be creatively employed by political actors in the light of their concern'.[83] Both writers anticipate nothing but enrichment from the employment of public law concepts in the realization of political goals.

It is true that observers of constitutional adjudication by continental courts have watched them evolve into 'adjunct legislators'.[84] But although they resemble specialized legislative chambers, this does not give them the unbounded political latitude feared by Griffith. Courts are permitted to intervene in the legislative process to control the *constitutionality* of legislation. In the exercise of this specialist function, they develop 'a formal discourse that serves to clarify the constitutional rules binding on the exercise of legislative power'.[85] The reception of these rules by the legislature and the language of its response forms the other side of a dialogue. Legal autonomy receives recognition in that the court's political legitimacy rests on the perception of its neutrality.

It is not a formal, functional separation of powers for which we should today be striving but for fluid arrangements which avoid concentrations of power in too few hands. A complex institutional map is evolving, in which a strong judiciary and independent professions will be an essential component. Law cannot endure as a world neutrally detached from the contests of political argument but must take its proper place as a facet of political society rather than as an autonomous and external force acting upon it. It is, and must be seen as, a necessary ingredient of the body of political ideas. This need not mean that its legitimacy will be impaired.

About the author

Carol Harlow, London School of Economics, Houghton Street, London WC2A 2AE, UK; email: *c.harlow@lse.ac.uk*

Notes

I am indebted to the comments of other authors in this book and to comments on earlier drafts from Rodney Barker, Neil Duxbury, Martin Loughlin and Richard Rawlings.

1 R. Barker, *Political Ideas in Modern Britain in and after the Twentieth Century*. London: Routledge, 2nd ed., 1997, p.101.

2 Ibid. Especially in the *Report of the Committee on Ministers' Powers* (the Donoughmore Committee) Cmnd 4050 (1932). W. Robson, 'The Report of the Committee on Ministers' Powers', *Political Quarterly* 3 (1932), 46, talked of the 'dead hand of Dicey'.

3 H. Laski, *A Grammar of Politics*. London: Allen and Unwin, 1925, containing chapters on sovereignty, property and the nature of rights, as well as the judicial process. For Laski's critique of legal sovereignty, see pp. 50–55.

4 Quoted by D. Sugarman, 'The legal boundaries of liberty: Dicey, liberalism and legal science', *Modern Law Review* 46 (1983), 102, (a review of R. Cosgrove, *The Rule of Law: Albert Venn Dicey, Victorian Jurist*. London: Macmillan, 1980) in which Sugarman criticizes Dicey's biographer for seriously underrating Dicey's political contribution.

5 For explanation of this usage see C. Harlow, 'Changing the mindset: the place of theory in English administrative law', *Oxford Journal of Legal Studies* 14, (1994), 419.

6 Sugarman, 'Legal boundaries'.

7 A.V. Dicey, *Lectures on the Relation between Law and Public Opinion in England during the Nineteenth Century*. London: Macmillan, 1905. The enduring influence of this book is attested by two collections based directly on it: M. Ginsberg (ed.), *Law and Opinion in England in the Twentieth Century*. London: Stevens, 1959 and R. Rawlings (ed.) *Law, Society and Economy*. Oxford: Oxford University Press, 1997.

8 Notably F.W. Maitland, *The Constitutional History of England*. Cambridge, Cambridge University Press, 1908.

9 W.T. Murphy, 'The oldest social science? The epistemic properties of the Common Law tradition', *Modern Law Review* 54 (1991), 182.

10 Lord Devlin, *The Enforcement of Morals*. Oxford: Oxford University Press, 1969.

11 Barker, *Political Ideas in Modern Britain* p. 101.

12 M. Oakeshott, *On History and Other Essays*. Oxford: Basil Blackwell, 1983.

13 Barker, *Political Ideas in Modern Britain* p. 101.

14 See his inaugural lecture, 'Can English Law be Taught at Universities?' (1883). See also R. Blackburn, 'Dicey and the teaching of public law', *Public Law* (1985) 679; D. Sugarman, 'Legal Theory, the Common Law Mind, and the Making of the Textbook Tradition', in W. Twining (ed.), *The Common Law and Legal Theory*. Oxford: Basil Blackwell, 1986.

15 M. Loughlin, *Public Law and Political Theory*. Oxford, Clarendon, 1992, pp. 17–23; H.L.A. Hart, *The Concept of Law*. Oxford, Clarendon, 2nd edn, 1997; N. MacCormick, *Legal Reasoning and Legal Theory*. Oxford: Clarendon, 1978 and 'The concept of law and "the concept of law"', *Oxford Journal of Legal Studies* 14 (1994) 141.

16 J. McEldowney, 'Law and Science', *Current Legal Issues*, 1998, 110, p.121, discussing notably the influence of Maine and Pollock.

17 I.W. Jennings, *The Law and the Constitution*. (London, University of London Press, 1959); W. Robson, 'The Report of the Committee on Ministers' Powers', *Political Quarterly* 3 (1932) 346; J. Griffith, *The*

Politics of the Judiciary. London: Fontana, 1977; F. Mount, *The British Constitution Now*. London: Heinemann, 1992.

18 K. C. Davis, 'The future of judge-made public law in England: a problem of practical jurisprudence', *Columbia Law Review* 61 (1961), 201, 202. See similarly L. Jaffe, *English and American Judges as Lawmakers*. Oxford, Clarendon, 1969. And see generally, P. Atiyah and R. Summers, *Form and Substance in Anglo-American Law, A Comparative Study of Legal Reasoning, Legal Theory and Legal Institutions*. Oxford: Clarendon, 1987.

19 Lord Hailsham, *The Dilemma of Democracy – Diagnosis and Prescription*. London, Collins, 1978, p. 106.

20 J. Summers, 'Pragmatic instrumentalism in twentieth century American legal thought – a synthesis and critique of our dominant general theory about law and its use', *Cornell Law Review* 66 (1981), 481; P. Atiyah and R. Summers, *Form and Substance*. And see N. Duxbury, *Patterns of American Jurisprudence*. Oxford: Clarendon, 1995.

21 S. Sedley, 'Autonomy and the Rule of Law' in R. Rawlings (ed.), *Law, Society and Economy*. Oxford: Clarendon, 1996, p. 311.

22 Discussed in a public law context by M. Loughlin, 'The Pathways of Public Law Scholarship' in G. Wilson (ed.) *Frontiers of Legal Scholarship*. Chichester: John Wiley, 1995). See also R. Dworkin, *Law's Empire*. London: Fontana, 1986.

23 See the sharp interchange between B. O'Leary, 'What should public lawyers do?', *Oxford Journal of Legal Studies*, 12 (1992), 404 and P. Craig, 'What should public lawyers do? A reply', *Oxford Journal of Legal Studies*, 12, (1992), 564.

24 *Public Law and Political Theory*, p. 4.

25 R. Miliband, *The State in Capitalist Society*. London: Quartet Books, 1973, pp.124-130.

26 W.S. Holdsworth, *A History of English Law*. London: Methuen, 1938, vol. X, p. 644. See also J. Allison, *A Continental Distinction in the Common Law, a Historical and Comparative Perspective on English Public Law*. Oxford: Clarendon, 1996, pp. 16–23.

27 T. Halliday and L. Karpik, *Lawyers and the Rise of Western Political Liberalism*. Oxford: Clarendon, 1997, p. 22.

28 P. Craig, 'Formal and substantive conceptions of the rule of law: an analytical framework', *Public Law*,(1997) 467, 468.

29 Reorganized for the first time into a unitary High Court by the Judicature Act 1873: see H. Arthurs, *Without the Law: Administrative Justice and Legal Pluralism in Nineteenth Century England*. Toronto: Carswell, 1985.

30 M. Vile, *Constitutionalism and Separation of Powers*. Oxford: Clarendon, 1967, pp. 212-238.

31 P. Dunleavy and B. O'Leary, *Theories of the State. The Politics of Liberal Democracy*. London: Macmillan, 1987.

32 H. L.A. Hart, *The Concept of Law*. Oxford, Clarendon, 2nd ed., 1997; H. Kelsen, *Pure Theory of Law*, transl. M. Knight. Gloucester MA: Smith, 1967).

33 Dicey, *Introduction*, p. 83.

34 Dicey, *Introduction*, pp. 81–2.

35 See *Introduction*, p. 81.

36 See R. Cotterell, *Law's Community. Legal Theory in Sociological Perspective*. Oxford: Clarendon, 1995, p.92.

37 See G. Teubner, '*Altera pars Audiatur*: Law in the Collision of Discourses' in R. Rawlings (ed.), *Law, Society and Economy*. Oxford, Clarendon, 1997.

38 J. Griffith, *The Politics of the Judiciary*. London: Fontana, 1977.

39 Lord Hailsham, *The Dilemma of Democracy: Diagnosis and Prescription*. London: Collins, 1978, p.107.

40 Promulgated by Lord Kilmuir in 1955 and reprinted in Public Law (1986) 383–6, this guidance was revoked by Lord Mackay in 1987: see Griffith, *The Politics of the Judiciary*. 5th ed., 1997, pp. 42–45.

41 *Report of the Royal Commission on Legal Services*. Cmnd. 7648, 1979, p. iii.

42 H. Arthurs, 'Public Accountability of the Legal Profession' in P. Thomas (ed.), *Law in the Balance, Legal Services in the Eighties*. Oxford, Martin Robertson, 1982).

43 The Courts and Legal Services Act 1990 and preceding White Papers, *The Work and Organization of the Legal Profession*. Cm. 570, 1989; *Contingency Fees*. Cm. 571, 1989; *Conveyancing by Authorized Practitioners*. Cm. 572, 1989.

44 Halliday and Karpik, *Lawyers and the Rise of Western Political Liberalism*, p.24.

45 *Civil Justice Review*, Cm 394 (1988), paras 5 (iii), 120 (i) and 2 (i). Since 1978, applications for judicial review, or public law cases, have been heard by a special administrative division of the High Court, in a special procedure laid down by Order 53 of the Rules of the Supreme Court (Order 53 procedure or the Crown list): see C. Harlow and R. Rawlings, *Law and Administration*. London: Butterworths, 2nd ed. 1997, ch. 16.

46 First in a Law Commission study of judicial review procedure which accepted the exclusive jurisdiction of the High Court: Law Commission, *Administrative Law: Judicial Review and Statutory Appeals*. Law Com No. 226 (London: HMSO, 1994) and more recently in Lord Woolf's recommendations for reform of civil procedure: Lord Woolf, *Access to Justice, Report to the Lord Chancellor on the civil justice system in England and Wales*. London: Lord Chancellor's Department, 1996.

47 Important contributions include: J. Laws, 'Judicial remedies and the constitution', *Modern Law Review*, 57 (1994), 213 and 'Law and democracy', *Public Law*, (1995), 72; S. Sedley, 'The sound of silence: constitutional law without a constitution', *Law Quarterly Review*, 110 (1994), 270; H. Woolf, 'Droit public – English style', *Public Law*, (1995), 57. Significantly, the traditional viewpoint was reasserted by Lord Chancellor in waiting, Lord Irvine, 'Judges and decision-makers: the theory and practice of Wednesbury Review', *Public Law* (1996), 59.

48 N. Browne-Wilkinson, 'The infiltration of a Bill of Rights', *Public Law* (1992), 397.

49 O. Hood Phillips, 'A constitutional myth: separation of powers', *Law Quarterly Review*, 93 (1977), 11. For rebuttal, see E. Barendt, 'Separation of powers and constitutional government', *Public Law* (1995), 599.

50 S. Sedley, 'Governments, Constitutions and Judges' in G. Richardson and H. Genn (eds), *Administrative Law and Government Action*. Oxford: Clarendon, 1994, p.41.

51 N. Browne-Wilkinson, 'The Infiltration of a Bill of Rights'; T. Bingham, '"There is a world elsewhere": the changing perspectives of English law', *International and Comparative Law Quarterly*, 41 (1992), 513 and 'The European Convention on Human Rights, time to incorporate', *Law Quarterly Review*, 109 (1993), 390; J. Laws, 'Is the High Court the guardian of fundamental constitutional rights?', *Public Law* (1993), 59; 'The constitution: morals and rights', *Public Law* (1996), 622 and 'The limitations of human rights', *Public Law* (1998), 254; S. Sedley, 'Human rights: a twenty-first century agenda', *Public Law* (1995), 386.

52 *R v Home Secretary ex p Brind* [1991] 1 AC 696. At common law, treaties are not automatically incorporated into the domestic legal system but require statutory authority.

53 *R v Home Secretary ex p. Leech* [1994] QB 198, *R v Lord Chancellor ex p. Witham* [1997] 2 All ER 779 (right of access to the court, ECHR Art 6(1)); *R v Ministry of Defence ex p. Smith* [1996] 1 All ER 257 (right of homosexuals to work in the armed forces, ECHR Arts 8 and 14); *Derbyshire County Council v Times Newspapers* [1993] 2 WLR 449 (free speech, ECHR Art 10); *R v Cambridge Health Authority ex p B* [1995] 1 WLR 898, *R v Secretary of State for Social Security ex p. JCWI* [1996] 4 All ER 385 (right to life, ECHR Art 1). See generally, M. Beloff and H. Mountfield, 'Unconventional behaviour? Judicial uses of the European Convention on Human Rights in England and Wales', *European Human Rights Law Review* (1996), 495.

54 [1997] 2 All ER 779 (Laws J).

55 H. Woolf, 'Droit public – English style' and 'Judicial review – the tensions between the executive and the judiciary', *Law Quarterly Review* 114 (1998), 579 at 581. See also J. Laws, 'Is the High Court the Guardian of Fundamental Rights?'

56 *Bringing Rights Home: The Human Rights Bill*. Cm 3782, 1997, now enacted as the Human Rights Act 1998.

57 C. Harlow, 'A Special Relationship? The American Influence on English Public Law', in I. Loveland (ed.), *A Special Relationship? American Influences on Public Law in the UK*. Oxford: Clarendon, 1995.

58 *R v Inland Revenue Commissioners ex p National Federation of Self-Employed and Small Businesses Ltd* [1981] 2 WLR 722; *R v Inspector of Pollution ex p Greenpeace* [1994] 1 WLR 570. And see Law Commission, *Administrative Law: Judicial Review and Statutory Appeals*, Law Com No 226. London: HMSO, 1994, pp.41–44.

59 *R v Secretary of State for Foreign Affairs, ex parte World Development Movement* [1995] 1 All ER 611. For political accountability, see F. White, I. Harden and K. Donnelly, 'Audit, accounting officers and accountability: the Pergau Dam affair', *Public Law* (1994), 526.

60 *Pepper v Hart* [1992] 3 WLR 1032. A note by D. Oliver, 'Pepper v. Hart: a suitable case for reference to Hansard?' *Public Law* (1993), 5, outlines the evolution of the rule and the steps taken by the House to overrule it.

61 C. Harlow and R. Rawlings, *Pressure through Law*. London: Routledge, 1992, especially ch. 7.

62 Reported as *R v Bow Street Magistrate ex p Pinochet Ugarte* (No 1) [1998] 3 WLR 1456; *R v Bow Street Magistrate ex p Pinochet Ugarte* (No 2) [1999] 2 WLR 272; *R v Bow Street Magistrate ex p Pinochet Ugarte* (No 3) [1999] 2 WLR 827.

63 H. Larsen, 'British Discourses on Europe: Sovereignty of Parliament, Instrumentality and the Non-Mythical Europe' in Jorgensen (ed.), *Reflective Approaches to European Governance*. Basingstoke: Macmillan, 1997, pp. 119–121.

64 See Lord Dilhorne, HL Deb., 2 Aug 1962 col. 420 and Lord Gardiner, HL Deb. 8 May 1967, col. 1197; *Membership of the European Community: Report on Renegotiation*. Cmnd 6003, 1974.

65 R. Rawlings, 'Legal politics: the United Kingdom and ratification of the Treaty on European Union (Part One)', *Public Law*, (1994) 254 – at 255.

66 The statute was the Merchant Shipping Act 1988, ruled incompatible with EC law in Case 246/89 *Commission v United Kingdom*, [1991] ECR I-4585.

67 Important stages in the litigation are reported as: *R. v. Secretary of State for Transport ex p. Factortame* (No. 1), [1990] 2 AC 8; *R. v. Secretary of State for Transport ex p. Factortame* (No. 2), [1990] 3 WLR 818; C221/89 *R v Secretary of State for Transport ex p Factortame* (No 3), [1991] 3 CMLR 709 and [1992] 3 WLR 288.

68 [1990] 3 WLR 818, pp. 857–8 (emphasis mine).

69 On accession, Member States agree to accept the *acquis communautaire*, which includes the existing jurisprudence of the Court of Justice.

70 Case 33/76 *Saarland*, [1976] ECR 1989. This would have been to assume the law to be settled, technically the doctrine known as *acte clair*.

71 On the failure of the Court of Justice to understand the questions asked and the consequentially flawed response, see A. Barav, 'Omnipotent Courts' in D. Curtin and T. Heukels (eds), *Institutional Dynamics of European Integration*. Dordrecht: Marinus Nijhoff, 1994, vol II, p. 268; Lord Donaldson, 'Can the judiciary control Acts of Parliament?', *Law Teacher*, (1991), 25, 4 at 7–8.

72 This is the celebrated *kompetenz kompetenz* debate, see further note 79 below.

73 P. Craig, 'Report on the United Kingdom' in A-M. Slaughter, A. Stone Sweet and J. Weiler (eds), *The European Courts and National Courts*. Oxford: Hart, 1998, p. 204 sees this as 'a move away from certain of the assumptions underlying what is taken to be the traditional view of sovereignty.' See also P. Craig, 'Parliamentary sovereignty of the United Kingdom Parliament after Factortame', *Yearbook of European Law*, 11 (1991), 221; H. W. R. Wade, 'The basis of legal sovereignty', *Cambridge Law Journal*, (1955), 172.

74 White Paper, *Scotland's Parliament*, Cm 3658 (1997), p.10.

75 R. Rawlings, 'The new model Wales', *Journal of Law and Society*, 25 (1998), 461 at 493–6.

76 A. Irvine, 'The development of human rights in Britain', *Public Law*, (1998), 221.

77 K. von Beyme, 'The Genesis of Constitutional Review in Parliamentary Systems', in C. Landfried (ed.), *Constitutional Review and Legislation. An International Comparison*. Baden-Baden: Nomos, 1988, p. 22.

78 *Crotty v An Taoiseach* [1987] 2 CMLR 666. For comment see, R. Rawlings, 'Legal politics: the United Kingdom and ratification of the Treaty on European Union (Part Two)', *Public Law*, (1994), 367 at 384.

79 BverfGE 89, 155, reported in English as *Brunner v. European Union Treaty* (1994) 1 CMLR 57. For comment see J. Weiler, 'Does Europe need a constitution? Reflections on demos, telos and the German Maastricht decision', *European Law Journal*, 1 (1995), 219.

80 D. Feldman, 'Public interest litigation and constitutional theory', *Modern Law Review*, 55 (1992), 44, at 70.

81 J.A.G. Griffith, 'The political constitution', *Modern Law Review*, 42 (1979), 1.

82 D. Feldman, 'The Left, Judicial Review and Theories of the Constitution', in W. Miller (ed.), *Socialism and the Law*. Stuttgart Franz Steiner, 1992, p. 176.

83 M. Loughlin, 'The Pathways of Public Law Scholarship'.

84 A. Stone Sweet, 'Constitutional Politics: The Reciprocal Impact of Lawmaking and Constitutional Adjudication' in P. Craig and C. Harlow (eds), *Lawmaking in the European Union*. London: Kluwer, 1998, p.112. See also, A. Stone, *The Birth of Judicial Politics in France, the Constitutional Council in Comparative Perspective*. Oxford, Oxford University Press, 1992.

85 A. Stone Sweet, *Constitutional Politics*, p. 130.

9

Sustainable Development: a New(ish) Idea for a New Century?

James Meadowcroft

It is an intriguing fact of late twentieth century life that just at the time when philosophers had proclaimed the final death of 'meta-narratives', the collapse of grand modernist dreams for re-moulding man and society and consciously shaping the human future – indeed, even the end of 'history' itself – international political leaders have come to identify themselves with an ambitious new project intended to act as the focus of human endeavour in the twenty-first century. This new project is 'sustainable development', and over the past decade international organizations, national governments, and local authorities have increasingly come to cite it as a fundamental objective of their activity.

In this chapter I would like to explore the character of this 'turn' towards sustainable development – particularly in relation to environmental policy-making in the industrialized countries.[1] The discussion will be organized in four parts. It will open with a conceptual and historical introduction to the notion of sustainable development. It will then move on to consider how the idea has been taken up practically by governments in developed states. The significance of the changes effected to date will form the focus for the third section. Finally some general observations will be offered about the (admittedly relatively brief) 'career' of sustainable development.

1. Sustainable Development: a Brief Introduction

Brought to international attention by the Report of the World Commission on Environment and Development (WCED) in 1987, sustainable development was formally endorsed by political leaders from more than a hundred and seventy countries at the Rio Earth Summit in 1992.[2] The WCED did not coin the expression 'sustainable development',[3] but it provided the term with a plausible content and a heady dose of legitimacy. Noting that a large proportion of the world's population still lived in poverty, that there were grave disparities in patterns of resource use between rich and poor countries, and that global ecosystems were already suffering acute stress, it called for an international consensus to re-orient economic activity in order to privilege the urgent developmental needs of the poor and to prevent irreversible damage to the global environment. For developing countries it proposed 'a new era of growth' to address poverty and under-development; for the more industrialized states it envisaged an intensive effort to increase energy and materials efficiencies and to shift economic activity onto less environmentally-burdensome lines. What was required was that all countries commit themselves to making development 'sustainable'. In a now famous passage the Report explained that sustainable development was:

> development that meets the needs of the present without compromising the ability of future generations to meet their own needs. It contains within it two key concepts: the concept of 'needs', in particular the essential needs of the world's poor, to which overriding priority should be given; and the idea of limitations imposed by the state of technology and social organization in the environment's ability to meet present and future needs.[4]

Although the Report was written 'by committee', and contains inconsistencies and contradictions typical of outputs of such a process, it was crafted carefully to accommodate various constituencies. The fundamental normative idea – that human societies will continue their quest for a better life, but that in doing so they should give priority to meeting the basic needs of the poor, while taking care not to 'foul the pond' for future generations – was intuitively appealing. Moreover, it appeared to offer a way out of the 'growth versus environment' polarity which typified environmental debate during the 1970s and early 1980s. It suggested that it was not a question of a choice *between* environmental protection and social advance, but rather a problem of selecting patterns of economic and social development compatible with sound environmental stewardship. The notion was one which could appeal to countries of both North and South – reflecting growing environmental awareness in the former, and the urgent development concerns of the latter.

Since memory of historical contexts is notoriously fickle, it is worth emphasizing that at the time the WCED was active there was grave concern about the debt crisis and economic stagnation in many poorer countries. The global consequences of environmental destruction were beginning to be widely perceived. Moreover East/West tension continued to preoccupy international decision makers. Sustainable development was therefore explicitly formulated as a *'bridging'* concept – as an idea that could draw together apparently distinct policy domains, and unite very different interests behind a common agenda. The title of the Report (*Our Common Future*) and those of its major sections ('Common Concerns', 'Common Challenges' and 'Common Endeavours') were meant in all seriousness – not as some later commentators have implied as a naive denial of opposed perspectives and interests; but rather as a deliberate attempt to transcend differences, construct shared understandings, and build a winning coalition for reform.

Key features of the approach championed by the WCED include the fact that it:

- focused on how to sustain a broad process of positive social change called 'development'. Such 'development' was understood as an advance in the material and moral circumstances of humanity – in a word, 'progress';

- employed the idea of 'meeting needs' to characterize the just aspirations of all peoples, but most particularly to emphasize the legitimate moral claims of (i) the world's poor and (ii) future generations. This priority on the needs of the poor, and the proviso that the ability of future generations to meet their needs must not be compromised, help define the nature of those authentic forms of 'development' which were to be styled 'sustainable';

- invoked an idea of environmental limits as a potentially serious obstacle to continued social advance. The authors stressed that the environment's capacity to support human activity was not fixed in any simple way – different limits held for different resources, and improved technologies and social organization could enhance environmental carrying capacity. But they also affirmed that there were 'ultimate limits', and they argued that in some cases these environmental limits had already been breached by human activity.

It is important to note that because what is to be sustained in sustainable development is the *process* of improvement rather than any particular institution, practice or environment, an activity that is not itself sustainable could be a part – even an essential part – of an ongoing movement that was sustainable. Thus patterns of production, consumption, investment, or behaviour which could not be continued into the indefinite future can be components of a process of social development that might be so continued. In other words, because sustainable development focuses upon the maintenance of developmental momentum, it does not necessarily entail the preservation either of existing environmental systems or of prevailing social structures and practices. On the contrary, 'development' implies the potential transformation of both. Of course, without the preservation of much – in terms of planetary life support systems and environmental resources (but also in terms of valued social institutions and practices) – continued improvement would be unimaginable. But just what should be preserved and what should be altered is open to argument. Moreover, the boundaries of what can or must be preserved/changed will undoubtedly shift over time as the nature of society, configurations of natural systems, and their inter-relation evolve.

Following publication of the Brundtland Report sustainable development was relatively quickly taken up by national governments as well as by an array of international organizations. Definitions of sustainable development have proliferated, and 'sustainable' and 'sustainability' came to be coupled with a vast array of other terms.[5] Over time, the mainstream understanding of sustainable development has evolved somewhat: it has become common to stress the triune nature of the concept (that economic, social and environmental factors must be assessed together); the idea of 'participation' in environment and development decision-making has been increasingly emphasized; and the notion of 'the common but differentiated responsibilities' of countries of the North and the South has been more explicitly formulated.[6] On the practical side, the Earth Summit agreements (including the Rio Declaration on Environment and Development, the Climate Change Convention, the Biodiversity Convention, and Agenda 21) have been taken to represent an international 'consensus' around the sort of orientation required to make sustainable development a reality.[7] Yet despite this evolution, the basic understanding of sustainable development formulated in the Brundtland report has continued to anchor subsequent international discussion.

As one might expect, as an idea which was formulated deliberately to function as a new norm for global conduct,[8] sustainable development has been subject to a wealth of criticism. Many environmentalists have decried its 'anthropocentrism', deploring the fact that it unashamedly takes the promotion of human welfare as its central value. They argue that rather than worrying about sustaining development, we should be more concerned with sustaining the natural environment.[9] Moreover they complain that the term obscures the essential contradiction between environmental limits and the modern growth economy. On the other hand, 'developmental' critics have argued that sustainable development is little more than a crude attempt to impose a Northern environmental agenda on the South – forcing countries whose primary concern should be economic advance to adopt inappropriate environmental measures which are really intended to protect the economic hegemony of the industrialized states or to assuage the environmental consciences of rich consumers. Within the social sciences, energy has been deployed in definitional arguments, in teasing out logical inconsistencies of the idea, or in attempting to establish whether or not the term adds something to existing technical vocabularies.[10] Many commentators have decried the ambiguities associated with sustainable development. Some have suggested the term is so vacuous that it could be invoked to justify virtually any policy. Others have complained that there are no incontestable procedures for operationalizing sustainable development in terms of policy priorities. These last criticisms are misplaced. To be precise, they fail to understand that conceptual ambiguities and competing decontestations are the staple of political argument; nor do they appreciate that the WCED deliberately construed (or 'designed') sustainable development in open-textured terms. Sustainable development was not formulated as either a logical construct or an operational maxim – but rather as a potentially unifying political meta-objective, with a suggestive normative core. As this core has been passed down in the international process extending through UNCED to its follow ups (such as the United Nations Commission on Sustainable Development, and the 1997 General Assembly Special Session to Review the Implementation of Agenda 21) it has been understood to embody ideas about promoting human well-being, meeting the basic needs of the poor and protecting the welfare of future generations (intra- and inter-generational justice), preserving environmental resources and global life-support systems (respecting limits), integrating economics and environment in decision-making, and encouraging popular participation in development processes.

2. Government Engagement with Sustainable Development in the Industrialized Countries

More than a decade after the publication of the Brundtland Report the notion of sustainable development has now been accepted into governmental idiom in many developed countries. A recent study of the responses of ten governments in the industrial world to the coming of sustainable development found that, with the exception of the USA, all of the central governments examined regularly invoked the idea of 'sustainable development' to characterize policy orientations.[11] The term appears in prominent statements of government intent, in the publications of official agencies and advisory bodies, and in national plans and strategy documents. Increasingly it is enshrined in legislative enactments. In the UK, for example, sustainable development has been integrated into the guidance central authorities give for local land use planning; it is included in the official remit of the newly created Environment Agencies; and it lies at the core of a strategy process which is intended to systematize and assess achievement with regard to environmental objectives. In Sweden sustainable development has appeared in several important laws, it helps define the objectives of the new Environmental Code, and it has recently served as the focus for a major (£2 billion) spending programme by the Social Democrat administration.[12]

While central governments place varying degrees of emphasis on sustainable development, and highlight slightly different dimensions of the concept, they typically relate their understanding explicitly to the Brundtland Commission and to the UNCED process and its follow ups. The theme of protecting the global environment is all pervasive; so too is the idea of integrating environment and economy in decision-making at all levels of society: when sustainable development is invoked, this much is almost always implied.

Environment ministries and agencies have generally taken the lead in engaging with the idea, but departments concerned with natural resources, industry, agriculture and transport have increasingly become active. Foreign ministries and international development agencies have also been involved in the externally focused dimensions of sustainable development. Some governments have specified that all branches of the central administration must review their operations in light of the new paradigm. In Canada, for example, federal government departments are now required to produce sustainable development plans every four years; and these plans are periodically audited by the newly created Parliamentary Commissioner for the Environment and Sustainable Development.[13] Governments have also set up a wide range of advisory, consultative, educational, and research bodies intended to assist the generation of the policy response, to raise public awareness of the issue, and to draw major actors into dialogue over the implications of sustainable development. For example, in the UK there have been organizations such as the British Government Panel on Sustainable Development, the UK Roundtable on Sustainable Development, and Going for Green. Norway has set up a National Committee for International Environmental Issues, the Centre for Sustainable Production and Consumption (GRIP), and the Environmental Home Guard.

Much of what governments have done in the name of sustainable development constitutes a 're-packaging' of traditional pollution control and nature conservation activities. Measures to improve air quality, to strengthen flood defences, to encourage energy efficiency, or to protect endangered species are hardly new – but all now figure in governmental accounts of their action for sustainable development. This cannot simply be dismissed as a cynical public relations exercise. When presented as part of a larger social effort directed at sustainable development traditional environmental programmes acquire a new rationale. And clearly their continuation is a necessary – if not a sufficient – condition for pursuing sustainable development. But in addition to such efforts at 'reinterpretation', governmental engagement with sustainable development in industrialized countries has been accompanied by a series of new initiatives related to the management of domestic environmental burdens.

There has been reform to *structures and procedures* of governance, designed to integrate environmental problem-solving into the workings of the main branches of the public administration. It has been accepted – at least in principle – that environmental policy can not operate as a *post hoc* corrective to normal (that is non-environmental) decision processes; rather the environmental dimension should be factored-in from the outset. Thus responsibility for environmental performance cannot remain the exclusive concern of a specialized ministry of the environment, but must be shared across the administration – in much the same way that the budgetary implications of policy cannot be left to the finance ministry, but must inform decision-making throughout government. In Norway reforms to formalize the responsibilities of sectoral ministries for environmental performance were introduced in 1988.[14] In Sweden such cross governmental responsibility was promoted by the Environment Bills of 1987/88 and 1990/91. In the UK a system of 'green ministers' was established whereby a junior-minister in each major department had responsibility for monitoring environmental performance. In Norway and the UK high level committees were also established to co-ordinate environmental decision-making across government (in Norway, the State Secretaries Committee on Environmental Issues; and in the UK, the Cabinet Committee on the Environment). In many countries this 'sectoral integration' of environmental management functions has been linked to broader efforts to promote 'green' government – for example, by improving the environmental performance of public bodies with respect to energy budgets, recycling, waste disposal, and transport. Public procurement policies have also been identified as a key route to leverage environmental gains. Examples here include Japan's 'Action Plan for Greening Government Operation' and the Swedish 'Green Purchasing Initiative'.

Another important change has been the tendency to initiate more comprehensive *strategy and planning processes* focused on the environment and sustainable development. In 1992, for example, Australia issued a National Strategy for Ecologically Sustainable Development (NSESD) which had been prepared on the basis of substantial public inputs and which signalled a new phase of State/Commonwealth co-operation in the environmental field.[15] Japan published its first Environment Basic Plan in 1994 under the provisions of its new Environment Basic Law. The Netherlands has adopted the most comprehensive and systematic planning regime through the three (and a half) environmental policy plans that have been adopted since 1989.[16] A somewhat different approach has been taken in Norway where, rather than preparing a formal plan, the government has issued a series of authoritative statements to parliament to orient sustainable development policy and has integrated environmental issues into the state budget planning routines. The Swedish government has also issued periodic strategy statements, and a sustainable development plan prepared by the Swedish Environmental Protection Agency has dealt with issues under this organization's remit.

By the close of the decade a substantial majority of OECD countries had launched some form of national environment or sustainable development strategy process.[17] In comparison with earlier ventures in environmental policy-making these plans and strategies adopt a more comprehensive approach, attempting to propose management options for a significant proportion of environmental burdens within the national territory. They also have substantial integrative ambitions: the idea is to match biophysical and social inter-dependencies with analytical, regulatory, and remedial strategies based on cross-disciplinary, cross-sectoral and cross-jurisdictional action. They adopt a longer range approach – focusing directly on the next 4 or 5 years, but considering possible scenarios 20 or 30 years into the future. Furthermore, the idea of 'sustainable development' provides a key conceptual anchor for these plans and strategies, furnishing a context for the integration of environment and economic decision making and emphasizing a pre-occupation with the life support and amenity functions of the environment, and a concern with the needs of future generations. Yet despite a common form and substantive points of similarity, these exercises are in other respects quite different. Important dimensions of variation include the range of issues brought within the strategy framework, the legal and institutional basis of the process, the nature of the qualitative and quantitative goals, the 'one-shot' or iterative nature of the process, the forms of social participation involved in plan development, and the degree of ongoing political salience.[18] In addition to such national plans, governments have also developed an extensive array of sectoral or thematic strategies for managing environmental burdens, including specific plans related to climate change and biodiversity. Recent additions in the UK, for example, include Local Environment Agency Plans (LEAPs),[19] and integrated transport plans being drafted by local authorities.

Another trend associated with sustainable development has been the effort to employ more systematic mechanisms for *measuring environmental effects, and monitoring the impacts of policy.* Compared with the situation in the mid-eighties considerable progress has been made with respect to 'state of the environment' reporting, the inclusion of environmental impacts into satellite national accounts, and the design of indicators. Work at the OECD and UN system organizations has popularized the pressure/state/response approach to sustainable development indicators, and governments are now increasing their capacity to track environment and development trends. The formal adoption of sustainable development as a policy objective, its emphasis on combining environmental, economic and social assessment, as well as a general political climate favouring performance measures in the public service, have encouraged this move towards quantitative monitoring. The entry into force of the Climate Change and Biodiversity Conventions have strengthened this trend, particularly with respect to source and sink inventories for greenhouse gases, and registers of biodiversity. From the early 1990s the UK has, for example, gradually committed itself to an increasing range of environmental performance measures. The Labour government recently proposed a set of 'headline' sustainable development indicators which in draft form included items for economic growth, social investment, employment, health, education and training, housing quality, climate change, air pollution, transport, water quality, wildlife, land use, and waste.[20] Recently the German Environment Ministry proposed an 'Environment-Barometer for Germany' which includes indicators and targets for six crucial environmental policy areas related to sustainable development: air quality (SO_2, NO_x, NH_3 and VOC emissions – with a 70 per cent reduction target for the period 1990–2010); soil (the increase in the area covered by human settlement and traffic routes – with the aim of reducing this increase from 120 hectares per day in 1997 to 30 hectares per day in 2020); nature protection ('ecological priority areas' – with a target to preserve 10–15 per cent of the land unsettled in 1998 to form a biotope network by 2020); water (chemical quality class – with a target that by 2020 all water will meet specified standards); energy productivity (GNP per unit of primary energy consumption – to be doubled between 1990 and 2020); and raw materials (GNP per ton of materials – to be increased 2.5 times from 1993 to 2020).[21]

There has also been movement with respect to the *policy instruments* invoked to secure environmental gains. While it is undoubtedly true that the core of environmental governance has been – and remains – regulatory (based around fixing standards, issuing permits, and legal enforcement), the coming of sustainable development has been linked to more negotiated or co-operative approaches. This has been taken furthest in the Netherlands where an intricate network of 'covenants' between the authorities and economic 'target groups' commit the latter to realize specified environmental objectives within a fixed time frame.[22] Other countries have not followed the Netherlands in adopting so formal or compre-hensive an approach to environmental agreements, but there has nevertheless been a broad proliferation of negotiative frameworks where public and private bodies interact to generate agreed approaches to sustainable development-related issues.[23] Another change has been an increased willingness to use taxes and charges to leverage environmental gains. Modest carbon charges have been imposed in number of the smaller European countries including the Netherlands, Norway and Sweden. In the UK the Conservative government of the mid-1990s introduced a landfill tax and fuel price escalator, and the Labour government is now carrying forward ideas for urban road-use and parking fees. The new German government has also taken recent (hesitant) steps towards 'ecological tax reform'.[24]

These are some of the more prominent innovations which governments have presented as part of their 'turn' towards sustainable development, but there are other noteworthy elements including:

- programmes to improve energy and material efficiencies, to increase re-cycling and improve waste management – particularly those involving ideas for radically increasing factor productivity ('Factor 4' or 'Factor 10'),[25] implementing product life-cycle management (from design to disposal) or ecocycle approaches (as in the 1993 Swedish Ecocycle legislation);

- the encouragement of 'sustainable cities' and 'Local Agenda 21' initiatives, focused on economic and social regeneration and managing the environmental loadings of urban living;[26]

- a more systematic effort to develop institutions for international environmental governance;

- the 'greening' of international aid, by vetting development assistance pro-grammes and projects; and

- the extension of activities and initiatives linked to the two major international conventions associated with sustainable development and the UNCED process – the Climate Change Convention and the Convention on Biodiversity.

3. Substance or Hyperbole?

In the proceeding section I have argued: first, that over the last decade the idea of sustainable development has to some significant degree been accepted into the politico-administrative vocabulary in many of the developed countries; and second, that sustainable development has been associated with a number of changes in the approach to environmental governance. Of course, causal links are hard to untangle here. It is difficult to prove that it is because governments began to talk of sustainable development that they then went on to adopt specific policies. What they are now describing as an orientation towards sustainable development is a complex mix of things that were already being done (but which have now been re-described in terms of sustainable development), new things which they might have done anyway (but which can be conveniently brought under the new label), and other initiatives which are more directly related to the international discussion of sustainable development. Nevertheless, the practical result is that since the late 1980s the idea of sustainable development has been linked by central governments to a broad portfolio of policies and initiatives. The fact that jurisdictions where the language of sustainable development has *not* been taken up are also those where practical activities of the kind described above are weak or absent is also suggestive. The USA is a case in point here: for it is not just that the term sustainable development has failed to make a mark on the US scene, but also that principles and approaches which (in other countries) have been associated with sustainable development have not – at least in terms of national politics – won widespread acceptance.[27]

One way to approach an assessment of the significance of this turn towards sustainable development is to consider the extent to which the perspectives and policies presented by governments actually embody the elements of the concept as it has been elaborated through international discussion. Looking at what governments in the industrialized countries have done so far, it is possible to identify three major elements which capture how sustainable development has been understood: first, the integration of environment and economy in decision making; second, the expansion of societal participation in environmental management; and third, the internationalization of environmental policy making. Each of these elements is present in the idea of sustainable development as it has been elaborated through the UNCED process, and each has been consistently emphasized by national governments. With respect to *'integration'*, the merging of environmental concerns into the responsibilities of line ministries discussed above is significant. But here the term is used in a wider sense to denote the various ways in which the environmental dimension can be factored into societal decision-making at all levels. This includes integrated assessment and management of environmental burdens across media (air, water, land), the integration of environment into the concerns of public bodies at all levels (for example in land use planning), the widened deployment of environmental impact assessment, the development of eco-audits and eco-accounting, and other measures to encourage economic agents (producers and consumers) to consider environmental consequences. With respect to *'societal participation'*, sound environmental governance has been held to imply increasingly complex patterns of public and private co-operation. The idea of 'partnership' has been regularly invoked to capture the extension of dialogue and collaboration to manage the interaction of economic, social and environmental factors as society comes to terms with the implications of sustainable development. With respect to *'internationalization'* key developments include: government participation in an ever more dense array of international regimes and negotiating processes intended to manage global environmental burdens; development of regional environmental accords (including the NAFTA side agreement and the extension of European Union competence into the environmental field); the formulation by governments of more explicit environmental foreign policy goals; and the 'greening' of international development assistance.

The planning and strategy processes discussed in the previous section provide an illustration of how these three strands converge in practice. National plans and strategies have an obvious 'integrative' component. At the very least they have been drawn up on the basis of inter-ministerial consultation, and often they are sponsored by several ministries or by government as a whole. More broadly they facilitate the adjustment of political and economic actors to anticipated shifts in environmental pressures and policy orientations. The 'participative' strand is evident in the tendency for strategy processes to involve widening networks of social consultation – important to ensure their salience and acceptability. Finally, 'internationalization' is manifest in the extent to which objectives agreed in multi-lateral forums, and concern to fix national priorities for future rounds of cross national collaboration, are a prominent feature of such plans and strategies.

In contrast, other dimensions of sustainable development appear less obviously present in governmental responses in the industrialized world. Two elements stand out in particular: first, the rather weak engagement with the theme of *international equity*; and second, the muted effort to engage with the idea of transforming patterns of *consumption and production*. Although governments all refer to supporting economic progress in the developing world, only a few countries – such as the Netherlands and Sweden – have made public education around the 'solidarity' aspects of sustainable development a priority. Overall, international aid budgets fell throughout the 1990s, and the largest countries in particular – such as Germany, the UK, and Japan – have failed to meet the UN objective of allocating 0.7 per cent of GNP to international development assistance. Although governments have taken cautious steps to improve energy efficiencies and to encourage reductions in conventional pollutant loadings, they have hesitated to address broader issues of consumption and production.[28] From a sustainable development perspective both issues – internationa*lism* and consumption – are crucial. They relate to the particular responsibilities which rich countries are expected to assume – (a) to assist, not just the environmental clean up efforts, but also the legitimate developmental endeavours of the poor states, and (b) to reduce the overall burden, not just the rate of increase of the burden, they place on the global environment – so that room can be made for the increasing resource and sink requirements of a developing South.

Another way to approach the significance of governmental engagement with sustainable development is to consider the salience, scale and stability of the changes effected under the banner of this concept. How pertinent are the policies? How much has really altered? How lasting are the changes likely to be? Consider the four topics raised in the previous section. With respect to the integration of environmental concern across government, it is unclear how far the new structures and procedures have actually altered decision making in sectoral ministries. There is also the worry that cohesion of environmental policy *across* the sectors does not seems to have been secured. Moreover the role of the environment ministry in a government where everyone is (supposedly) concerned with environmental consequences remains unclear. The idea of an environmental 'super-ministry' riding-herd on other departments (as finance ministries sometimes do through their budget control functions) has not found favour. In some jurisdictions 'integration' has been almost entirely at the level of rhetoric – in Japan, for example, production oriented ministries and plans operate in parallel to organizations and plans centred on environmental sensitivity; and in the European Union the environment has remained marginal to key spending programmes such as the Common Agricultural Policy and the Structural Funds.[29] Elsewhere the integrative ideal has been more thoroughly pursued – in the Netherlands or Norway, for example. Yet generally, structures and procedures remain in flux. With respect to national planning and strategy processes a similar story can be told. Great variation exists among governments. Most initiatives remain relatively unstable. Canada, for example, tried a national Green Plan,[30] and a broad-based visioning exercise (the *'Projet de Société'*), before settling on the current departmental strategy regime. But the new system has yet to pass through a full cycle of planning/action/assessment, so judgements about its effectiveness or long term survival are premature. In Australia, a recent parliamentary review was sceptical about much of the governmental follow-up to the NSESD. Even in the Netherlands it is unclear whether NEPPs will remain a semi-permanent feature of Dutch politics, and debate continues about whether future plans should be merged with the land use planning system, or should incorporate other issues (such as international assistance). With respect to measurement, much of the work is exploratory, reliable runs of data have not yet accumulated, and specialized units remain vulnerable to periodic campaigns to reduce state expenditure. With respect to policy instruments, the jury is still out on the effectiveness of more inclusive and negotiated approaches. There is evidence that negotiations often result in stretched time frames and diluted environmental objectives; on the other hand, the Dutch covenants have succeeded in meeting many of their targets. Efforts to extend carbon taxes in Europe are frozen for now, and wider plans for 'ecological tax reform' have been slow to bear fruit. In short, a sceptic could claim that so far the salience, scale and stability of the reforms which have gone on under the banner of sustainable development are unimpressive.

Behind this discussion lurks an even broader question: to what extent are the policy responses elicited so far likely to lead to ultimate outcomes which are congruent with the long term objective of sustainable development? In other words, are the measures taken adequate to secure the stated objectives? To formulate a systematic strategy to address this question would take us well beyond scope of this essay. But the impressionistic evidence is not especially encouraging. If one considers the major sustainable development questions of climate change and biodiversity, the policy response so far has had a scarcely discernible impact on environmental loading across the OECD. Detailed mechanisms of the international climate change regime continue to be elaborated at successive Conferences Of the Parties, but most of the richest countries will fail to meet their original UNCED target of stabilizing emissions at 1990 levels by the year 2000. Those which do so will often have met the objective as a by-product of pursuing other (non climate-related) ends.[31] It is not that policies implemented around climate change have failed to secure any emission reductions, but rather that efficiency gains have been swamped by emissions from increased economic activity (especially in the transport sector). As things stand, many countries will have serious difficulties achieving their Kyoto targets without heavy reliance on extra-territorial reductions secured under the Convention's 'flexibility mechanisms'. For its part, the Biodiversity Convention is not in good shape.[32] Despite progress in building up domestic competences on the issue in the industrialized countries, there is no discernible evidence 'on the ground' of any slowing in the pace of biodiversity loss globally, or in the developed world. Climate change has significant implications for biodiversity, but so too does the ever expanding space required by human activities. And in this regard the 'development' juggernaut continues to roll forward, even in the most environmentally conscious countries of the North.

4. Conclusion

The first part of this essay introduced the concept of sustainable development and described its entry into international political debate. The second considered how governments in industrially developed countries have engaged with sustainable development since it was popularized by the WCED in 1987. The third presented a tentative assessment of the character of this policy response. In conclusion I would like to offer some general reflections on the career of sustainable development to date. Clearly a comprehensive review of the impact of this idea would require examination of its reception by international bodies, by business and environmental groups in the developed countries, and by all levels of state and society in the developing world. Nevertheless, the more limited enquiry undertaken here can provide the basis for some observations.

The relatively rapid uptake of the idea of sustainable development by governments in the industrialized world is worth emphasizing once again. It is actually rather rare for a new normative concept to gain widespread cross-national acceptance – not just as a term of art deployed by international negotiators, or a specialist term accepted by a particular disciplinary or professional group – but as an idea that is absorbed into domestic political interchange across a variety of national polities. Yet sustainable development has achieved just such acceptance in little more than a decade. Remarkably, this is a notion which was explicitly formulated by an international body (but on the basis of ideas which were already rooted, or taking root, in certain national contexts and discursive communities), and which then proliferated 'downward' through transnational channels into national jurisdictions and sub-national politics.

Also of note is the sweeping nature of this ideational construct, which operates as a multi-dimensional bridging concept which links environment and development; local, national and international scales; present and future generations; efficiency and equity; government and societal actors; and so on. By combining notions of 'development' (which during the period after the Second World War became accepted as a central political objective for the poorer two thirds of the globe) and of the 'sustainable' (which during the 1970s became linked with environmental critiques of conventional social trajectories) the result has been a concept of broad sweep and ambition, which can be presented as a long term meta-objective of government.

Reasons for this relative 'success' include its rather open texture – which draws together key concerns about environment and development, while leaving ample room for different interests to contest their implications. Intimating both change and continuity, it urges the abandonment of inequitable and environmentally unsound practices while avoiding any suggestion of a direct assault on established centres of political and economic power. Strength is drawn from a core appeal to the notion of 'progress' – after all, it is the process of progressive social change called 'development' which is to be carried forward over time. Sustainable development therefore embodies an upbeat and positive message that contrasts with the perspectives of ecological (or developmental) doomsters.[36] Although the idea of progress has taken something of a beating during the twentieth century, and today intellectuals often like to snicker at the naive self-confidence of our Victorian forebearers, the idea of progress remains deeply embedded in our culture. The fact is, alternatives to progress are unpalatable. And sustainable development offers an image of progress suited to an increasingly inter-dependent world, where millions remain in poverty, and the rupture of ecological limits threatens future social advance. There is an underlying confidence in technological progress, but also a faith in the power of human reason to apprehend problems and to consciously re-mould social institutions and practices.[37] There is little doubt that the particular combination of concerns with equity and efficiency, growth and conservation, progress and stability, national responsibility and international co-operation displayed by sustainable development resonates strongly with the social democratic tradition. It is hardly coincidental that some of the more important figures involved in preparing the WCED report, as well as the countries which have taken up sustainable development with particular enthusiasm, are linked to social democracy. Yet sustainable development would not be the first normative idea to have had original affinities with one political tradition but later to have won acceptance across the ideological spectrum.

When considering the possible future of this concept – whether the discourse of sustainable development will (so to speak) turn out to be 'sustainable', or whether the idea will prove more ephemeral – it is worth keeping in mind that its resilience may be greater than many observers assume. Consider some of the charges levelled against the idea. One argument is that sustainable development needlessly complicates discussion of environmental issues by mixing together different sorts of problems – particularly by introducing issues of equity into the analysis of environmental burdens. Of course this appears to 'complicate' things – but the insight suggested by sustainable development is that equity issues *are already* entwined with the environmental problematic: that is to say, any approach to environmental management necessarily confronts distributional issues; and a refusal to engage with these simply results in an uncritical acceptance of received distributions of costs and benefits. A related charge is that sustainable development posits a simplistic relationship between poverty (or equity) and environmental sustainability, suggesting that poverty (or injustice) causes environmental destruction and that the elimination of poverty (or inequality or injustice) would therefore be good for the environment. There is no doubt that causal inter-linkages between poverty and environmental destruction are part of the sustainable development equation, but the main tenor of the Brundtland report was to link equity and the environment in another way. It argued that (a) there could be no valid moral foundation for refusing the peoples of the developing world the life chances offered to those in the rich countries; and (b) since human activities were already pressing on the frontiers of the environmentally sustainable; then (c) all countries should seek an alternative development trajectory which would bear more lightly on the planet; and (d) the rich countries had a particular responsibility to assist development in the South, while dramatically reducing their own environmental loadings. Parallel to this reasoning there was a similar chain of argument relating to the entitlements of future generations. In other words, equity was valued as an independent ideal (not primarily because of its 'functionality' for environmental sustainability); and considerations of equity, combined with observations about the environmental consequences of current economic activities, created imperatives for change.

Another line of criticism focuses on the human-centred character of 'sustainable development' – that sustaining the environment is *not* given centre stage. Several points can be made here. While human welfare is at the core of sustainable development, environmental concerns are clearly essential to its purview. First, and most obviously, the environment appears as a constraint on development decisions: environmental processes provide an essential foundation for human development, both in terms of broad planetary life-support systems, and the more specific environmental assets and amenities on which economic activity depends. Thus a substantial degree of environmental protection is required to keep development sustainable. Second, environmental issues are crucial to arguments about the character of authentic 'development'; specifically, with respect to determining the kinds of human/environment interaction that are most conductive to human well-being. A great range of preservationist measures can be justified as necessary to protect species, ecosystems and natural phenomena valued by humans and/or important for human welfare. Third, space can even be made to accommodate non-instrumental reasons for valuing nature: for it can be argued that authentic 'development' cannot be based on moral wrong, and so it must provide adequate recognition (where this is due) to the intrinsic value, and/or the rights, and/or the entitlement to ethical consideration of non-human natural entities. The Brundtland report was not so entirely anthropocentric as critics sometimes claim, and it makes explicit reference to ethical objections to the despoliation of nature. Of course the primary emphasis is on meeting human needs, and on sustainable use of the biosphere; but openings do exist to advance a less instrumental agenda within the discourse of sustainable development. Moreover, sustainable development does not have to be accepted as a hegemonic project, displacing all other ethical norms. It does not of itself provide an adequate environmental ethic, and for this we must look elsewhere. All this said, however, it should be appreciated that the human focus of sustainable development is one of the features that has permitted it to acquire the influence that it has had. Unsurprisingly, human beings remain mostly concerned with human ends. And to the extent that sustainable development has contributed to moderating environmental destruction it has been able to do so precisely because it reflects this pre-occupation.

Others have complained that sustainable development mistakenly assumes that all environment and development problems can be converted to win/win scenarios. In fact within the Brundtland report, and in the national and international discussions it sparked over the past decade, there is a clear recognition that hard choices and trade-offs must often be made. Other critics complain that sustainable development is not sufficiently radical in orientation for – at least on the dominant interpretation – it does not explicitly demand root and branch reform, the complete transformation of existing economic and political structures, a decisive shift in world views and a revolution in social practices. And yet sustainable development does call for fundamental structural reform to national and international systems so that the development process may be carried forward, so that poverty may be eliminated and breaches of the thresholds of physical sustainability avoided. More-over sustainable development poses no *a priori* limits on the depth or breadth of the economic and political reforms that may be required to realize this objective. Not surprisingly governments have begun cautiously. But most already acknow-ledge that sustainable development will imply further profound changes to social practice. And in the longer term, policy failure and contradictions generated by partial solutions may lead to bouts of social learning and to the implementation of reforms that extend far beyond those initially envisaged by the political leaders of today.

Many of these lines of criticism actually reveal the potential resilience of sus-tainable development, and suggest why it continues to attract attention. Among its most important strengths are its focus on global issues, on linking economic and environmental decision making, on inter- and intra-generational equity, and on achieving structural reform while leaving it open to experience to establish the ultimate parameters of the required change. Such features help explain why sus-tainable development has been much more widely taken up than similar ideas such as those of 'eco-development', or 'ecological modernization'.

To date the changes governments have wrought in the name of sustainable development are in some senses remarkable and profound; but in others barely scratch the surface of the phenomena they purport to address. Sustainable develop-ment is, after all, just an idea and its future depends on what people actually do with it. If those who invoke it shy away from some of the more potent, but dis-concerting, dimensions of the concept – especially those related to international equity and to the reduction of the environmental loading imposed by the North – the idea may yet be discredited with many constituencies. In particular, it is unclear whether developing countries will show continued acceptance of a concept which may be deemed to have failed to live up to its promise. One thing of which we can be sure, however, is that the sorts of environment and development issues which sustainable development was formulated to address are destined to be at the centre of international political argument in the coming century.

About the author

James Meadowcroft, Department of Politics, Unversity of Sheffield, Elmfield, 132 Northumberland Road, Sheffield SH0 2TY, UK; email: *j.meadowcroft@sheffield.ac.uk*

Notes

This chapter (especially the argument in sections 2 and 3) draws on insights gained during a three year collaborative study of governmental responses to sustainable development. The project 'Implementing sustainable development in high consumption societies: a comparative assessment of national strategies and initiatives' (COMPSUS) was co-ordinated by William Lafferty and James Meadowcroft. Other members of the team were Susan Baker, Christiane Beuermann, Gary Bryner, Katarina Eckerberg, Oluf Langhelle, Marie Louise van Muijen, Elim Papadakis, Glen Toner, Miranda Schreurs, and Stephen Young. The project was funded by ProSus (The Centre for Research and Documentation for a Sustainable Society, Oslo) and the UK Economic and Social Research Council (R000221956). The full findings of this project are to be presented in Lafferty and Meadowcroft (eds) *Implementing Sustainable Development* (Oxford: Oxford University Press, forthcoming). I would like to thank the members of the project team, and in particular William Lafferty, for helping clarify my perspective on issues discussed in this chapter. Any errors or inaccuracies are solely the responsibility of the author.

1 As the subsequent discussion will make clear, sustainable development is not just an 'environmental' concept, and it can be invoked as a normative meta-objective across the whole of government. It also has quite specific implications for international development policy, a point to which I will return in due course. Nevertheless, governments in the developed countries typically have argued that in light of their generally robust economies and established social welfare systems it is with respect to managing environmental burdens that the concept can be of most use. Some governments have made efforts to draw the idea of sustainable development into decision making across a broad range of areas. On occasion the expressions 'ecologically sustainable development' or 'environmentally sustainable development' are employed to make explicit the primary concern with environmental constraints.

2 World Commission on Environment and Development, *Our Common Future*. Oxford: Oxford University Press, 1987. 'Sustainable development' is cited in eleven of the 27 'principles' of the 'Rio Declaration on Environment and Development'. The full title of the action programme adopted at the United Nations Conference on Environment and Development (UNCED) in Rio was: 'Agenda 21: A Blueprint for Action for Global Sustainable Development into the 21st Century' (United Nations Conference on Environment and Development, *Agenda 21*, New York, United Nations, p. 13.)

3 References to 'sustainability' and the 'sustainable society' can be found in radical environmental literature from the 1970s. 'Sustainable development' was famously invoked in the *World Conservation Strategy* issued in 1980 by the International Union for the Conservation of Nature, the United Nations Environment Programme and the World Wildlife Fund. For a discussion see W. Adams, *Green Development*. London: Routledge, 1990.

4 WCED, *Our Common Future*, p. 43.

5 Early reviews of the literature on sustainable development can be found in D. Mitlin, 'Sustainable development: a guide to the literature', *Environment and Urbanization*, 4 (1992), 111–124; J. Pezzy, 'Sustainability: An Interdisciplinary Guide', *Environmental Values*, 1 (1992), 321–62; and S. Lele 'Sustainable development : a critical review', *World Development*, 19 (1991), 607–621. For a more analytical approach to understanding different approaches to sustainability see A. Dobson, 'Environmental sustainabilities: an analysis and a typology', *Environmental Politics*, 5 (1996), 401–428.

6 Arguably each of these ideas is already present within the Brundtland report, but subsequent international discussion centred on the UNCED process made their centrality to sustainable development more explicit.

7 For a discussion of the Earth Summit see M. Grubb, M. Koch, K. Thompson, A. Munson and F. Sullivan, *The Earth Summit Agreements: a Guide and Assessment*. London: Earthscan, 1993. For an overview of the UNCED process consider D. Reid, *Sustainable Development: an Introductory Guide*. London: Earthscan, 1995.

8 For sustainable development as an international norm see W. Lafferty, 'The politics of sustainable development: global norms for national implementation', *Environmental Politics*, 5 (1996), 185–208.

9 See, for example, W. Sachs, 'Global Ecology and the Shadow of "Development"', in *Global Ecology : a New Arena of Political Conflict*. London: Zed, 1993, pp. 3–21; and D. Richardson, 'The Politics of Sustainable Development' in S. Baker, M. Kousis, D. Richardson and S. Young (eds), *The Politics of Sustainable Development: Theory, Policy and Practice within the European Union*. London: Routledge, 1997.

10 For an interesting exchange consider W. Beckerman, 'Sustainable development: is it a useful concept?', *Environmental Values*, 3 (1994) 191–209; and M. Jacobs, 'Sustainable development, capital substitution and economic humility: a response to Beckerman', *Environmental Values*, 4 (1995), 57–68.

11 COMPSUS project. For full details see unnumbered note.

12 K. Eckerberg, working paper for COMPSUS project, 1999. One of the more important laws is: 'Targeting sustainable development: implementation of the UNCED decisions' (Prop. 1993/94:111). See also: Ministry of the Environment, *The Environment Code*. Stockholm, 1998.

13 Government of Canada, *A Guide to Green Government*. Ottawa: Minister of Supply and Services, 1995; and, G. Toner, working paper for COMPSUS project, 1998.

14 M. Reitan, 'Norway: A Case of "Splendid isolation"', in M. Andersen and D. Liefferink (eds), *European Environmental Policy: the Pioneers*. Manchester: Manchester University Press, 1997; and O. Langhelle, working paper for the COMPSUS project, 1998.

15 B. Dalal-Clayton, *Getting to Grips with Green Plans: National Experience in Industrial Countries*. London: Earthscan, 1996; and E. Papadakis, working paper for COMPSUS project, 1998.

16 These are the National Environmental Policy Plans: NEPP (1989), NEPP+ (1990), NEPP 2 (1993) and NEPP 3 (1998).

17 M. Janicke and H. Jorgens, 'National environmental policy plans and long-term sustainable development strategies: learning from international experiences', *Environmental Politics*, 7 (1998), 27–54.

18 For discussion of dimensions of variation see Janicke and Jorgens, 'National environmental policy plans'; and J. Meadowcroft, 'The politics of sustainable development: emergent arenas and challenges for political science', *International Political Science Review*, 20 (1999), 219–237.

19 For an example, see Environment Agency, *Local Environment Agency Plan: Severn Vale*, Consultation Draft. Tewkesbury, Glos.: Environment Agency, 1999.

20 Department of the Environment, Transport and the Regions, *Sustainability Counts*. London: DETR, 1998.

21 Federal Ministry of the Environment, Nature Conservation and Nuclear Safety, *Sustainable Development in Germany; Draft Programme for Priority Areas in Environmental Policy: Summary*. Bonn: 1998. Note the contrast in emphasis with the UK approach, which has recently stressed drawing together the economic, social and environmental dimensions of sustainable development, while the German government chose to focus particular attention on the environmental themes.

22 For more on the Dutch covenants see P. Glasbergen, 'Partnership as a Learning Process: Environmental Covenants in the Netherlands', in P. Glasbergen (ed.), *Co-operative Environmental Governance: Public-Private Agreements as a Policy Strategy*. Dordrecht: Kluwer, 1998.

23 For a discussion of the implications of such approaches see J. Meadowcroft, 'Co-operative management regimes: collaborative problem-solving to implement sustainable development', *International Negotiation*, 4 (1999), 1–30.

24 For a general discussion of eco-taxation see M. Andersen, *Governance by Green Taxation*. Manchester, Manchester University Press, 1994.

25 Factor productivity refers to the output per unit of resource input. Factor 4 refers to getting 4 times more output per input (ie increasing materials and energy efficiency four fold). Factor 10 is a still more ambitious objective. See for example: E. Weizsacker, A. Lovins and L. Lovins, *Factor Four: Doubling Wealth, Halving Resourse Use, the New Report to the Club of Rome*. London: Earthscan, 1997.

26 On Local Agenda 21, see H. Voisey, C. Beuermann, L. Sverdrup and T. O'Riordan, 'The political significance of local Agenda 21: the early stages of some European experience', *Local Environment*, 1 (1996), pp. 33–50; and W. Lafferty and K. Eckerberg (eds), *From Earth Summit to Local Forum: Studies of Local Agenda 21 in Europe*. Oslo: ProSus, 1997.

27 G. Bryner, working paper for COMPSUS project, 1998.

28 Governments have shown little enthusiasm for programmes to alter consumption patterns. Some steps have been taken on eco-labelling, and consumer education – particularly in Germany, the Netherlands, Norway, and Sweden. Norway in particular has assumed a leadership role on the international level by supporting a work programme around 'sustainable production and consumption'. For results of a recent initiative financed by Norway see N. Robins and S. Roberts, *Consumption in a Sustainable World*. London: IIED, 1998.

29 S. Baker, 'The Evolution of European Environmental Policy: from Growth to Sustainable Development?', in Baker *et al.*, *The Politics of Sustainable Development*.

30 On Canada's Green Plan see G. Toner and B. Doern, 'Five political and policy imperatives in Green Plan formation: the Canadian case', *Environmental Politics*, 3 (1994), 395–420; and E. Darier, 'Environmental governmentality: the case of Canada's Green Plan', *Environmental Politics*, 5 (1996), 585–606.

31 For useful discussions of climate change see T. O'Riordan and J. Jager, *Politics of Climate Change: a European Perspective*. London: Routledge, 1996; and U. Collier and R. Lofstedt (eds), *Cases in Climate Change Policy*. London: Earthscan, 1997.

32 D. McGraw, 'The Convention on Biological Diversity at the Cross-roads', paper presented to the workshop on 'Implementing policies of sustainable development: examining actor relationships and negotiating processes', 25–26 May 1998, Geneva.

33 Ministry of Housing, Spatial Planning and the Environment, *Third National Environmental Policy Plan: the Summary*. The Hague: 1998.

34 Whether *global* resource and pollutant burdens associated with domestic consumption in these countries have decoupled from growth is another question. To ascertain that one would have to take account also of the displacement of certain productive sectors (for example, ship building) towards the developing world.

35 OECD, *OECD Environmental Data: Compendium 1997*. Paris: OECD, 1997. For an informed discussion of the environmental performance of industrialized states see M. Janicke and H. Weidner (eds), *National Environmental Policies: a Comparative Study of Capacity Building*. Berlin: Springer, 1997.

36 J. Dryzek, *The Politics of the Earth*. Oxford: Oxford University Press, 1997.

37 For a further discussion of this point see J. Meadowcroft, 'Planning for Sustainable Development: What can be Learnt from the Critics?', in M. Kenny and J. Meadowcroft (eds), *Planning Sustainability*. London: Routledge, 1999.

Notes on Contributors

Stephania Abrar is Equalities Officer for the National Lottery Charities Board. Previously she was a Research Assistant in the Government Department, London School of Economics. Her publications include 'Feminist intervention and local domestic violence policy', *Parliamentary Affairs*, 1996 vol. 49 no. 1.

Rodney Barker is Reader in Government at the London School of Economics and Political Science. His books include *Political Ideas in Modern Britain In and After the Twentieth Century; Politics, Peoples, and Government: Themes in British Political Thought Since the Nineteenth Century* and *Political Legitimacy and the State*.

Steve Bruce taught from 1978 to 1991 at The Queen's University of Belfast. He is now Professor of Sociology at the University of Aberdeen. His most recent works are *Conservative Protestant Politics* and *Choice and Religion: a Critique of Rational Choice Theory*.

Andrew Chadwick is Lecturer in British Politics and Research Fellow in the Centre for Social and Economic Research (CESER) at the University of the West of England. His publications include: *Augmenting Democracy? Political Movements and Constitutional Reform during the Rise of Labour, 1900–1924* and 'A "Miracle of Politics": the Rise of Labour, 1900–1945' in Brian Brivati and Richard Heffernan (eds), *Labour's First Century*.

Michael Freeden is Professor of Politics at Oxford University and a Fellow of Mansfield College, Oxford. Among his books are *The New Liberalism, Liberalism Divided, Rights*, and *Ideologies and Political Theory: a Conceptual Approach*. He is the founding editor of the *Journal of Political Ideologies*.

John Gray is Professor of European Thought at the LSE. Until 1998 he was Professor of Politics at Oxford. He has been a Visiting Professor at Harvard, Yale and other universities. His books include *Mill on Liberty: a Defence, Beyond the New Right, Isaiah Berlin, & Enlightenment's Wake*.

W. H. Greenleaf is Emeritus Professor of Political Theory and Government, University of Wales, Swansea. He is the author of *The British Political Tradition*

Carol Harlow is Professor of Public Law at the London School of Economics and Political Science. Her books include *Law and Administration*, and *Pressure through Law*, both with Richard Rawlings. She writes regularly about administrative law and European public law.

Joni Lovenduski is Professor of Politics at Birkbeck College. Her jointly edited or authored books include *Women in Politics; Political Recruitment in Britain; Gender and Party Politics*; and *Contemporary Feminist Politics*.

Helen Margetts is Reader in the School of Public Policy at University College London. Her publications include *Information Technology in Government: Britain and America* and (with P. Dunleavy and S.Weir) *The Politico's Guide to Electoral Reform in Britain* (London, Politicos Publishing, 1998); *Making Votes Count: Replaying the 1990s General Elections under Alternative Electoral Systems*

James Meadowcroft is a Senior Lecturer in the Department of Politics at the University of Sheffield. His research interests are focused upon environmental politics, political ideologies, and the history of political thought. His publications include *Conceptualising the State* and *Democracy and the Environment: Problems and Prospects*, co-edited with W. Lafferty.

INDEX

utilitarianism   2, 3–4, 8, 12, 95, 96
utterances, addressivity of   74

value-pluralism   103, 107–9, 110
interpretations of   103–6
values, Christian and pluralism   57–8
Verwoerd, Hendrik   122
Victim Support   25
Viguerie, Richard   41, 45, 46
Volosinov, V. N.   73–4

Wainwright, Hilary   11, 12
Wallace, George   45
Warner, John   43, 50
waste management   155
Watson, S.   18
Wattenberg, M.P.   46
ways of life
   rivalries between   107–8, 109–10
   see also modus vivendi
Webb, Beatrice   68
Weber, Max   49
Welsh Assembly   142
Weltanschauungen   93

Weyrich, Paul   41
White, H.   76
wife beating   22
Wittgenstein, Ludwig   103
Women Against Violence   20
Women's Aid Federation   20, 25, 26, 31
women's liberation movement   20
Women's National Commission   20
women's studies movement   20
Woolf, Lord   139
World Commission on Environment and Development (WCED)   148, 149–50, 160
world peace   126
World War I   119

zealot politics, and democracy   41–60
zealotry
   advantages of   51
   disadvantages of   52–5
Zero Tolerance   20
Zionism   54